An Unexpected End
The lessons I learned through faith, marriage, and divorce

A Memoir

ALEXA C. FAITH

Published by KHARIS PUBLISHING, imprint of
KHARIS MEDIA LLC

ISBN-13: 978-1-946277-08-4
ISBN-10: 1-946277-08-8

All KHARIS PUBLISHING products are available at special quantity
discounts for bulk purchase for sales promotions, premiums, fund-raising,
and educational needs. For details, write:

Kharis Media LLC
709 SW Elmside Drive
Bentonville,
AR 72712
Tel: 1-479-903-8160
info@kharispublishing.com
www.kharispublishing.com

The events in this book are true. However, names of individuals have been changed to protect their identities. The author's name has also been changed.

The Bible verses quoted are taken from the following translations:

AMP   *Amplified Bible*®
Scripture quotations marked "AMP" are taken from the *Amplified Bible*®. Copyright © 1954, 1958, 1962, 1964, 1965, 1987 by Lockman Foundation. (www.Lockman.org) Used by permission. All rights reserved.

AMPC   *Amplified Bible, Classic Edition*®
Scripture quotations marked "AMPC" are taken from the *Amplified Bible, Classic Edition*®. Copyright © 1954, 1958, 1964, 1965, 1987 by Lockman Foundation. (www.Lockman.org) Used by permission. All rights reserved.

EXB   *The Expanded Bible*®
Scripture quotations marked "EXB" are taken from *The Expanded Bible*®. Copyright © 2011 by Thomas Nelson Inc. Used by permission. All rights reserved.

NASB   *New American Standard Bible*®
Scripture quotations marked "NASB" are taken from the *New American Standard Bible*®. Copyright © 1960, 1962, 1963, 1968, 1971, 1972, 1973, 1975, 1977, 1995 by Lockman Foundation. (www.Lockman.org) Used by permission. All rights reserved.

NKJV   *New King James Version*®
Scripture quotations marked "NKJV" are taken from the *New King James Version*®. Copyright © 1982 by Thomas Nelson Inc. Used by permission. All rights reserved.

NLT   *The Holy Bible, New Living Translation*®
Scripture quotations marked "NLT" are taken from *The Holy Bible, New Living Translation*®. Copyright © 1996, 2004, 2007 by Tyndale House Foundation. Used by permission. All rights reserved.

MSG   *The Message Bible*®
Scripture quotations marked "MSG" are taken from the *Message Bible*®. Copyright © 1993, 1994, 1995, 1996, 2000, 2001, 2002 by NavPress Publishing Group. Used by permission. All rights reserved.

When a Bible verse is a direct quote, it is in quotation marks and is cited with the book name and number for the chapter and verse. The translation is identified before or after the quote in either of the following formats:

"Hope deferred…" (Proverbs 13:12, NKJV).

Proverbs 13:12 says, "Hope deferred…" (NKJV).

When a Scripture is paraphrased, the book or chapter of the Bible verse may be included next to the statement, before the end of the sentence, but will not have quotation marks and will not include a reference to a translation, such as:

God hates divorce (Malachi 2:16).

The term "Scripture", and variations of it, always refers to the Scriptures from the Bible.

Apart from the chapter headings, any words of Scripture appearing in italics is the author's emphasis; this is only noted here, rather than next to each verse where italics are used.

The content of the Bible translation is always preserved; however, the format has been changed at times to create continuity within the format of this book:

- o Any superscript characters, such as letters denoting a study note or cross reference verse, have been removed from the Scripture quotations.
- o Punctuation has been changed to flow better with the text/layout of this book.
  - o Lower case letters are used unless the word is a proper noun or is at the beginning of a sentence.
  - o God, and references to Him, is considered a proper noun. Even if a translation does not capitalize the pronouns used to refer to God: "He", "His", "Him", "Who", or "Whom", they are capitalized consistently throughout this book to express respect and importance for the Lord.
  - o If the Scripture passage ends in a comma, a period might be used, particularly if that Scripture is used to end a sentence.
  - o "Heaven" is capitalized because this is considered a proper noun.
- o Space marks have been removed from the verses quoted from the EXB version.

There is not a ™ or ® used when mentioning the brand name of a product, per the recommended guidelines of APA and MLA.

DEDICATION

This book is dedicated to the Lord, who has walked with me through everything. It is also dedicated to those in my life who have lifted me up when I needed their support.

"And we know that all things work together for good to those who love God, to those who are called according to His purpose."
(Romans 8:28, NKJV)

Unexpected endings may occur in life, in a variety of ways. There can be things we don't see coming, that leave us disappointed. Although not all things in our lives happen as a result of God, the Bible says He can bring good out of anything we experience. I am holding Him to that promise.

CONTENTS

ACKNOWLEDGMENTS

I want to thank my parents and the rest of my family for their steadfast support through the years and for showing me what it means to be loved unconditionally.

Thank you to those with whom I've fellowshipped over the years—your prayers and encouragement have been invaluable! Many sisters in the Lord have prayed for and encouraged me as I attempted the task of capturing my experiences in writing.

Thank you to those who reviewed the content of this book and provided great suggestions! Over 25 people, comprised of friends and family, reviewed portions of this book and several individuals reviewed my entire manuscript. Each person provided valuable feedback.

An anonymous friend helped me tremendously with editing, as did J. Wilday, who proofed an earlier draft of my manuscript for me. Both of these people provided great feedback.

Thanks is also due to all those whose ministries, songs, and teachings have influenced my walk with the Lord. Several of these are referenced in the *References* section at the back of this book.

I would also like to acknowledge Kharis Publishing for their assistance in making this book a reality.

All of these people helped make this book what it is; I couldn't have done this without them.

FOREWORD

This memoir captures many of my experiences from 2009 to 2015. Those six years were the birthing ground for many realizations in my life. The events during that time served as a catalyst for my maturation.

I am transparent in sharing the events captured in this book because I want others to learn from my experiences. When I tried to select which moments in my life should be included, I was hesitant at times to share certain things because they were so personal. At one point, I said, "That's too personal, God," and His response came immediately: "I am a personal God." As one might anticipate, with a response like that, I decided to include that section anyway.

This book captures many of the *kairos* (strategic timing) moments that have occurred in my life. There have been many times when God has spoken and provided direction. Several of these experiences, as well as the corresponding lessons learned, are captured in this book so you can take encouragement from them and hopefully avoid some of the mistakes I made.

I am far from perfect and have been greatly humbled as God has dealt with me since my divorce. Acts 10:34 says, "God shows no partiality" (excerpt from NKJV). That means if He's been faithful to provide guidance to me as I sought Him, He will also provide guidance to others who seek Him. God wants to be involved in each person's life.

My hope in writing this is so you will know:
o   God loves you and He is faithful.
o   Jesus died to forgive you of your sins.
o   No matter what you are going through or how imperfect you are, you can reach out to the One who made you.
o   If you draw close to God, He will draw close to you.
o   God desires to speak to you, be personally involved in your life, and do great things through you.
o   A wife needs to respect her husband because that respect is a life-source for him. This was something I should have been more aware of during my relationship.
o   Feeling justified in a decision does not make it right, nor does it make it the best choice.

1. THE CRAZY NIGHT

In the midst of crisis, one can always turn to God.
There is power in prayer.

"He who dwells in the secret place of the Most High shall abide
under the shadow of the Almighty. I will say of the Lord,
'He is my refuge and my fortress; my God, in Him I will trust.'"
(Psalm 91:1-2, NKJV)

"They have a gun?! Do you want me to call the police?" I asked.

Jacob sounded desperate, "No, please don't call the police."

I felt helpless. It was 2 a.m. and I was in my living room in my pajamas. As I listened to what my husband was describing to me on the phone, I pleaded with God to intervene and resolve this crazy conflict.

Twelve hours earlier, my husband, Jacob, had confessed adultery. The news had not come as a surprise—we had been separated for about eight months. It had been heavy on his conscience, and he decided it was finally time to confess. I had not seen him attend church often, but our paths crossed there on that particular Sunday, and he told me he wanted to talk. Shortly after our chat began, I could see why he had wanted to talk so badly. As we sat on cushioned chairs in a quiet, dimmed room after church, Jacob began his confession, "I have been unfaithful to you…"

Even though I was not shocked, I didn't know what to say in the moment. He almost left me the previous year for an ex-girlfriend. Although their interactions hadn't culminated in adultery, there had been other women Jacob did meet with. My husband explained that he had reached out to women online for the sole purpose of physical intimacy. There had also been inappropriate relations with an acquaintance.

I finally have biblical justification for a divorce.

Based on my understanding of the Bible, marital unfaithfulness seemed to be a legitimate reason for divorce in God's eyes. Though I'd desperately wanted our marriage to last and moved out with good intentions, I had come to anticipate that a divorce would be in our future.

My husband didn't appear to be revealing these things because he wanted to restore our relationship. It seemed the confession was more about getting right with God, and he knew it was important to confess his infidelity to me because I was his wife.

The way he said, *"IF* we get back together..." caught my attention. As I considered the implications of his tone, I was mildly surprised. *It's not his expectation that we will restore our marriage?*

Jacob eagerly described how he wanted to get things right with the Lord. He had an immediate action plan. When he got home he was going to throw out his La-Z Boy because it had contributed to him being a "lazy boy." Additionally, he planned to take down the blanket over the sliding glass door. Jacob explained, "I've literally turned day into night."

He seemed so sincere as he described the changes he wanted to make in his life. For a few minutes, I saw a glimpse of the passionate man I had fallen in love with six years earlier. Although I saw his sincerity, I couldn't help but feel unsure. *This is too soon.*

Since moving out eight months ago, I'd prayed often for Jacob to get right with God. Finally, after months of praying, in July of 2010, God told me in a dream that Jacob would begin to get right with Him around July of the next year, 2011. It was only September 2010. I pondered this in light of what Jacob had just shared. *Well, if Jacob gets right with God sooner than next July, that's great! But I really believe it was God that revealed to me the time frame of next July. That's nine months from now.*

As time would tell, my dream had indeed been accurate.

Little did I know that within hours of my husband's confession, he was about to face turbulence in his life that would again set him back in his walk with the Lord.

The Crazy Night

Several hours after sitting me down to confess marital infidelity, my husband called and confessed in more detail. As we talked and Jacob shared the details of his indiscretion, he became convinced the residents in the apartment below had heard our whole conversation and were very upset with him.

Jacob then began to describe a very strange scenario:

The man in the apartment below had a cousin over, an ex-Marine in his mid-thirties who had a gun. They'd heard Jacob's confession and were planning to shoot him for what he had done. They knew one of the women with whom he had inappropriate relations and decided to get revenge.

A little while later, the ex-Marine started running around the parking lot of the apartment complex singing the "Brass Knuckle Rapture." *Who would sing that song and run around a parking lot?*

Afterward, he began to hotwire Jacob's car. *Why would he be hotwiring his car? What is he going to do with it, steal it?*

Next, the ex-Marine's 12-year-old son had been directed to come in through the sliding glass door and steal Jacob's blanket out of the living room. Confused, I thought, *Couldn't the sliding door to the living room be locked?*

I was mystified. *Why would they want this adolescent boy to steal a blanket?* Nervous, I was listening intently to every update.

The boy then began to climb up the side of the apartment complex to get onto Jacob's second-story porch. *Will he be able to get up there?*

Contemplating the weird string of events that had been described, I concluded, *These people are nuts.*

As Jacob updated me, I prayed fervently, asking God to intervene. While praying, the Lord gave me two insights. The word "create" came to mind, and I saw an image of a triangle, which I knew was somehow associated with "right angle." Unsure of what to do with either of those insights, I asked God for more understanding, "What does 'create' mean? 'Create' what?" There was no further clarification, so I gave it my best guess and tried to incorporate those into my prayers. "Lord, create a victory in this situation. Thank you that You see things from the right angle..."

At one point Jacob called the police. The officer paid a visit to the neighbors below, then told Jacob they were asleep when he'd arrived. Scoffing, Jacob told me about this and shared his conclusion, "The neighbors *pretended* to be sleeping."

It was nearing 2:00 a.m.

The neighbors were now going to make the 12 year-old boy come and shoot him. Jacob overheard their whole conversation. The ex-Marine's son had been given a hand-gun, with orders to use it. *Why would they make him do that?*

After some time passed, the kid began approaching Jacob. Armed with his own weapon—a shotgun—but not wanting to fight, my husband was prepared to defend himself. I heard Jacob call out into what I assumed must be the apartment stairwell, "I don't want to hurt you!"

In the moments that followed, there was the sound of a gunshot, then another. I listened in stunned despair.

Next, Jacob screamed, "No! No!" *CRASHHHH!* Breaking glass was the last thing I heard.

Someone must have just died. I was horrified.

Immediately, I grabbed my oversized, yellow rain jacket, pulled it over my pajamas, shoved my feet into some shoes, and climbed into the car. Taking off down the road, I kept the house phone in hand—not because it would get reception—but because I was desperate. I wanted it with me just in case, somehow, I might hear something—anything—to give me a clue as to what was happening.

As I sped toward Jacob's apartment I was listening carefully for anything the Lord might reveal to me. I'd read in the Bible that God's children can hear His voice, and I knew this to be true. However, there was no new revelation. "Create" came to mind again.

Crying out to God, I pleaded for His intervention. *God, please, please intervene! Somehow be glorified by this. Don't let it be in vain. What do I do? No. This can't be.*

Ten minutes later, I finally arrived at the apartment complex.

Upon pulling into the parking lot I saw the lights off in the apartment, and a hole in Jacob's bedroom window. A flashlight was being manipulated inside the dark apartment. My heart raced even harder as I noted the moving beam of light in the apartment. *I think they only do that when someone is dead.*

I ran inside and found a police officer looking around in the apartment with Beth, who'd leased the apartment to us four years earlier.

Seeing Beth, I exclaimed, "What happened?!"

She took a few steps closer to where I stood in the middle of the living room, made eye contact and tenderly told me, "He's gone."

No. No! Everything in me didn't want that to be true. I had to know more, "What do you mean he's gone?!"

"He's not here. The ambulance took him," Beth said.

A wave of relief washed over me. *I can't believe she picked those words!* I was so thankful that he wasn't truly *gone!*

What happened?

After rushing to the hospital, I found Jacob. There, I learned he had been hallucinating throughout the night. During the "gun fight" Jacob moved the dresser to serve as a duck-and-cover while he and the imaginary kid had a shoot-out. For some reason, the shoot-out took place from his bedroom into the hallway that led to the spare bedroom. It had not been in a stairwell or outside, like one might guess. Firing his shotgun into the hallway, he'd shot up the apartment, doing damage to the walls and splintering the wooden bedroom door.

When Jacob ran out of shells for his shotgun, he dove out of the bedroom window—while it was still closed. Ten or fifteen feet below, he landed on the ground. His fall was slightly cushioned by a small bush. Incredibly, all he had was a broken finger and a need for about 50 stitches from the glass cuts, primarily on his arms. I thanked God. It was amazing no one else had been hurt and Jacob had only minor injuries. I was so grateful no one had been killed!

His blood sugar levels were quite high—around three times what they should have been. As a brittle diabetic there was a constant risk of Jacob's blood sugar going too high or too low if he did not take care of himself. Extremely high blood sugar can cause hallucinations, as can severe alcohol withdrawals. Jacob had been a heavy drinker for the last few years, but the week prior to the incident he'd been refraining from alcohol for at least a few days. I don't know how much the withdrawal effects had to do with what Jacob experienced, but his blood sugar levels were definitely high!

After talking with the police officer on the scene and seeing Jacob later at the hospital, I learned the scenario Jacob had described to me on the phone that night was *created* in his mind, and he was not seeing things from the *right angle*. Finally, I made sense of the insights from earlier that night.

How much I wished I had the complete picture before arriving to the apartment! But when God reveals things it is often only a bit at a time. As 1 Corinthians 13:9 says, "Now our knowledge is partial and incomplete, and even the gift of prophecy reveals only part of the whole picture!" (NLT). In other words, God rarely reveals every detail of a situation at one time, this creates a continual need to seek God and rely on Him.

I was grateful to have been in communication with Jacob that night because it provided me with a solid opportunity to intercede for him when there was an urgent need. I attributed prayer to be part of the reason Jacob was alive after the episode.

The Hospital Visit

Filled with compassion and concern for my husband, I felt the need to stay with him at the hospital. That morning I called into work, "I have a family emergency and won't be coming in today." Jacob's parents began the long trip from out of state as soon as I contacted them. I planned to transfer care of their son to them when they arrived.

Nearly 12 hours after arriving at the hospital, still in my pajamas and large rain jacket, I'd decided to stick around for the evening also—I didn't want to leave his side. However, when I called my Bible study facilitator, Ruby, and explained why I wouldn't be coming to Bible study that night, she did not think it was a wise choice for me to stay. She told me plainly, "You need to extract yourself from that situation."

Ruby knew about much of what had taken place in my marriage, and she knew that I'd followed the Lord's prompting to separate myself from Jacob for a while. Taking on the responsibility of talking to the doctors could get me intertwined in taking care of Jacob, at least to some degree. In the months leading up to this day, the interactions between my husband and I had been minimal. Staying at the hospital would make it more difficult for me to maintain my distance. Ruby was a trusted mentor and her counsel held a lot of weight with me. So, I considered her advice in the midst of these difficult circumstances and chose to leave. Thankfully, Jacob's parents would be at the hospital very soon. Otherwise, I would have felt like I was abandoning him.

At Bible study that night a friend pulled me aside upon my arrival. She prayed for me and said, "I see the Lord standing with His hands behind His back. He says you keep getting in the way of what He wants to do." The woman telling me this had a great gift of hearing from the Lord. I considered what she shared and believed it was from God. I understood the message. I needed to let Jacob face the music on his own and stay out of the way so God could deal with him. Change would never come to Jacob's life if he didn't experience the consequences of his own decisions. If I served as a buffer to those consequences, it would not be advantageous for Jacob and could interfere with what the Lord wanted to do in Jacob's heart.

Jacob's terrible experience that night was not necessarily something God directed to happen. It is the devil who comes to steal, kill, and destroy. But I knew *somehow* God could bring good out of the situation. For many years when difficult times had come, I'd held onto the promise in Romans 8:28 which says, "And we know that all things work together for good to those who love God, to those who are called according to His purpose" (NKJV). That does not mean everything happens because God orchestrates it. Romans 8:28 is simply saying that when situations, however difficult, are given to the Lord, He can bring something good out of it. I concluded that because I love God, I could hold Him to His Word and ask for good to be brought of the situations that arise in life—both for me and my loved ones.

After my friend's prayer, we went through our Bible study lesson. Partway through our study, there was a moment when I closed my eyes and again sensed the Lord revealing something to me. This time, the message was clear, not partial like it had been during Jacob's hallucination. I saw a picture of me standing on cement stairs, trying to move forward, but I simply could not take the next step while holding onto Jacob. This vision answered the question posed in Amos 3:3, "Can two people walk together without agreeing on a direction?" (NLT). The answer was definitely no. When one person is moving forward while attached to someone going the opposite direction, they cannot move together.

I *had* to let go of Jacob. How hard! He seemed so needy and vulnerable. As I lay in bed that night, I kept seeing Jacob in my thoughts and was tormented at the thought of him needing me.

Following Jacob's incident, I would need to be intentional to follow the advice from Proverbs 3:5-6 which says, "Trust in the Lord with all your heart, and lean not on your own understanding; in all your ways acknowledge Him, and He shall direct your paths" (NKJV). Since learning that Scripture early in my Christian walk, I'd tried to apply it consistently in my life. Even though I didn't understand the "why" behind everything that took place, I needed to trust the Lord and lean on Him. Despite my understanding that God is faithful, it was still very difficult to let go of my husband and entrust him completely to the Lord.

Together Forever?

I reflected on the months leading up to this moment. After various conflicts had arisen between my husband and me, I moved into my own place. During that time of separation, I had come to believe my marriage would not last. Now, with Jacob's confession, I felt like I had biblical justification for a divorce, but the idea of permanently ending my marriage terrified me.

I loved God too much, Jacob too much, and myself too much not to do what was necessary. Jacob was the man I had entrusted with my heart and the one to whom I was committed. In my heart, I wanted my marriage to be reconciled. But even more than that, I wanted God's will to be done— whatever that might be. Eventually, I would come to understand what it meant to be an enabler to an unhealthy relationship.

This was not the ending I had anticipated.
None of this had been.
How did this happen?

2. IN THE BEGINNING

The future held much excitement!
I met the man I would marry.

"And the Lord God said, 'It is not good that man should be alone;
I will make a helper comparable to him.'"
(Genesis 2:18 NKJV)

Before meeting Jacob, I encountered the Lord and He captured my heart.

Early On

It was freshman year of college. Excited that a very attractive friend suggested we meet weekly for lunch, I prioritized it in my schedule. He was nice, athletic, and loved the Lord. Those weekly lunches became a turning point in my life. My friend would say things like, "I'm trying to give God more of my life, to invite Him into areas of my life that I have withheld from Him until now." This was a new concept. Fascinated, I listened intently to what he shared and determined I wanted to give my life to God.

Although I'd been to church before, I never understood how to give my *daily* life over to God. After meeting with my friend, I began to understand what this could look like. It was about surrendering things to the Lord. Trusting Him. Living to follow Jesus' ways. *What could I surrender? Fear.* The words from my childhood friend's scary story echoed in my mind, "And then, something grabbed her toes while she was on the bed." *Ever since I heard that story when I was young, I have always needed to have my feet covered. Okay, God. I trust you. Tonight I won't cover my feet when I go to sleep.* It was a small step, but it was the first time I began to practice trusting God and not letting fear reign over me. Gradually, I surrendered more and more of my heart to the Lord.

At the turn of the semester, I joined a women's Bible study at the prompting of a friend. I soon began reading the Bible for myself, and God became very real to me. Reading the Word of God and being connected with people who loved the Lord helped me as I developed my own relationship with God.

Attending weekly church services became a part of my new routine. Growing up, I'd believed, intellectually, that Jesus died for my sins, but I didn't know what it meant to surrender my life to Him. I had never sought God before or tried to listen to the Holy Spirit. Put simply, although I had known *about* God while growing up, I did not *know* God until college. After beginning my personal relationship with Jesus freshman year, I learned the importance of prayer and the Lord continued to show me what it looked like to follow Him.

A few months after beginning my walk with the Lord, a classmate made a comment that stumped me, "I would only date someone if he was Christian." Perplexed, I asked, "Really? Why?" I didn't understand her perspective. *What's the big deal? I almost dated a Hindu, but his parents wouldn't approve of a cross-cultural relationship, so we agreed to be friends. I'm a Christian and we got along fine.*

As I continued to grow in my faith, I encountered the Lord and He transformed my heart. Eventually, I too wanted only to be with a Christian man. Being with a Christian man would allow God to be at the center of our relationship, allow us to grow together in our faith, and ensure we shared many of the same values.

A Desire Fulfilled

While attending a campus church service one day, I saw Jacob for the first time. Immediately, he caught my attention. I hoped for the opportunity to spend time with him. He was incredible—very intelligent, gifted with music, and super passionate. During my junior year of college, we became friends.

I was drawn to Jacob. He was one of the most passionate people I had ever known. I admired him and imagined what it might be like if we were together someday. There was a spark he had that was contagious when he shared his faith with others. When I was around Jacob, I believed anything was possible.

The idea of being more than friends with Jacob seemed almost too good to be true. From the time I was a little girl, I both hoped and expected to one day have a husband and children. But feelings of inadequacy mixed with deep insecurities caused me to feel like it was fitting if men didn't notice me. I didn't think I was someone who Jacob would ever see as more than a friend. However, after being friends for a couple years, Jacob did see me as more.

Once we were engaged, the fear of being unloved was eased. I had found my match. Surely, we would have an amazing future together.

Jacob and I looked forward to our lives together. I would be graduating college in May and we reasoned it would be best to get married immediately following my college graduation. During the several months of our engagement, I completed my schooling, planned for the wedding, and prayed often about our life together.

It became common in my prayer life for the Lord to show me mental pictures. I often did not know how I should respond or what exactly to pray for when I saw those. Finally, I realized I should ask God what those images meant. The images were usually symbolic—providing insight into a particular situation, showing me the state of someone's heart, or prompting me to pray for certain things.

There Will Be Hard Times Ahead

Oddly, on three different occasions when I prayed about my future with Jacob an image came into my mind of a bumpy dirt road. As I pondered the bumpy dirt road, I understood this to be God showing me it would be a hard road ahead. With almost no hesitation I responded, "That's okay Lord, I still want to marry Jacob."

Each Sunday volunteers offered to pray with people after church service. Reasoning that prayer was not reserved for only major requests and understanding God cared about every area of each person's life, I often went forward for prayer. My requests varied. Sometimes I requested prayer for family, health, direction in life, or anything else that seemed like a good idea to pray about.

One day, halfway through my engagement to Jacob, I went forward after service and the person who prayed for me said the Holy Spirit brought an image to mind of a rose bush during the prayer. Realizing the Holy Spirit is the part of God that brings people insight regarding God's heart, I understood that He speaks to people through a variety of ways and can provide direction, guidance, warning, encouragement, or confirmation. So, I was attentive to what this man of prayer told me. Making eye contact with me, he explained, "Roses have thorns and that is symbolizing there will be tough times ahead." I did not want to believe that could be true. *I am about to get married. Things will be great.* In actuality, though, what the man shared was confirmation to what the Lord had already shown me—it would be a difficult road ahead. I guess I just didn't fully comprehend how Jacob and I would face difficult times because I was still star-struck at the idea of marrying him.

During most of our friendship Jacob had been dedicated to following the Lord. However, shortly before we became engaged, Jacob moved to an area about 40 minutes away from his Christian friends. That time of seclusion was difficult for Jacob; he wasn't consistent about following the Lord when he was isolated from other Christians.

One day when I was visiting him at his apartment, Jacob said, "When I was in the shower, the Lord asked me, 'Will you not make a sacrifice for the Kingdom [of God]?' I know God was referring to drinking." Assuming Jacob's answer to the Lord had been yes, I decided to aid him in this goal of not drinking and vowed that I would never drink alcohol again. *No sense in him being tempted because I am having a glass of wine or something. We will be getting married in a few months. Since God asked Jacob to give up drinking, I should do the same. That will make me a supportive wife.*

I knew Jacob had been struggling in his walk with the Lord but believed his heart for God would be rekindled as we began preparing for married life. It was obvious to both of us that God had great plans for Jacob. We believed he would be called to the ministry someday.

Married Life Begins

After a short, five-month engagement, the day came. June 17, a beautiful day for a wedding. It was a sunny and hot, somewhere between 80 and 90 degrees, but perfect! I hurried about, finishing up the last minute odds and ends, then slipped into my ivory wedding dress with delicate blue flower beads and sparkles sewn on top. Next came the veil my mom and family friend had created for me. I was ready to meet my groom.

On cue, the pianist began "Here Comes the Bride!" Walking down the aisle, I was in awe of the wonderful fact that I would be able to spend my life with this man. I was marrying the man of my dreams! After some time of worship music, speaking to the guests, and the exchange of vows, my groom lifted the veil and kissed me. Jacob tenderly held my face in his hands so we wouldn't bump noses.

In the movies, I'd seen grooms carry their brides. I thought all grooms were supposed to hold their bride that way at some point during their wedding day. Apparently Jacob hadn't gotten the memo. When I jumped into his arms unexpectedly, it was obvious my new groom was struggling to hold me up. Taking him by surprise the way I did, I was fortunate he didn't drop me! Thinking all grooms picked up their brides was just a silly example of the many misconceptions I had going into marriage.

When the honeymoon week was over, I moved into Jacob's apartment and we began married life together. While Jacob worked in town, I studied for my upcoming teaching certification test and ran errands. Each day, I looked forward to my husband's return. *I wonder what we will do tonight when Jacob gets home.* A few options were likely. Swimming in a nearby pool or venturing to the lake were a couple ways we escaped the summer heat. Sitting in the living room of our small apartment while Jacob strummed his guitar and sang was something we both enjoyed. He was an awesome musician. Other times, we would walk around the local video store. The new releases were too expensive so we would usually select an old flick to watch for the night. Spending time with my husband was so special to me. When we went places together, I lit up because I was proud to be his wife.

Occasionally, I tried my hand at cooking. Making dinner was a special way I could serve my husband. Household chores were no bother to me because I was happy to serve Jacob. It was a privilege to be his helpmate.

Seeing myself as a helpmate is a concept I got from the story of Adam and Eve. After God created the first man, Adam, He said, "It is not good for the man to be alone; I will make him a helper suitable for him" (Genesis 2:18, NASB). God then made Adam's helpmate, Eve. Like Adam, Jacob would not have to be alone anymore, and I was glad to be the one chosen to keep his company.

As his helpmate, at first, I thought I should meet Jacob's every need. But I simply wasn't able to. My lack of athleticism proved that. He wanted to feel challenged when he played sports. One day I told Jacob I didn't feel I could give him everything he needed. To my relief, he explained I didn't need to be the source for *everything*. For example, he had friends who challenged him when he played tennis.

The concept that *I* didn't need to be his source for all things—whether it was challenging him at sports, discussing literature, encouraging him, or providing fellowship—may have been obvious to most other people. However, I did not understand that until after Jacob pointed it out to me. It made sense when I thought about it. Of course he would need others in his life who related to him differently than me. For example, he had male friends who were able to mentor and encourage him in ways I couldn't. A weight was lifted off my shoulders with the realization that I was not responsible for meeting Jacob's *every* need.

Opposites Attract

Often, opposites attract. That was the case with Jacob and me. My husband and I were different from each other in multiple ways—personality, gifts, and hobbies. We complemented each other well. For example, I hated dust, dirt, and grime; Jacob hated clutter. Together, we kept a clean home. Jacob was intellectual and had a passion for books, whereas I was relational and had a passion for people. He was mechanically inclined and I appreciated the fact that he could do basic maintenance on our vehicles. I also admired his athleticism. It was fun having him teach me how to play racquetball at the gym. When he considered training for a marathon, I thought it was a great idea. Surely he could run a marathon; he could do anything! I believed with all my heart Jacob could accomplish anything he set his mind to.

I loved that my husband was musically gifted, playing both the acoustic guitar and djembe very well. He used his gift sometimes to serve on the church worship team. I vividly remember Jacob playing his guitar for me one day when I was very sick and he didn't know what else to do for me. Laying nauseous on the floor, I felt comforted by the music and really appreciated his kind gesture.

We both shared the belief that the Bible is true. Jacob was gifted in the prophetic, meaning that he often heard from the Lord. Often, Jacob discerned what things needed to be prayed over people. One day after we'd prayed for my college roommate, she looked at me and said, "He prayed everything that was in my heart." I wasn't surprised. Jacob was sensitive to the promptings of the Holy Spirit and He knows everything that is in a person's heart. My experience was different. Dreams and visual images were a significant way God spoke to me. Together, we made a good team to minister to others. Having different giftings equipped us well for that.

Growth in Spiritual Gifts

During my college years, I'd spent time with Christians who operated in a variety of spiritual gifts and saw the importance of having a spiritual mentor. I realized people may hear from God in a variety of ways, and came to understand that visual images could be a way the Lord speaks to someone in prayer. I also learned about the gift of prophecy—where someone hears the Lord speak and shares what He is saying.

One day at church, a visiting pastor who had the gift of prophecy heard the Lord say I would have dreams and visions. In my heart I responded, *Yes, God, I want You to give me dreams and visions!* Eagerly anticipating when the Lord would speak to me in those ways, I told Him how much I wanted those gifts.

After a couple months, I decided that I'd waited long enough. *Everyone's gone tonight. I am going to insist that God give me dreams.* In the empty house, I began to cry out to God. Shouting, I declared, "You have dreams for me. I want dreams!" I understood sometimes prophetic words should be prayed so they can come to pass. My approach may have seemed a bit irreverent, but I was desperate for more of God. I wanted everything He had for me, including dreams. That night, I dreamed my ears were being cleaned out. Afterward, I began to dream more and more often.

Journaling my dreams became an important part of my day. I was careful not to dismiss dreams without evaluating them and coming before the Lord. I felt the need to consider every dream because I did not want to miss something God might be revealing. I realized a person's subconscious can influence dreams and understood not every dream is a message from God. Journaling and prayer helped me discern what was from God and what wasn't. I longed to be close to God, to hear from Him. In addition to journaling my dreams and further developing my personal prayer life, I also made a point to read the Scriptures.

Teaching Job

A couple months following the wedding, I received my teaching certification and prayed about my job situation. The same night I prayed about what God had for me with regard to a teaching position, I had a dream that I was on the phone with someone named Ryan talking about a job. After getting up the next day, I pondered the dream and decided to call a colleague of mine from college named Ryan. I'd not seen him in a while and assumed he was pursuing a teaching job. No sooner had I greeted him before he told me about a school district who was looking for science teachers. Pleased to hear his comment, I said, "I thought you would know about a job opening for me," and told him about my dream.

I applied for the high school science teacher position in the district Ryan told me about and got hired merely four days before the school year began. Agreed that I should take the position, Jacob and I were excited for our new venture. Quickly, we prepared for our move across the state.

Although hurried and a bit stressed, we managed. While I was at the school, Jacob apartment-hunted. Within a week of starting the new job, we found the apartment that would be perfect for us. After moving everything into our new apartment, we looked around and let out a satisfied sigh, knowing our future was being shaped by this move.

The New Environment

Relocating made us dependent on my salary until Jacob found a job in our new community. Before we moved, Jacob had been working as an alarm technician. With his skill-set and variety of work experience, we assumed that him finding a job would be no problem. Jacob had a good work ethic and took pride in his work. He loved to be challenged and learn new things.

I didn't realize until later—when jobs were hard to find—how much working was a factor in Jacob's self-confidence. Thankfully Jacob did find some work in our new location, but the jobs he found were seasonal or temporary. Sometimes those jobs came with challenging environments where he worked with people who were not edifying to be around. One of his bosses even dealt drugs on the side.

Knowing the importance of my salary gave me the strength to go into work each day, even when I did not want to. Being a new, young, female teacher in an inner city school was quite difficult! There was a lack of resources, challenging students, and a cultural environment to which I was not accustomed. Many of the students came from broken homes, and had concerns like whether or not they would eat later that day or need to fight someone after school. Having basic needs not met and an underlying sense of insecurity made it hard for my students to retain much academically. I was confident the Lord had placed me there, and hoped to help my students see that life didn't have to consist of teenage pregnancy and fighting.

School became my life. I didn't want my job to be all-consuming. I would have rather spent time with my husband. But I didn't know how to separate myself from my work. Between being new, not feeling confident in my abilities as a teacher, having very limited resources, and grading student work, I felt a constant tug to be working on lessons and things for school. This imbalance in my life took away a fair amount of attention from my husband.

At times, I felt slighted by the breadth of all my responsibilities, especially with my husband not working the majority of the time. Jacob didn't usually take initiative by asking if he could help somehow. It was hard not be frustrated. *He should be offering to help me grade. I have so much work to do and he is just sitting there reading.* Sometimes I would ask for his assistance, but he didn't seem eager to help. Yet, there were some glimpses of my husband's thoughtfulness, like the day he came by the school and dropped off flowers for me. Those flowers were a nice addition to my classroom.

Unstable Work

My second semester of teaching, the school district redistributed the students and my original teaching position was eliminated. So, I substitute taught for the remainder of the year. During that time, funds were very tight.

The temporary jobs Jacob worked helped with our finances. However, his jobs were not long-lasting and were sometimes weather dependent. My husband wanted to work but felt discouraged by the lack of jobs available. When there was work, if it didn't incorporate Jacob's acquired skills, that also disappointed him. He wanted to apply himself to something.

Provision

During that first year of teaching, Jacob and I had seen God provide for us both through job opportunities as well as generous gifts from others. As the weekend of our first anniversary approached, we scarcely had enough to make ends meet. Our one-year anniversary fell on a Sunday, so we attended church as usual. A woman, whom we'd seen at the church once or twice, was in the pew behind us and asked us to speak with her after service. Unsure of what she wanted with us, we were astounded when she handed us a card containing a check for $350! She barely knew our names and knew nothing about our situation, but the previous week, the Lord had spoken to her. In the card was a verse the Lord had given her to share with us, Jeremiah 29:11,

"For I know the thoughts that I think toward you, says the Lord, thoughts of peace and not of evil, to give you a future and a hope" (NKJV). We were very thankful for the Lord's provision in our lives. He provided for us in a variety of ways, and each month we had enough to pay our bills.

Time Together

As the school year came to a close, I got to see first-hand the new project Jacob started. He took that summer to fix his purple and silver 1983 Honda Magna motorcycle. Jacob had never done anything like this engine repair before. However, using just his natural talents, the motorcycle manual, and an occasional phone call to a friend, he managed to dismantle and reassemble the entire thing! That was a big project, especially because we were in an upstairs apartment and didn't have a garage. He and his buddy had taken all the engine parts up the stairs of the two-story apartment complex and set them in our spare bedroom. My desk became Jacob's workshop. At times my husband would fall asleep with the manual on his chest. He worked very hard on that engine repair, and I was proud of him. To me, this was just a tangible example of how he could accomplish *anything* he put his mind to.

That motorcycle was his baby. Taking rides together on the motorcycle was something we both really enjoyed. Riding near the vineyards in the fall was especially nice. The aroma of ripened grapes saturated the air while we cruised down the paved back roads.

Spending time with friends from church was also something we enjoyed. There were two couples our age whom we considered some of our best friends. All of us got along very well and looked forward to our get-togethers. For about two years, we built a friendship with those couples and invested in each other's lives. My husband's knowledge of the Bible allowed him to make a great impact on people as he challenged them to apply the concepts in Scripture.

Over time, I saw the growth in my friends' husbands as they became more rooted in their faith. It was incredible to see their spiritual growth when they accepted Jacob's challenge to memorize Romans 12:1-2, "I beseech you therefore, brethren, by the mercies of God, that you present your bodies a living sacrifice, holy, acceptable to God, which is your reasonable service. And do not be conformed to this world, but be transformed by the renewing of your mind, that you may prove what is that good and acceptable and perfect will of God" (NKJV). Memorizing Scripture and applying the concepts they discovered took their faith walk to a new level. The changes in them were due to a combination of prayer, attending church, and receiving mentorship from Jacob as the men spent time together.

Things Begin To Change

In the fall, I began a new teaching job at a neighboring district, which served as a stable source of income for us. We were grateful for the financial security. However, me serving as the primary provider caused stress in our relationship. Over time, things changed considerably between us and various challenges arose.

After coming home from work, I would often become a bit irritated. *Couldn't he clean while I am away?* Seeing the dishes in the sink, the laundry undone, or various other tasks not completed made it hard not to be upset with the way he spent his time. Not all of his time was ill-spent; it just felt like he didn't do the things I would have if I had been in his position.

Besides burning through several books in a week, Jacob also enjoyed playing videogames. Eventually, not having a consistent job became a great weight for him. To fill his time and dull the dissatisfaction of his circumstances, he took to unhealthy habits like viewing pornography and drinking. It would be a year before he told me about those sins in his life. Sin refers to breaking God's commandments or doing something contrary to the Lord's heart. It is sin that separates mankind from God, which is why Jesus died to pay for the sins of humanity and reconnect mankind to God. As drinking and pornography entangled Jacob, those addictions became a virus not only to his own personal relationship to God, but also to our marriage.

After opening Jacob's Bible one day, I noticed an inscription he had written, "Either this book will keep you from sin, or sin will keep you from this book." I contemplated how profound that statement was. Then, I watched Jacob's life unfold as the truth of that inscription became more and more evident.

3. THE DRINKING BEGAN

I had no idea my husband had a drinking problem, until one evening when he surprised me by informing me he had been drinking for most of our marriage.

"O God, You know my foolishness;
and my sins are not hidden from You."
(Psalm 69:5, NKJV)

Odd Behavior

At times, I noticed odd, erratic behavior. Suddenly, my husband would be very loud or say bizarre things. *Where is this coming from? This is so strange.* We would be in our apartment and Jacob would behave obnoxiously—for no good reason. I remember one particular phone call he made to the heating company and watching him overreact. Jacob's response surprised me. *That seemed so unnecessary.* He was diabetic, so I would sometimes suspect abnormal blood sugar levels to be the culprit. After pricking his finger and touching the tester, though, his blood sugar was rarely out of whack. Most of the time, there just seemed to be no good explanation.

What?!

One night, after attending a women's conference at church, I called my husband to say I would be home soon. Shortly into our phone conversation, Jacob said, "There is something I need to tell you." From the tone in his voice, I could tell that it would not be favorable news. My heart began to pound. *What could it be?* I braced myself in the remaining minutes of the drive down the local highway.

Entering the apartment, I found Jacob in the living room. Very concerned, I asked, "What is it? What's the matter?" Jacob then told me he had been drinking heavily for the last year. *What?!?!* This was a blow I hadn't anticipated.

I tried to take in and process what he just said. I had not seen this coming. *How did I not know? I feel like such a doofus. We have been married for a year and a half! How could I have been so dumb to not know?* A long time later, I learned that others had known for quite a while. They could smell it or see it in his behavior. I lived with him—how did I not know?.

This explained the erratic behavior I had seen and not understood. Questions swirled through my mind: *Who is Jacob with low blood sugar? Who is he with high blood sugar? Who is he when he's drunk? When he's sober with normal blood sugar levels?* This was so hard. I felt so dumb. And now, I didn't even know who my husband was. What was his personality really like? We got married as soon as I finished college. I had not spent that much time with him to *really* get to know him.

Before we got married I knew there'd been excessive drinking in Jacob's past. But while we were engaged, God had asked him to give up drinking. I thought back to the question posed to him two years earlier, "Will you not make a sacrifice for the kingdom?" I realized then, Jacob had probably never purposed in his heart to stop drinking, even though *I* had been diligent to refrain from alcohol since that day. Although a commitment for me not to drink was not a huge sacrifice, since I was never a big drinker, I had been rash in making a vow to never drink again. Naïvely, I'd *assumed* that Jacob's answer to God's request to give up alcohol had been something like, "Yes, Lord, I'll not drink anymore." I have since learned to never assume!

Thankfully my husband decided to reveal to me what had been happening. Keeping his behavior a secret would have prolonged his feeling of shame and become a rift between us. When Jacob was forthcoming about his drinking and told me he needed my help, that was a pivotal moment. The way I responded could determine the direction of our marriage.

In my attempt to help Jacob do the right thing, I responded in a way I later regretted. Instead of thanking Jacob for his confession, sympathizing with him for the struggle he'd faced, praying for him, and having a dialogue about our options to get help or counsel, I tried to control the situation.

During his confession, I'd keyed in on his comment, "I need your help." Standing in the middle of the living room, I tried to process the situation while Jacob sat on the couch looking forlorn. After I asked how I could help him, Jacob looked up, vulnerable and discouraged, and simply said, "I don't know." Since he didn't have an immediate answer, I came up with my own idea. In the minutes following his request for my help, I did the most logical thing I could think of—I took charge of all the money. This way, Jacob wouldn't be able to purchase alcohol, thus aiding him to stop drinking. That approach eventually backfired.

Money, Money, Money

The system I put in place would go like this: Jacob was not allowed to spend any money unless I monitored the purchase. Resentfully, Jacob agreed to let me be in control of our money. Then, the games began. Trying to sneak things without me knowing became my husband's way of life. Hiding his antics from me had already become routine with his addiction; now it would be financially also. He viewed life as a game. And I had just become one of his opponents.

Only a few people knew about my decision to take control of all our finances. Jacob's mom challenged me saying, "He will feel emasculated." Not giving much consideration to her concern, I justified my decision. *I have to do this. Otherwise, he will use money to purchase alcohol.*

Perhaps it could have worked to have an account where my husband could have accessed a small amount of money for running errands. It's hard to know for certain what the best approach would have been. Some people looking at our situation would say it was appropriate for me to take steps to protect my financial assets. After all, the joint person on the bank account was not contributing much financially and could have potentially emptied the account. However, to not allow Jacob *any* access to money restricted him too much. I never removed his name from our shared bank account, I just made it clear that I needed to be the one to handle all the cash.

As my husband, Jacob was supposed to be the designated leader of our relationship, but having monetary restrictions imposed on him stripped him of his ability to make basic decisions. This made it more challenging for him to function in the role of leader. Me calling all the shots and limiting my husband's access to finances did leave him feeling emasculated. Without access to money, Jacob was not able to make purchases—or certain decisions—and he felt powerless. Denying him the ability to freely use our funds for a while ended up not being such a good idea after all. That arrangement only prompted rebellion.

Wife or Mother?

My attempt to control Jacob's behavior altered our relationship significantly. At times, our relationship was more like a mother and son than a wife and husband. The transitional role I had entered—as a mother rather than a wife—made our relationship worse instead of better. This new dynamic created an emotional distance between us. Desperate to see Jacob's behavior change, I tried to force a change. However, that did not work. When there was something imposed on Jacob that he did not want to do, he rebelled.

My experience with Jacob was similar to what parents experience when their teenager resists control, craves independence, and rebels. Rather than realizing we were on the same team, Jacob viewed our relationship as "me vs. you" instead of "us".

Not only did Jacob's addiction to alcohol consume his time, focus, and heart, but so did a growing addiction to pornography. As the tentacles of those addictions latched onto him more tightly, the bondage in his life became more and more evident. Jacob's resentment of me also grew.

Jacob Goes To Bible College

Getting a college degree meant a lot to my husband. He wanted to feel accomplished. Although Jacob took some courses after high school, he hadn't completed college. Eagerly anticipating the accomplishment of getting a degree, my husband enrolled in Bible college. Initially, we agreed that school would be a priority for him over working until he was finished with his education.

Bible college was a logical next step for Jacob. He was already well-versed in the Scriptures. Aiding in his ability to know the Bible very well was Jacob's ability to read anything very quickly and remember most of the text. This allowed him to memorize great portions of Scripture with little effort. This became apparent one night when I randomly picked a book from the Bible and began reading. While Jacob played video games, I read aloud a line of Scripture from Philippians chapter two. Playfully, I said, "Tell me what comes next." Almost verbatim, he told me what came after it. *Wow!* I continued this game for a while longer. Stunned at his accuracy, I processed the remarkable ability he had. *When was the last time he read Philippians chapter two? Probably not for a while. What a gift he has!*

My husband loved to read so much that when I told him about an elderly man at the nursing home who couldn't read because he needed new glasses, Jacob's compassion was stirred. Considering the man's situation, he said, "I can't imagine not being able to read." And, with my blessing, Jacob found the man I'd told him about and paid for him to get new prescription glasses.

Jacob placed a great deal of value on learning and wanted to be intellectually challenged. He looked forward to majoring in Greek because that's the language the New Testament was originally written in. Jacob believed that by knowing Greek, he could more thoroughly understand the Scriptures. He had a long commute, but school was very important to him. Twice a week, he got on his motorcycle and rode an hour and half to class. At times his commute was kind of intense. One day, he came home and said, "Someone tried to kill me today! I was riding in the far left lane and a truck moved into my lane. I almost had nowhere to go!" Despite the dangers and stress of commuting in the city traffic, Jacob *loved* riding his motorcycle.

21

Shhhh…

As time progressed, we seldom had friends over because I wanted to showcase the best side of Jacob. If friends came to our house, it was always possible that Jacob had been drinking and would act strange. Here we were, a couple in our twenties without children, and we rarely spent time with friends. There were many people I would have loved to have invited over for dinner or spent time with, but I was cautious before making commitments. Arrangements for entertaining company were generally made at least a day or two in advance. That way, Jacob could be on his best behavior and hopefully stay sober for their visit.

I tried to keep Jacob's drinking a secret and did not ask others for their input. Primarily, I didn't want people to know about Jacob's unfavorable lifestyle. Secondly, I didn't want them to say my husband's drinking was an issue that he couldn't help and come up with excuses for his decisions. Although desperate for the problems to go away, I wasn't too keen on obtaining advice from others.

Hiding my husband's alcoholism was not because I didn't trust the people around me. It was because I wanted them to see Jacob as a man of God—as the person he was supposed to be, the person I knew he could be without the bondage he was wrapped up in.

Only my siblings and a couple other carefully selected people knew about Jacob's excessive drinking. Keeping the struggles of my marriage a secret limited my access to wise counsel. My siblings, although wonderful, had little experience with this kind of situation.

Over the years I'd heard people say alcoholics couldn't help themselves. I utterly detested the thought that someone might justify Jacob's behavior. *They are going to try to tell me he can't help it. Well, that is unacceptable. Drinking is a choice, plain and simple!* I was desperate for Jacob's drinking to stop and believed it was simply a matter of Jacob getting right with God. The thought of pursuing counseling was not one I considered. Either I honestly didn't think it would help, or when it was suggested I quickly dismissed it because I was not interested in what some person had to say about the situation—I wanted God's intervention.

Rehab

Several months following his initial confession to me about his drinking, my husband enrolled in a month-long rehabilitation program. That June, while he stayed at the off-site rehab program about an hour from home, I was able to visit him twice. One visit was to celebrate our second anniversary. To make it special, we had a picnic outside, next to the facility. Jacob described some of the ways drinking and its associated bondages had impacted the people in the program. He particularly noted one of the people he met who hallucinated as a result of the extreme alcohol withdrawals. We winced at the thought of how terrible it would be to be affected that way.

After finishing rehab, it was not long before Jacob resumed drinking. Eventually, he tried to quit again, but the physical repercussions made it hard. Refraining from the hard liquor made his blood sugar levels run high. Jacob also experienced delirium tremens, a horrible withdrawal effect that made his hands shake. Sometimes the shaking was fairly minor, other times it was extreme.

Watching Jacob's hand rapidly waver back and forth as he tried to drink from a glass one day made it apparent how much those shaky hands were affecting the simple tasks of daily life. Going through withdrawal symptoms was awful. Attending school became especially difficult. How could he take notes or write with shaky hands? Withdrawal symptoms like that served as a strong negative reinforcement, making it very difficult for him to quit drinking.

Bible School Ends

Diligently, Jacob attended Bible college for about a year and a half. I noted how his daily lifestyle did not uphold the values of his Bible college. It enraged me to see the hypocrisy in his life. Although it was school policy for enrollees to refrain from drinking alcohol, Jacob still drank. The frustration from his shaky hands that accompanied his occasional sobriety, coupled with a lack of self-restraint, meant it was only a matter of time before Jacob would return to drinking and be dismissed from the school. Surely his drinking would eventually come to light. And it did.

Devastated one day, Jacob came home and sat in his golden-yellow arm chair. He then told me how the school staff discovered he had been drinking. By attending that school, he had knowingly entered into an agreement that he would not drink during the time he was enrolled there.

Despite his blatant disregard for their policy, the school was quite gracious in their response to Jacob. One of the senior college staff had spoken with my husband and was willing to work with him. They wanted success for Jacob but believed there had to be accountability for his actions. The staff discussed the option for Jacob to return to school. If he would take the steps necessary to stop drinking, they were willing to allow him to come back under certain conditions. He implemented some of their recommendations, but not all, and did not return to school.

My husband felt like he'd failed. For years, he held onto this incident and perceived it as a grave failure. Jacob, like many people, didn't respond well to failure. The disappointment he experienced seemed to provide an excuse for why he shouldn't try to succeed at something else. Shame from failure can be a strong hindrance to moving forward and trying something again. Sometimes people are unable to forgive themselves or feel unworthy of a second chance. Other times, fear of failure (or even a fear of success) keeps someone from trying again.

4. EROSION

Being angry and simply wanting something to change doesn't mean it will.

"For the wrath of man does not produce the righteousness of God."
(James 1:20, NKJV)

Ambulance Calls

Alcohol not only caused issues in our marriage and Jacob's school, but also affected Jacob physiologically. The impact of hard liquor on Jacob's body became apparent to me after some time.

One morning I was getting ready for work and came to the bedroom. Standing in the entranceway, I looked over and saw my husband awake in bed. He looked terrified! Jacob's eyes were opened very wide and his jaw was clenched. *What is it?* Worried, I tried to understand what was happening and asked him, "What's the matter??" Offering no response to my question, he just laid there. *Why is he is so scared?!* I tried to quickly assess what it was that could be frightening him but didn't know. Then it hit me. *His blood sugar must be very low.*

I called 9-1-1 and retrieved the glucose serum from our cupboard that his family had instructed me to use if this ever happened. Distraught, I tried to draw the sugar solution into the syringe. Only half of the serum could be drawn out of the bottle because of how the needle was positioned. *I can't get all the serum out! Ugh. The needle is too long. Half of the serum will have to do.*

As I approached Jacob with the syringe, he tried to roll away from me. Even though he had not been able to respond to me or my questions, it seemed he was able to recognize the needle! Doing my best to hold him down, I plunged the needle into Jacob's left buttock and injected the serum.

He had a bruise for days. I later realized that although it had been a fight to give him the injection, I didn't need to be so forceful about it.

When the medics arrived and checked his blood sugar they determined it was not necessary for him to go to the hospital. The serum took about 20 minutes to get his levels up to where he could get something to eat and get stabilized. I was so thankful he was ok!

Trying to draw up all the serum into the syringe and not being able to extract all of it had been so frustrating. It was not until I was sitting at work later that day, that I suddenly realized if I had lowered the needle, I could have drawn up all the serum from the bottle. What was obvious to me under normal circumstances was not at all apparent to me while I had been in the midst of such a stressful situation. Stress, like many emotions, can cause someone to not think clearly.

Two or three weeks passed and a similar incident occurred. Immediately, I recognized what was happening and called 9-1-1. This time, we didn't have the glucose serum, so I grabbed chocolate cake frosting and squeezed some onto my finger. Using my best attempt to open Jacob's mouth while he kept maneuvering away from me, I rubbed the frosting on his inner cheek. That way the sugar would dissolve and get into his system. It was quite the struggle! Soon there was chocolate frosting smeared all over the bed.

Several minutes after the medics arrived, Jacob's blood sugar had risen enough that he gained clarity of mind. He was deeply disturbed as he looked to the area around him on the bed and asked, "What happened?" *Ohhhh. He must be thinking that he lost control of himself and had an accident in the bed.* At that point, I realized brown frosting had not been the best choice because it bore a close resemblance to the color of certain body functions. I made a mental note to choose purple or neon blue frosting in case something like that happened in the future. That way, when Jacob regained clarity of consciousness he would not be accosted with a similar concern.

Finding my husband unresponsive on two mornings in less than a month's time troubled me deeply. I'd just started a new job, making twice what I had as a teacher. Jacob and I were excited about the financial blessing this would be for us. However, I had not yet been there long enough to have medical insurance.

If Jacob needed to take a trip to the hospital, it could be very costly. That weighed on my mind a bit, but what really troubled me was knowing I worked Monday through Friday and could not always be there to check on him. Concerns reeled through my mind. *How will I know if Jacob is ok? He rarely gets up when I do, so I won't know how he is doing before I leave for work. It almost seems like I should be home every day to make sure my husband is all right. What if this happens and I am not here, or I don't know if his sugar is running low?*

As a Type 1 Diabetic, Jacob was constantly faced with the need to maintain an appropriate blood sugar level. Something about the hard liquor made his blood sugar run low. When he stopped drinking, his levels would spike. Spikes in blood sugar can cause the body to release ketones. Persistent elevated blood sugar where ketones are released can eventually cause nerve damage; this happens when diabetics are not vigilant about controlling their blood sugar. Some diabetics eventually get amputations of their fingers or toes, or even hands or feet, due to extensive nerve damage. Many diabetics do not maintain control of their blood sugar, regardless of alcohol.

Jacob had been a diabetic since before the age of 2 years old. So, he grew up knowing the importance of taking care of his body and was usually able to keep his blood sugar levels under control. Eventually, though, his addiction to alcohol seemed to override his obligation to health. It was difficult seeing someone I love make such destructive choices.

Frustrations

Though desperate to see transformation in Jacob's life, I didn't know how to help him. I watched as the course of his life continued to turn in an unfavorable direction. I knew no one could be perfect. However, my attention kept getting drawn to my husband's shortcomings and the disappointments I had in my marriage. Seeing that drunken look on Jacob's face made it difficult not to feel discouraged and angry.

Thinking about the fact that I often had to drive if we went *anywhere* stirred up even more disappointment. Knowing I needed to drive was frustrating because I wanted to use the long commutes when visiting relatives or going on vacation to be productive, to complete my reviews for work or study for training. For shorter driving distances to visit friends or go to the store, I wanted to at least have the option of having Jacob drive. It was my opinion that if he drove when we went somewhere—particularly to a friend's house—it would subtly present him as the leader of our relationship. I longed for my husband to step into his role as the head of our home but felt like I needed to step up instead.

I wished I could go places with Jacob, but his behavior was unpredictable. Before going out in public with him, I first weighed the risk. When he had been drinking, there was no telling what he might do. One extreme example that comes to mind was when we went to visit relatives across the state. During the long drive—going at least 70 miles per hour down the highway—Jacob decided to make an obscene gesture to a truck driver nearby (I am still not sure why). The passenger window of our van was broken, so in order to make sure the truck driver saw him, Jacob opened the passenger door to stick his hand outside of the vehicle. Shocked, I yelled out, "What are you doing?! Close the door, please!" His destructive lifestyle and the unpredictability of his behavior grated on me. I wanted my husband to be in his right mind!

Jacob's decisions brought him deep into bondage. It seemed he couldn't break free from the need to drink or the anger and depression he felt. I understood that God had purchased freedom for each person. My husband did not have to be bound by addictions forever. *Jacob knows the Bible, he should press in for deliverance.* Ultimately, it was up to Jacob whether or not he embraced the forgiveness, healing, and peace that God could release to him. To lay hold of those things, Jacob would need to ask God for them and be obedient to what the Lord directed. I often wondered, *When will he get free from his bondage?*

My husband's lifestyle was not what I thought it should be. Frustration constantly bubbled under the surface of my emotions. I fluctuated between being infuriated and devastated. To me, it seemed very simple—he should just stop buying alcohol and stop drinking. Although I tried to control the money, I wasn't 100% successful. Jacob still purchased alcohol often enough to fuel his frequent habit. Our marriage was indeed going down a bumpy road.

Productivity Gradually Fades

Drinking seemed to overtake Jacob's life in many ways, but he still tried to be productive at times. For example, shortly after returning from rehab, Jacob was feeling motivated and built an awesome wooden bookcase from scratch. He worked diligently to ensure the angles and measurements lined up just right. Our small apartment served as his workshop and inevitably sawdust got on our living room carpet, but that didn't bother me much. I knew he was focused on the project at hand. He kept me updated me on the project and I was always happy to see what he'd accomplished.

After explaining that he needed to put feet (wooden pegs) on the bottom of the bookshelf, an idea was sparked between the two of us to put actual wooden feet at its base. I loved the unique bookshelf, with what looked like someone's feet poking out from underneath it. I was thankful Jacob had done something constructive with his time and was very impressed with his accomplishment.

As time passed, my husband's productivity gradually faded. Jacob pulled into his own personal shell. I knew what God intended for Jacob's life was much different than the state of bondage he was living in. One of many Bible passages indicating that God had more for Jacob and wanted to bring him out of the darkness, is 1 Peter 2:9, "But you are a chosen generation, a royal priesthood, a holy nation, His own special people, that you may proclaim the praises of Him who *called you out of darkness into His marvelous light*" (NKJV). God's marvelous light encompasses truth and freedom. It is the complete opposite of bondage.

Constant Monitoring

Eventually, Jacob drank about two bottles (a fifth of a gallon each) of whiskey during a given week. Sometimes he would go through a bottle and a half in just a few days. Sneaking and checking the levels of his liquor bottles was almost an obsession to me at times. As I focused on how frequently he drank, I seethed with anger.

Seeing the glazed look in his eye that washed over him each time he drank grated on me. I wanted my husband back, not this drunken man. Living his life inebriated wasn't going to help Jacob accomplish his God-given destiny or allow him to utilize his talents or gifts to the full extent. Hearing the lid to his blue, wooden storage box open and shut throughout the day made it easy to figure out where he hid his liquor. In our small apartment, I could hear him retrieve his bottle of whiskey as soon as I left the room.

One day I finally said, "No more alcohol in the apartment." He would need to keep it somewhere else if he was going to keep drinking. Thankfully Jacob honored that request and began keeping his liquor supply in his car. He then made frequent trips outside to the parking lot of our apartment complex. After my husband exited the apartment, I would go to the bedroom window. Pulling back the blinds, I would watch him go out and sip his liquor. I spied on him like that fairly often. This fueled my anger, making me feel like I had a stronger case against him.

Instead of seeing Jacob as someone who needed help, I was self-righteous and did not understand why he simply didn't stop drinking. Angry and despairing, I wallowed in self-pity because I was married to a man who knew the Word of God inside and out but didn't have a surrendered heart to the Lord. There were many days that I felt *intense* frustration. Waking up ready to be offended makes for a miserable existence.

Anger Simmers

While attending a Christian concert with some friends one night, Jacob began to worship the Lord. Immediately, when I saw him I started thinking about the lifestyle my husband maintained and it made me angry. Rather than being thankful he was reaching out to the Lord, I stood in front of him so I wouldn't have to look at him.

Instead of getting upset at the concert, I should have been rejoicing. God loves when people who are struggling reach out to Him—He loves when anyone reaches out to Him. I knew full well that the whole reason Jesus came and died was because God knew people would have imperfections and struggles. My husband's addictions had not taken God by surprise. The Lord wanted to meet Jacob right where he was in life, and show him how to walk in freedom. I knew this. But my heart was hard. Self-righteousness and resentment sometimes won the battle in my heart over logic.

My bondage was not to alcohol; it was to a host of negative emotions and a poor attitude. Instead of separating myself emotionally from the detrimental decisions Jacob made, I was tormented with frustration and anger. I hated feeling the way I did but had no idea I could be set free from those feelings. Rather than ruling over my emotions, at times I was a slave to them. Yielding to negativity and staying in that place of emotional turmoil, is not where I ever want to be again. Living with an undercurrent of anger steals my joy, can keep me stuck in the past, and causes me to squander the present. I would much rather let God, in His grace and wisdom, fully guide my heart.

One day the Lord dealt with me about my constant stream of anger—it was as though cold water had been splashed on my face. I was struck by these words: "the wrath of man does not produce the righteousness of God" (James 1:20, NKJV). Reading that verse, I suddenly realized being angry would not bring about the changes I desperately wanted to see in my husband.

Light and Darkness

Reflecting on my relationship with Jacob, I can see the wisdom in not marrying someone who is in a very different place spiritually. To those who follow Jesus, it is said, "Do not be unequally yoked together with unbelievers. For what fellowship has righteousness with lawlessness? And what communion has light with darkness?" (2 Corinthians 6:14, NKJV). This Scripture indicates that someone who has a close relationship with Jesus and follows Him should not enter into a marriage together with a person who does not. Mentally acknowledging Jesus is real is not the same as being in a relationship with Him.

If a believer is partnered with an unbeliever, the believer's passion for the Lord can easily become diminished. The unbeliever may not be interested in the things of God or may not support the believer's desire to foster a relationship with the Lord—attend Bible study or church, read the Bible, listen to worship music, pray, or follow the Lord's promptings—thus, hindering the believer's growth in the Lord. Additionally, complications can arise when trying to raise children in the faith.

Both Jacob and I believed that Jesus is the Son of God, but without each of us being surrendered to the Lord, we were, in a way, unequally yoked. My husband and I seemed to have very different values. This made us frustrated with each other. Jacob often resented me and detested any words of correction I offered.

Because we each felt hindered by the other person, Jacob and I were both miserable. We got along well when we watched a movie together, but most other times there seemed to be a constant tension. Still, I loved my husband. I desperately wanted to see him set free from the bondage that encased him and was certain that someday he would be delivered.

Although it did not do any good, I would try to reason with him and explain that he had to stop viewing pornography and drinking. *Maybe if I tell him this time, he will listen and decide to change.* At times, he didn't disagree. He knew he needed to stop those things, but he either didn't know how or lacked the intrinsic motivation and self-discipline necessary. Jacob once commented that when he spent time reading the Bible he was able to refrain from drinking. Unfortunately, reading the Bible was not something he did consistently.

My words rarely seemed to have any impact on my husband. *Me* realizing something and pointing it out to him did not produce change in his life, he needed to come to *his* own realization.

One day, I was reading the Bible and saw these words: "He who disdains instruction despises his own soul, but he who heeds rebuke gets understanding" (Proverbs 15:32, NKJV). Naturally, my thoughts turned to Jacob. Later that day, I asked him, "Do you like yourself?" Unfortunately, his response aligned with what I'd read, "No, I hate myself." I realized then, how much self-disdain was influencing Jacob's decisions.

5. HINDSIGHT IS 20/20

There was hardship living together.
Having different values made it difficult to get along.

"Nevertheless let each one of you in particular so love his own wife as himself,
and let the wife see that she respects her husband."
(Ephesians 5:33, NKJV)

Trying to Force a Change

After knowing about Jacob's drinking for nearly a year, frustrations had accumulated and someone very close to Jacob recommended I consider moving out. This person reasoned it would help Jacob come to grips with his drinking issue. *Perhaps me leaving for a while could help my husband face his lifestyle choices.* Because this opinion came from an individual who loves Jacob very much and was a Christian, the suggestion held a lot of weight with me. I prayed about it for a couple minutes, opened the Bible, laid eyes on a Scripture from Jeremiah that mentioned foreigners and figured it could be applied to this situation because I would be "leaving my land." I had no witness in my spirit that I should leave or that God was actually speaking that verse in response to my situation. But, in the five minutes I gave God to answer me, I didn't hear Him say, "No."

So, I grabbed one of Jacob's bottles of whiskey and went to confront him. Holding up the bottle, I faced my husband while he stood next to his vehicle and said, "You have to make a decision. Either me or this bottle. What's it going to be?" Astounded at what a difficult choice it was for him, I watched as he looked longingly at the bottle. After a few moments, he concluded that he couldn't give up drinking. Disgusted, I went back inside.

Immediately, I began making arrangements with an elderly couple from our church who had an upstairs I could rent. *Their place will be perfect. The new location will be a little farther from my work, but I must move out if Jacob is going to get over his drinking.* I told the couple I planned to move in within the week. However, two days before I was supposed to move into the new place, the Lord gave me a dream which I interpreted to mean that I should not depart from my husband. I refer to that dream as the "Helicopter Dream."

Helicopter Dream:

There was a big helicopter (like a mama) flying through the air, carrying a smaller (baby) helicopter. Then, the big helicopter let the smaller one go. When this happened, the small helicopter crashed and burned. Eventually, the big helicopter also crashed.

Upon waking, I pondered the dream.

Before dismissing a dream as nonsense—even when it seems very strange—I have found that I should always ask God if a dream is from Him. Discerning which dreams are from the subconscious or from God can be difficult. Praying is usually necessary to determine the source. Sometimes I know instantly if a dream is from Him. Other times, it is not as clear.

In the case of the helicopter dream, I knew right away it was from the Lord. Immediately upon waking, the interpretation was clear, "If I let Jacob on his own now, he will crash and burn. After that happens, eventually, I too will crash and burn. Those helicopters represent us. I am the mama helicopter and Jacob is the baby helicopter."

Undoubtedly, God can provide guidance in dreams and could reveal whether or not it's wise to move to another location. Scripturally, there is an example of this in Matthew 2 with Joseph. After Mary gave birth to Jesus, her husband Joseph was warned in a dream to leave to Egypt because King Herod was going to try to kill baby Jesus. Then, after King Herod died, Joseph had a dream indicating it was time to return to Israel.

As a result of my helicopter dream, I canceled my plans to move out and recognized how destructive it could be to leave prematurely. I then determined in my heart that I would not ever leave my husband unless I *knew* that God had released me. Making the decision to leave so suddenly had been impulsive and would not have been wise.

God's heart for spouses to stay together and support each other can be seen in 1 Corinthians 7:10-11, "…A wife must not leave her husband. But if she does leave him, let her remain single or else be reconciled to him. And the husband must not leave his wife" (NLT). Unless God directs a wife to move out and provides scriptural support, it is probably His heart for them to continue dwelling together.

Family

In my heart, I really wanted things to work between Jacob and me. Grateful, I noted the effort my family made to connect with Jacob and include him. From the beginning of our relationship, they did their best to embrace Jacob. One way my parents actively tried to make Jacob feel like part of the family was including us on their family vacations.

A hero status had even been granted to Jacob by my mom after a family excursion to Bryce Canyon National Park in Utah. After we'd all been hiking one day, we became concerned about my mom. She had been hot and tired when we started out that day, so she and my dad took the short-cut. Then, after our lengthy hike, there was no sign of my parents' return. We knew my dad would be fine. He was in great physical shape. But my mom was not.

Realizing that my mom might be having a hard time somewhere on the trail—it was Jacob to the rescue! Gathering his rescue rope, a cold soda, and a granola bar he began jogging down the trail. Soon, Jacob came across my folks and gave my mom the soda (her favorite). Although he was prepared to do an intense rescue mission, and only a mild one was needed, my mom developed a deep appreciation for him that day. For the longest time she told the story of how Jacob came completely prepared to rescue her. He had many good qualities that not only I, but also my family, appreciated about him.

I hoped his tendency to drink would lessen following our vacation to Utah, but that did not happen. After returning from that trip, Jacob still had self-hatred and a measure of depression which enticed him to continue drinking. Looking at one of the photos of Jacob and me during our time in Bryce Canyon, I see his small, insincere smile. Progressively, his smile had faded in our photographs together. It was apparent that Jacob's joy decreased as his bondage increased.

The Respect Effect

A factor impacting Jacob's level of joy was how respected he felt by those around him, especially me. If I'd been asked to define respect, I would have said, "Listening to Jacob when he asks me to do something and presenting him in a good light to others."

I had no idea verbalizing criticisms and sharing my concerns with my husband would be so detrimental. Neither did I realize making those comments made him feel disrespected. I wasn't trying to make Jacob feel bad about himself. Bringing up issues to discuss, and letting my husband know my opinion, seemed like the logical thing to do. It seemed to me that not confronting Jacob about areas where change was needed could enable him to continue making unhealthy choices. However, explaining to Jacob on multiple occasions that he had to change his lifestyle made him feel defeated and worthless because he felt powerless to change the situation.

R-E-S-P-E-C-T

"Men need respect." I'd heard this during the first couple years of my marriage. However, I didn't understand how to effectively address this need. If I'd better understood how to show respect to Jacob, I think it would have breathed life into him. Being more intentional to encourage him may have also built up his self-confidence and motivated him to make some positive changes.

In my heart, I respected my husband and absolutely believed in him. I'd even determined that I would respect him whether or not he deserved it. Tucked away in the corner of the café one day, I shared with a friend about my situation and she said, "He needs to earn your respect." Challenging that statement, I asked, "Where is that in the Bible?" I had already given the topic considerable thought and was fairly certain there was not much, if any, scriptural support for the idea that respect needs to be earned by a husband. Sharing my conclusion, I explained, "Because he is my husband, he is to be given respect, regardless of whether or not he earns it." I meant those words. I had purposed in my heart to respect Jacob.

And yet, resentment oozed out of me in response to Jacob drinking, not actively applying for a job, and not doing the things I wanted him to such as washing the dishes or taking care of other household responsibilities. When Jacob saw something that seemed like a good idea *to him*, he would do it. If I asked him to do something, though, he rarely got to it. If our roles had been reversed, and I was home most of the time, I would have taken care of the things that needed to be done around the apartment. I kept it no secret that he was not meeting my expectations. I did not constantly nag at him, but it showed in my attitude that I was displeased with his lack of contribution.

Dr. Eggerichs, author of *Love and Respect*, makes the case that a wife needs to unconditionally *respect* her husband the way a husband is to unconditionally *love* his wife.[1] Although I'd been exposed during my marriage to the material presented in *Love and Respect*, I still failed to realize how my actions probably appeared to Jacob. Without even realizing it, I deprived my husband of respect. Although I respected my husband in my heart and was trying to demonstrate respect for him, I didn't know what that should look like. My perspective and way of understanding things was very different from his.

Unintentional

Unintentionally, I did things that implied Jacob was not good enough. One example of this was when we said grace before dinner. The only time we routinely prayed together was when we said grace. So, I would often extend the prayer of thanks Jacob said over our dinner and add a prayer of my own, thinking it was an opportune time to pray. One day after saying grace, Jacob looked at me and, with narrowed eyes and accusation in his voice, said, "My grace isn't good enough for you." I was surprised at his reaction. I never meant to imply he said grace inadequately. I tried to explain there were things I thought we should pray for and it seemed like a good time to lift up those requests. Looking back, I can now see why he thought I viewed him as inadequate. I never imagined at the time that he would have perceived my extension of saying grace at dinner as disrespectful.

Since better understanding the importance of respect, I have pondered which other times I might have come across as disrespectful to Jacob. Two instances in particular come to mind. In both instances, I made a comment in front of someone else that really seemed to upset my husband. One was disagreeing with a quote he shared, saying I thought he'd stated something inaccurately. Another was saying I had been bothered by the way he made lasagna (it was totally different from mine). If I'd made the comment in jest and he had known that, it probably would have been no big deal, but my comment was not stated in a joking way.

Eventually, I realized that correcting him in front of others or making a negative comment about how he did something was perceived by Jacob as disrespectful. Hurting my husband by making the comments I did was never my intention! I was simply saying my thoughts aloud. However, those comments probably came across to my husband like I was challenging him and suggesting that he was inadequate. I have since come to understand that when a man is determining self-worth, he asks himself, *Am I adequate?* Being viewed as inadequate can breed feelings of disrespect. It is a man's deepest need to *feel* respected.

Doing everything I could for him—not intentionally ridiculing him in front of others and trying to be attentive to the comments he made about small things such as not leaving the hair dryer on the living room floor— were ways I tried to show him respect. Hiding his drinking was one of the ways I attempted to protect his reputation and demonstrate I respected him. Later, I came to understand the secrecy simply enabled him. In reality, my attempts to demonstrate respect were futile if Jacob didn't *feel* respected. Jacob's idea of respect was different from mine.

I loved the man and was trying to do everything I could to make sure we (he included) did the right thing. But trying to force him to make good decisions didn't produce good results. Taking control, expressing disappointment and frustrations every so often that Jacob didn't have a job (especially when he wanted one but couldn't find one), and verbalizing criticisms all chipped away at my husband's self-esteem. Instead of empowering him, many of my interactions with him enhanced the feelings of inadequacy that he already had.

As Jacob's wife, I should have been his biggest cheerleader, but I wasn't a very good one. My husband didn't know how much I was rooting for him because what he saw were pom-poms of control in one hand and resentment in the other. Intermittently, between shaking those pom-poms, I told my husband how much I cared about him and praised him for the things I could see that he did well.

Never once did I stop believing in him. On the contrary, I believed in him with everything in me. But I don't think he knew that. I probably never overtly said to him, "I believe in you, Jacob, no matter what." If I had, I think that statement would have breathed life to a part of him that had died inside.

There was no question in my mind that it was possible for Jacob to pursue his calling. I believed all things were possible with God and knew my husband had it in him to overcome his struggles. I saw good qualities in Jacob. He had so much potential; he was smart, athletic, well-read, musically talented, and gifted in the prophetic. Many people benefited when Jacob ministered to them and explained things to them about the Christian faith and the Scriptures. Lots of people (myself included) had been inspired by his passion at times. His passion was my favorite quality. It was contagious when Jacob was passionate about something.

I had high hopes for my husband. Optimistically, I assumed he would overcome whatever obstacles got in his way—even when circumstances seemed dismal. Jacob wanted to get out of the rut he was in and change, but he either didn't know how or didn't think it was possible. Eventually he developed a feeling of hopelessness. "Hope deferred makes the heart sick." (Proverbs 13:12, NKJV). Hope deferred zaps someone's emotional strength and uses discouragement, disappointment, or hopelessness to dissipate the inner motivation that could otherwise make change happen.

The Quills Come Out

On many occasions when I tried to have a mature conversation with my husband or point something out that was unfavorable, my efforts back-fired. Similar to how a porcupine releases its quills when it feels threatened, Jacob would attack (with words) if he felt I was somehow approaching him with ill intent. There was an ever-present assumption that I was coming to him with the intention to attack.

Often, I simply wanted to talk with him about something. However, Jacob's heart was full of hurt and disappointment from various experiences throughout his life, and it was as though he wasn't able to absorb what I was saying. Until he dealt with the issues causing him pain, and allowed those hurts to be healed, his capacity for being able to take ownership of his decisions or respond to criticism in a healthy way was extremely limited. One of his favorite responses was, "Oh yeah, make me out to be the bad guy." It was like there was no room for Jacob to take in any negative feedback, particularly from me or his family. Like many people who carry hurt, disappointment, or rejection in their heart, Jacob operated by the sporting strategy of "The best defense is a good offense." He would often act like he was a victim or dismiss the unfavorable comments and point out the short-comings of the person who said them.

Feelings of justification propelled me to tell Jacob how he needed to change. Unfortunately, feeling so justified to share my concerns and criticisms also kept me from realizing how my husband was perceiving our interactions.

Almost Sucked In

Focusing on the things in Jacob's life that disappointed me fostered a great deal of negative feelings. I *hated* the sin and addiction in his life. When I considered my husband's habit of viewing pornography, I felt inadequate. I longed for *me* to be enough for him.

In some ways, Jacob was like a Bible scholar. He knew God's Word and could even quote Scriptures about how people are designed to be a temple of the Holy Spirit, yet he pursued a lifestyle contrary to that. *Jacob is not only defiling himself through that behavior and viewing those sites, he is also feeding into the multi-billion dollar pornography industry.* Thinking about the exploited men and women featured on those websites and the hurts, insecurities, and broken pasts that landed them there, saddened me.

Although not hard-wired to be as visually stimulated as men, women can still become hooked on pornography, especially with exposure over time. For a short time, I too started to get drawn into pornography, even though I hated what it did.

After arriving at work one day, I noticed Jacob left his computer in my car. Suspicious, I turned it on and reviewed the computer history. That evening I decided to investigate the websites Jacob had been viewing. Seeing the pornographic content on those sites fueled my anger and frustration. Although I was utterly disgusted by it, somehow I found myself being drawn in by what I saw and began developing an unhealthy interest. Additionally, I started to screen the movies he rented to verify there was no nudity. Thankfully, the couple movie rentals I reviewed were fairly clean.

A few days after I'd begun the investigations of the websites, I went to church. After church service, a friend came up to me and said, "Alexa, I had a dream last night. [In the dream] someone said, 'Something terrible has happened to Alexa.'" I closed my eyes for a moment, breathed in, and responded, "I know what it means. Thank you for sharing that with me." In God's faithfulness, He was calling me out. My friend didn't have the details, nor did she need them. Instantly, I knew that dream was the Lord's way of getting my attention to stop investigating those websites. Viewing those images and becoming drawn in by them was not pure. That behavior was opening the door to sin in my life. I knew that's not what God wanted. He desires holiness. "Be holy for I am holy" (1 Peter 1:16 NKJV). Holiness is a state of purity that takes place when there is absence of sin. I needed to close the door to pornography before I got entangled in it.

Why did God deal with me and not just let me continue investigating pornography until the point where it became a bondage to me? I believe it was because of prayer (either my own or someone else's). I've heard it said before, prayer is the muscle that moves the hand of God, and I believe this to be true. Thankfully, my friend sharing her dream helped snap me out of the tendency I was developing. I am grateful for how the Lord intervened!

Unnecessary

One of my more shameful moments in responding out of my "justified" anger toward Jacob was when we were driving to Timothy's funeral. Timothy had been wonderful to Jacob and me. In addition to leading us through pre-marital counseling, he performed our wedding ceremony and even paid for our honeymoon cabin! Jacob had a deep respect for Timothy, and we were both sad that he was now gone.

As we began the three hour trip to the funeral location, we reminisced about Timothy and his wife, appreciating their generosity and how they'd made an investment in our lives. While going down the road, I asked Jacob pointedly, "What would Timothy think if he knew what you've been doing? That you've been looking at pornography and drinking?" He was *so* mad at me. I had intended for my comment to somehow produce conviction which would then spawn change. In reality, all it did was stir up anger in Jacob. A little further into the drive, we stopped for food and Jacob almost left me at the restaurant. As I made my way outside, I discovered he had pulled out of the parking space and was about to exit the parking lot without me. The irony seemed glaring. *We are on the way to the funeral of the man who married us! I can't believe he would leave me here!* Fortunately, it was only a minute or two before he came back.

During most of our marriage, I rarely made sharp comments; I really tried to never do that. But the resentment I carried was breeding grounds for negative thoughts. It was only a matter of time before some leaked out and became destructive comments.

No person is bullet proof. Everyone has different tolerance levels for the amount of negative interactions they can take before they react. Jacob's threshold for absorbing unfavorable comments was very low. Admittedly, I posed a question that wasn't going to be beneficial, so it should have been no surprise I got the reaction I did. The tone I'd used was more one of accusation than curiosity. If it had been a sincere question, maybe things would have turned out differently in that conversation.

6. TRIP OUT WEST: SHENANIGANS

In the midst of disappointment, God was faithful to sustain me.

"My soul follows close behind You;
Your right hand upholds me."
(Psalm 63:8, NKJV)

The Return From Out West

The sun was setting on a nice June evening, and the night seemed so peaceful. Soon, Jacob and I would celebrate our third wedding anniversary. I had just arrived to my car after attending a Wednesday evening church service and was appreciating the view. Jacob would be home soon. My phone rang. *This must be him.* Jacob was returning from his motorcycle trip across country. The journey had lasted for a month and a half—that was a long time for him to be gone.

While out west, Jacob visited his family, then continued his travels to see a friend in California. As I went to pick him up from the train station, I felt for him. His motorcycle had finally kicked the bucket. When it happened he had been only a state and a half away, at the tail end of his return home. Another five hours of driving and he would have made it all the way back to our apartment. However, it seemed taking the 2,000-plus mile trip was all that motorcycle could endure. That motorcycle was his prized possession and now he was returning without it.

I pulled up to the train station in my dented, but durable, purple minivan and Jacob hopped in. After getting home, we each pulled up a chair to the kitchen table, and he began to tell me about his trip. To my surprise, he told me he had almost met up with his ex-girlfriend, Cammi. She had contacted him via social media while he had been visiting his folks out west. Jacob then recounted how poor my timing had been with a phone call a few weeks prior.

I remembered that phone call. During that conversation, I announced there would need to be changes when he returned. I wanted our home to be a place of purity, where I felt comfortable with what was in our home. That meant no more porn and no more alcohol. Additionally, I didn't want his horror movies to remain in our home—he could keep them in the car. Even though he rarely watched them, just knowing they were there made me uncomfortable.

I'd laid that ultimatum (a difficult one) on him the same day he had made the appropriate, but sacrificial, decision not to meet up with his ex-girlfriend. Although she was married, she wanted closure for their previous relationship that had ended several years before Jacob and I got married. He knew if they met up it would quickly turn into something physical—despite the fact that she was married, with three children.

My Chest Hurts

The morning after laying down those ultimatums over the phone, I discovered my heart physically hurt—particularly when I bent at a certain angle. This pain occurred prior to Jacob telling me about Cammi and did not stop for several months following his return from out west. Later, this was diagnosed as pericarditis (inflammation of the lining of the heart) which couldn't be explained.

Eventually, I gained some insight to what was causing the heart issue. After church one day, an image of a woman I'd spoken with a couple times before popped into my mind while I was praying. I believed that image was from the Holy Spirit. Concluding that I should seek her out to talk with her, I began to look for her, hoping she had indeed come to church that day. I was pleased to find her in the next room.

A simple greeting of, "Hello," was all it took. I don't even think the woman knew my name, but she immediately began to tell me about her relationship woes and the serious heart condition that required her to have a pacemaker. Her husband, for quite some time, had been in an ongoing relationship with another woman. But she did not want to let her husband go, so they still remained married—even though he was living with the other woman.

As I listened to the woman at church tell me about her situation, I made the association between her painful and twisted relationship with her husband and the severe physical issues she had with her heart. Her situation seemed like tangible evidence that someone's emotional state can have an impact on one's overall health. I believe the Lord wanted me to see what happened to her and what could happen to me if I chose to stay in my sorry emotional state. I needed to make sure God had my heart and that I didn't hold onto emotions that would torment me.

The Other Woman

Days prior to Jacob's return from his big adventure out west, a friend felt led to give me her old running shoes. When she gave them to me, she explained how they symbolized the difficult times she'd faced in her marriage, and how God had brought her through them. It was not until after Jacob returned that I understood why she had given me that gift. God knew I would need encouragement regarding the situation with Cammi. Looking at those shoes gave me hope for my marriage.

When Jacob first told me about Cammi, I thought I should reach out to her and try to avert her interactions with my husband. I asked Jacob for the phone number and called her. I explained that if she ever needed something she could come to *me* and I would be happy to pray for her or help her in some way but she really shouldn't go to Jacob for things. Perhaps I was too nice, or maybe she really just didn't care, I don't know. Within minutes, she was on the phone with Jacob telling him all about our conversation. *Seriously? Maybe I shouldn't have called her after all.*

As the weeks passed, I watched as Jacob's heart longed for Cammi. However, he was stuck with me. I told him I would never divorce him—no matter what. One evening, I stated matter-of-factly, "I am sticking to our [marriage] covenant. If you did leave me to go be with her, I would wait for you. I wouldn't divorce you. Eventually, you would come back to me." In retrospect—even though I meant it—I shouldn't have told him I would be willing to wait for him. A statement like that can grant someone permission to go astray.

Thankfully, Cammi lived hundreds of miles away. The distance helped a bit, but with present day technology, communicating frequently was not difficult. My husband and I were technically together as lovers, but not in his heart. I knew the Lord could relate to my pain because He says in Matthew 15:8 that there are people who, "honor Me with their lips, but their hearts are far from Me" (NLT). Likewise, even though my husband was still together with me, his heart was far from me.

Living through this time helped me understand why the Lord says, in Revelation 3:16, "But because you are lukewarm—neither hot, nor cold—I am ready to spit [vomit] you out of my mouth" (EXB). I always figured God wanted as many people in Heaven as possible and wondered, *Why couldn't He include the lukewarm ones in that population?* However, after going through what I refer to as the "Cammi-Era" I came to understand why God spews out those who are lukewarm. It can be nauseating and heart-wrenching to know a person claims to have a connection with someone when, in reality, that person's heart is dedicated to another.

I was absolutely committed to Jacob, but he had come to resent my presence in his life. He viewed me as a hindrance to being able to pursue pleasure without accountability. At one point Jacob told me, "I am beginning to hate you." I was heart-broken. The same man, who had been so loving to have once told me not to say anything bad about myself because he didn't want anyone (even me) talking badly about his wife, no longer wanted anything to do with me. I'd had such grand dreams about what our lives would be like and how amazing it would be to be married to this man. However, as our marriage continued to erode, it became difficult for me to see my husband through a perspective not colored by disappointment or resentment. Similar to how the grease on a mechanic's hands can leave marks on anything he touches until he washes his hands, resentment can contaminate everything in its path if someone holds onto it.

Continuing On Day By Day

Most evenings, I felt angry or distressed about the situation with Jacob. There was one night in particular where I really believed I was as close as humanly possible to going crazy without actually crossing that line. That was one of my worst moments ever. Enraged and deeply distraught, all I could do to express my emotions that night was scream and cry. Sitting on my bedroom floor, with my back against the bed, I came before the Lord with my mix of intense emotions and cried out to Him. Jacob was concerned about me but didn't know what to do. Perhaps the only reason I didn't actually go crazy that night was because I went to the Lord with my duress instead of simply fall apart underneath it. Thankfully, the intensity was only so extreme that one night. There wasn't even one particular event that brought me to that point. I was just completely fed up with Jacob's shenanigans.

Many nights were difficult for one reason or another. Often, I didn't think I could go in to work the next day. Yet, morning came and somehow I would get up and face the day. I don't know how I continued to operate in the normal world, except by God's grace. Only one or two people at work knew anything about my home-life situation. At work, I was able to fully function. Then, I would come home and succumb to the negative emotions that awaited me as I focused on the situation with my husband.

Despite how broken I was throughout the season of my life where Jacob pursued Cammi, I was not constantly depressed. Even though I was hurting over my husband's decisions, I found that joy was still within reach. Sometimes I didn't access the joy of the Lord as often as I should have, but it was not uncommon for coworkers to comment on how I was always so happy. Despite what I experienced with Jacob, I often walked in joy. How was that possible? Joy is not purely dependent upon someone's circumstances. Joy is a fruit of the Holy Spirit and it is a part of the Kingdom of God.

The times I didn't walk in joy were when I would focus too much on the situation with Jacob and let my thoughts linger there. Although I felt sad and frustrated when I contemplated the situation with Jacob, I was still hopeful. *I'm certain Jacob will have a change of heart. I just need to wait it out.* Every day, I was dependent on the Lord for strength. Many days, I felt tapped out emotionally. At times, I did not have the strength, or perhaps the discipline, to come before the Lord formally with prayer, but I would feed on the Lord's faithfulness. Feeding on God's faithfulness is mentioned by King David in Psalm 37:3, "Trust in the Lord, and do good; dwell in the land, and *feed on His faithfulness*" (NKJV). To do this, I would sometimes just say, "You're faithful. Lord, You're faithful." That simple phrase connected me to the Lord and fed my spirit. Even though I felt tired, I could still muster the energy to speak that phrase as a way to confess my trust in the Lord.

Thankfully, God upheld me during that difficult time. I could relate to the words in Psalm 63:8, "My soul follows close behind You; Your right hand upholds me" (NKJV). The Lord was upholding me and a big part of that was due to the prayers lifted up on my behalf. I cherished each prayer offered up by my friends. I remember one phone call in particular, when one of them called to tell me, "The Lord is saying, 'Cast your cares upon Him because He cares for you.'" This was a reference to 1 Peter 5:7. That word of encouragement meant so much to me. I certainly did have a lot of cares, and the Lord was faithfully reminding me that I could cast them upon Him.

Cammi's Husband

About a week following Jacob's return from his trip out west, Cammi's husband, Randall, and I got in touch. I'd asked Jacob to please get me the phone number for Cammi's husband. Jacob wasn't excited about the idea, but he did it. So, I began touching base with Randall and tried to encourage him, "Hang in there. Don't give up." The purpose in connecting with Randall was to see how he was doing and to share what we knew about what our spouses were up to. Given the fact that his spouse was pining after mine, I figured it made sense to communicate. We had some general conversation, vented a bit about the shenanigans of our spouses, and discussed the importance of maintaining our faith in the Lord and staying committed to our spouses. Voicing how committed I was to Jacob, I explained that we just needed to wait this out and believe our spouses would come to their senses. Standing in faith together, we waited.

Unfortunately, the communication between Randall and me made our spouses feel even more justified in their own interactions with each other. When I was going to be out of town, I informed Cammi's husband so he would know if his wife disappeared, she had probably come to be with my husband.

Talking with Randall made me feel validated and gave me a sense of satisfaction I didn't usually have when I spoke with my husband. Even though Randall and I didn't talk very often, to ensure emotional distance between us, and avert frustration in our spouses, it would have been helpful to keep our phone conversations shorter and more focused. Perhaps email may have even been a better source of communication to use because it is not as personal as a phone call.

The Woman at the Well

During the escapades with Cammi and my husband, there came a particular moment where I gained insight regarding why Cammi was pursuing him. This clarity came while listening to our church's pastor share a message about the story of the Woman at the Well, documented in John 4. In this scenario, Jesus spoke with a Samaritan woman at a well who'd had several husbands. The pastor explained that those men were that woman's life-source—men were the well she tried to draw her life from. Upon hearing this, there was a witness in my spirit so intense that I felt like a volcano erupted within me. I almost stood on the pew and shouted, "That is Cammi! Men are her life source!"

Considering this, I felt some compassion for Cammi, but I still wanted her to keep a good distance from my husband. In her heart, she had never let Jacob go; there were still soul ties that drew her to Jacob. Soul ties were something I didn't understand until long after Cammi tried to reconnect with Jacob. Basically, a soul tie is a deep connection, or a tie, between two people's souls, or emotions. These can occur between lovers or even close friends. Soul ties are not always bad. Spouses should have soul ties to one another— because of the connection between them established by intimacy and close relationship. However when a relationship ends, if the soul ties are not broken it can hinder someone's ability to receive healing from the hurts affiliated with that relationship.

I got the John 4 message on cd after church that day and sent it to Cammi anonymously. *If only she'd realize that God wants to be her life source. That would fill the void she has inside of her.* I hoped Cammi would come to realize her search for value was misplaced.

7. THE PURSUIT CONTINUES

Jacob's interest in Cammi lingered.
I did my best not to lose heart.

"Come to Me, all who are weary and heavy-laden, and I will give you rest."
(Matthew 11:28, NASB)

Interest in Cammi Continues

When will this ridiculousness end? Absolutely holding onto the hope that things would end between my husband and Cammi, I was convinced I just needed to wait this out. Jacob would indeed get his heart right with the Lord, get free from all the bondage he was in, and enter into the calling God had placed on his life—to bring the Word of God to the nations. I was certain of this.

While Jacob and I were in the living room one day, he informed me, "Cammi makes me feel good about myself." After briefly considering what her comments to him might entail, I wondered to myself, *What does he do that is worthy of praise?* Unfortunately, there wasn't much good I could think of to say to Jacob. Part of the draw to Cammi was because she fed his ego and let him know he was desired. Cammi did not seem to share my same frustrations or concerns about Jacob. I was in awe. *Doesn't she care if he is bound to alcohol?*

Telling Songs

Over time, Jacob's heart became hardened. Within a year or so of confessing his drinking to me, Jacob's heart became so numb it seemed like he didn't want to change. Eventually, he listened over and over to the same two songs—"Behind Blue Eyes" by The Who and "Comfortably Numb" by Pink Floyd. Both of these songs reflected how Jacob felt. In the song, "Behind Blue Eyes," the line that resonated the most with Jacob was the lyric that said, "No one knows what it's like to be the bad man. The sad man."[1] In "Comfortably Numb" there was a line that said, "And I-I-I have become comfortably numb."[2] Jacob's heart was indeed sad and he was numb to many things. Ignoring the inner promptings that come from the Holy Spirit, which let someone know that a wrong choice is being made, will harden one's heart. Eventually, it can make a person feel numb.

After my brother commented on how often Jacob listened to "Behind Blue Eyes" and "Comfortably Numb" those songs became a joke in my family. So, on the next family outing when someone sat in a wad of gum at a carnival, the gummed individual lifted his shirt for all to see the gum stuck to his backside and began to sing, "Nobody knows what it's like to have a gummed butt. A gummed butt." Those lyrics were a spin off "Behind Blue Eyes." Then he made up a different song, this time to the tune of "Comfortably Numb," "And I-I-I have become uncomfortably gummed." We still laugh about that years later. Sometimes humor helps lessen the pain of dark situations.

Hot Pursuit

Jacob may have been numb to conviction in many ways, but his sensuous desires were alive and well. Those desires fed his interest in Cammi, and she encouraged his pursuit. They sometimes texted each other at late hours.

Staying up long into the night had become quite normal for Jacob. Without consistent work, his schedule was very flexible. He almost never went to bed at the same time as me and that bothered me. Even if he came to bed and read for a while, at least he would be next to me. However, the motivation to join me just didn't seem to be there. Many nights, that empty place in the bed left me sad and longing for my husband.

Every morning, I scouted out where Jacob's phone was. If Jacob wasn't *still* awake in the morning when I was getting ready for work around 6 or 7 a.m., I would see if any texts had been exchanged with Cammi. It became an obsession for me. I wanted to know what they were saying to one another and be aware of any plans the two of them might have. Each night when I went to bed, I would hope Jacob wasn't still awake when I got up in the morning. It was not uncommon for him to still be up when my alarm went off. When this happened, I would try to take extra time getting ready before work, hoping he might wander off to bed so I could sneak a look at his phone.

Seeing their messages to one another was devastating. I saw the pictures she sent him, one of which was topless. I heard the song he made up for her and had recorded. For Jacob, there was no greater way to express love for someone than to sing that person a song. I read about the sexual encounter they wanted to have and the innuendos in Cammi's texts to my husband.

One text in particular was burned instantly into my memory upon reading it. In that message, Cammi wrote, "If you don't want to leave your wife to be with me because you are afraid that your marriage will fail, the Bible says 365 times 'do not fear.' We love each other and love comes from God." It's true God doesn't want people to have fear, and He commands His followers to love one another, but she was taking those concepts sorely out of context! I was utterly disgusted. *How twisted and manipulative! The Bible is clear sexual relations outside of marriage are wrong! Plus, both of these people are already in a marriage covenant. "Do not commit adultery" is one of the Ten Commandments!* As expected, she refrained from quoting the parts of the Bible which would not help her accomplish her agenda. This experience showed me that when Scriptures are taken out of context, they can be twisted to say anything someone wants. Because of this, I am always careful to examine scriptural context.

In another text, Cammi mentioned following her heart. Jacob responded by paraphrasing Jeremiah 17:9, which says, "The heart is deceitful above all things, and desperately wicked..." (NKJV). She didn't reply to that specific text message. Referencing that verse had indeed been fitting. Following the heart without restraint can potentially lead a person into immoral things. Sometimes people want things they shouldn't have.

Jacob texted her in another message, "Woman, you are tempting me." But that only invited more suggestive talk and smooth words from her. To Cammi, a statement from someone stating he was tempted only meant she was that much closer to a breakthrough, not that she should back off and refrain from pursuing him.

Although there were moments when Jacob resisted Cammi, he did not effectively distance himself from her. I watched as the lust in Jacob's life served as a snare, and I could see that my husband was trapped. I wished he would totally separate himself from Cammi.

The Draw

Jacob knew the Bible. He was familiar with the passages of Scripture (like Proverbs 2 and 5) which warn against the adulteress woman and her smooth words. In the end, that path is the way to destruction. Yet, many go there. Temptations to pursue impure relationships are something many face. My husband was standing at the crossroads of that path.

Although many men might be lured by that kind of woman, I wasn't going to let my husband go. I was intentional to uphold intimacy in our marriage. I briefly contemplated denying him unless he was sober, but realized because he drank every day that wouldn't be practical. Intimacy is an important part of marriage that helps maintain the bond between a husband and wife. I did my best to be a gatekeeper and keep Cammi at bay.

My intentional effort at maintaining the intimacy in my marriage was a major reason that Jacob did not just pick up and move away with her to Ohio. For some reason, that was their chosen destination in the event they both left their spouses.

Jacob knew his interactions with Cammi were wrong, but he liked the attention she gave him. She desired him, and that made Jacob feel worthwhile. He did not have a job at the time and drank quite a bit. There were few things which strengthened his self-esteem. Cammi's interest in Jacob provided him with a false basis for self-worth.

Frustrated, I would think to myself, *Why doesn't he just get it? He should know better than this.* He was living a life so contrary to what he was called to be as a man of God. Like many people do, Jacob was choosing the immediate reinforcement of pleasure instead of doing what he knew to be right.

It was clear to me that Jacob did not understand his true identity, which is founded in Jesus Christ. If my husband realized how valued he was, and truly believed in his heart that God made him for a purpose, I think he would have made different decisions. In the early years of our friendship, Jacob seemed to understand God's love for him. Over time, though, Jacob's focus shifted off the Lord, and he lost sight of who he was created to be.

Perhaps I should have made more of an effort to speak encouragement and purpose over my husband. That could have sparked life within Jacob, and may have empowered him to believe in himself and embrace who he was called to be. However, it seemed like there was nothing I could say to penetrate his heart and prompt a positive change. At times, even when I talked about God's love and forgiveness, it didn't have much impact because Jacob felt as though he was not eligible for God's grace. The only exception to this would have been if the Lord gave me a very specific message to share and I correctly discerned the timing for when to share it. Otherwise, his heart was not open. To be completely honest, it was difficult for me to have compassion for Jacob, or to speak words of life over him. There were many moments where all I saw when I looked at Jacob was a man of great potential, wasting his days.

As the situation with Jacob's drinking progressed, he gave in to temptations such as pursuing Cammi, getting violent, and indulging laziness. While his heart continued to grow hard, I wallowed in my own self-pity and wished things were different. I tried to hide the situation concerning Jacob and Cammi from most of the people we knew. I was waiting for the situation to get resolved on its own and didn't actively seek out the counsel of others.

In actuality, counseling and mentorship are important. Older men and women in the faith are supposed to serve as examples for others. Rather than fixating on my husband's poor choices, I should have been more intentional to encourage him to find the mentorship and counsel of a godly man. Many of Jacob's choices could have been discussed if he was meeting consistently with a godly man who could provide him with wisdom and mentorship. Jacob did meet with a pastor for a while but never attained the long-term accountability he needed.

At one point, the pastor and two friends from church came over in a surprise visit to our apartment to encourage Jacob and help him understand how to recognize and deal with alcoholism. Both of us appreciated their attempt to reach out and offer us support. Their hearts were in the right place. They wanted to see Jacob get the help he needed and be set free, as did I.

A Desire to Change Roles

In my heart I longed for Jacob to be the primary provider for our household, and to be the head of the home. Routine tasks such as doing the dishes and sending checks for the bills were often left up to me—not because Jacob couldn't do them, but because the motivation to contribute to our home was gone. It seemed as though the breadth of responsibilities for our household fell primarily on my shoulders. In many ways, I felt as though I was the head of the home, even though I knew that was supposed to be Jacob's place, as the husband. Serving as the head of the home means the husband has the final say on issues where there is not consensus, and I assumed this also entailed shouldering the responsibility of the household as a whole and making sure it functioned.

I *really* wanted to one day have the option to be a stay-at-home mom. Instead, we were in no place in our lives to have children. I didn't want to bring kids into a dysfunctional family, nor did I want to bring children into an environment where I was the only parent who worked. Subsequently, I often needed to guard against resentment when I came across stay-at-home moms or met wives who didn't have to work.

Instead of focusing on others, I simply needed to be faithful with what I had been given. I needed to remind myself that life isn't all about me. What mattered was doing what God asked of me. In everything—including in my work—I needed to honor the Lord. Colossians 3:23-24 says, "Whatever you do [whatever your task may be], work from the soul [that is, put in your very best effort], as [something done] for the Lord and not for men, knowing [with all certainty] that it is from the Lord [not from men] that you will receive the inheritance which is your [greatest] reward. It is the Lord Christ whom you [actually] serve" (AMP). Although I'm familiar with this verse, there have been times when my flesh has gotten in the way, and I have copped an attitude about my situation.

Gentle Reminders

Not having balance in my life between work, family, friends, my studies, working out, eating healthy, and getting proper rest was a constant challenge. I didn't know how to have balance. I desperately wanted it, but felt like true balance in my life, where I could focus on everything I should, was always out of reach. No matter how busy life got, I knew I was without excuse to not take time for cultivating my relationship with God through spending time in His Word and praying. Yet, sometimes it was still difficult for me to prioritize time with the Lord.

On occasion, the Lord asked me to spend time with Him. One day, a friend called and said, "I feel like the Lord is saying He misses you." It was true. I had not been spending time with Him daily. I often thought about God and I loved Him, but I hadn't been actively seeking the Lord by pulling aside daily to spend time reading the Scriptures and praying.

Another day, I was in the living room with Jacob when, entirely out of the blue, a song lyric—"Come away with me."[5]—came to mind. I believed it was from the Lord and felt He was asking me to remove myself from the hustle and bustle of daily responsibilities and spend time with Him. My experience that day reminded me of the Scripture in Song of Solomon 2:10, "My beloved speaks and says to me, rise up, my love, my fair one, and *come away*" (AMPC). God wanted to draw me close. In His presence, I could be ministered to, refreshed, and focus my heart on Him. He longs for that.

Job Application for Ohio

Since my husband's return from out west, Cammi had commanded Jacob's heart and attention. One of the hardest things for me to process was discovering he'd applied for a job in Ohio. Instantly, I felt a sense of betrayal and abandonment. Many things had not been easy to deal with during Jacob's interactions with Cammi, but this was especially hard to stomach. *He is trying to get a job to support Cammi? I work so hard to provide for both of us. I've wanted him to work for so long.* I had not seen an effort from Jacob in a long time, to pursue a job in our geographic area to support the two of us. If Jacob did apply for jobs he never informed me about it, and I assumed he hadn't been submitting job applications.

Proverbs 31

Tending to odds and ends in the bedroom one day, I noticed Jacob in the doorway and could tell he wanted to talk. Pensively, he said, "When I was in the bathroom today, what came to me was, 'Charm is deceptive.' Cammi is charming." I listened intently. He had my full attention, "And 'Beauty is fleeting.' Cammi is beautiful." I stood there waiting, hoping that was not all he would say. After a moment, I concluded that was indeed where his revelation ended. Those were phrases I recognized; they were from Proverbs

31, a passage in Scripture entitled *The Virtuous Woman*. Miffed, I thought about the very next line of Proverbs 31:30 which essentially said that a woman who fears the Lord should be praised. Proverbs 31:30 says, "Charm is deceitful and beauty is passing, but a woman who fears the Lord, she shall be praised" (NKJV). *Didn't Jacob consider the last part of that Scripture? How frustrating! If he'd thought about the last line, perhaps he would have associated that line with me. I love the Lord and certainly have a reverential fear of Him.*

I was thankful God's Spirit was trying to deal with Jacob, but I was disappointed my husband was so short-sighted. Perhaps it was only the first two lines he needed to be thinking about and I should not have felt slighted. At the time, I was angry that despite my best effort to follow the Lord and be a good wife I was overlooked by Jacob. Instead of seeing me as a virtuous woman, I think he saw me as a rule maker and a hindrance to his freedom.

Getting Through

One night in bed, the Lord brought to mind Philippians 4:4, "Rejoice in the Lord always. Again I will say, rejoice!" (NKJV). As I pondered this, I thought, *I don't want to rejoice. I know I should, but I just don't want to. I don't feel like rejoicing.* Unfortunately, I did not push aside my feelings and rejoice the way I should have; I succumbed to those feelings instead. Like rejoicing, joy is often a decision.

Thinking about things that stir anger or depression is the complete opposite of choosing joy, yet it was a natural tendency for me when I was around Jacob. Meditating on negative thoughts provided no benefit. I knew this. But there were still times I didn't make myself snap out of that mentality right away. Focusing continually on everything that has gone wrong or what is lacking could waste years of someone's life. I needed to be careful not to let that happen to me.

I held onto the Lord with all my heart during Jacob's pursuit of Cammi, but I was weary and lacked emotional energy. Occasionally, I thought back to the vision of the bumpy dirt road I'd seen three times prior to getting married. The Lord had told me it would be a hard road ahead. But I hadn't realized how hard. Thankfully, God is able to give rest to the weary and hope to the hopeless. Because the Lord wants to refresh His people and come alongside them, He says, "Come to Me, all who are weary and heavy-laden, and I will give you rest" (Matthew 11:28, NASB). I've been grateful to know that I can come to the Lord whenever I feel tired and burdened!

8. ENCOURAGEMENT THROUGH A DREAM

Nothing I experienced would be in vain.
God was going to bring good out of the challenges I had faced.

"Be strong and of good courage, do not fear nor be afraid of them;
for the Lord your God, He is the One who goes with you.
He will not leave you nor forsake you."
(Deuteronomy 31:6, NKJV)

Meaningful Encouragement

On July 19, 2009, my Bible study group decided I would be the facilitator for the next topic we studied. For each new topic, the present facilitator would provide a gift and a prophetic word to the next person selected to lead the Bible study sessions. My heart was touched as I listened to the word that God had given my friend Crystal to share with me. She presented me with a tallit (Jewish prayer shawl), an encouraging word, and a beautiful mustard seed bracelet with Scriptures etched into it.

The group prayed for me, and Crystal told me the Lord said I was a Deborah (described in Judges 4). She was a woman in leadership, as a judge over Israel, who led a military leader named Barak to victory as he fought for Israel. Everything shared with me that evening was very meaningful. Previously, someone else had spoken over me that I was a Deborah. Hearing it for the second time was confirmation that there were characteristics she and I shared.

That night, I had a dream that really encouraged me concerning the situation with my marriage. In my dream, there was a woman named Hannah, and a broken shell with oil dripping from it. Having Hannah in my dream symbolized the importance of prayer (in the Bible, a woman named Hannah prayed with all her heart before the Lord). Prayer would help me to endure the hardships I faced, and eventually allow me to receive the anointing God had for me.

In Scripture, the anointing is often associated with oil. An example of this is found in Genesis 35:14, "Jacob set up a stone pillar to mark the place where God had spoken to him…and *anointed the pillar with olive oil*" (NLT). When making olive oil, there must be a pressing or squeezing to get to the substance within the olive. Obtaining an anointing from the Lord can be similar to creating olive oil. At times there can be a difficult process people go through—where they feel like they are being crushed and broken.

Pondering the dream, and the broken shell I'd seen with oil dripping from it, I came to the clear conclusion, *Brokenness leads to the anointing.* By anointing, I mean the outpouring of God's Spirit that would equip me to fulfill the role He has for me. A book entitled *The Master Builder's Apprentice* defines the anointing as "the power and presence of God manifested in a committed vessel yielded to the Holy Spirit."[1] God's presence and His power are associated with the anointing.

As I journaled the dream and pondered its details, I received more of its interpretation. I believed the Lord was showing me there would be another year or so of dealing with difficulties in my marriage. No specific details were given to me about how those would end or if new ones would arise.

I believed God was showing me that He would use my experiences with Jacob to bring me to a place of great brokenness and then the anointing would flow. Ultimately, this dream was showing me that God's presence would be able to move through me more freely as a result of all that I would experience. Going through those experiences would eventually remove some of the blockages in me and allow more of the Holy Spirit to flow through me.

If God is going to entrust someone with power, that person must have the character to handle it. Going through trials and testing is the primary way character is developed. Romans 5:3-5 says, "tribulation produces perseverance; *and perseverance, character*; and character, hope" (NKJV). Tribulations are never easy, but if someone responds to those in the right way, it's possible for them to make someone stronger and build character.

Taking much encouragement from that dream, I called Cammi's husband and shared the dream with him. Filled with hope and finding purpose in my marital chaos, I explained how God could use the mess we were experiencing with our spouses to help each of us become more established in God. Deeply thankful, I relayed how the Lord could bring good out of our situation, such as developing an anointing in us. Our difficult times did not have to be in vain!

As the weeks passed, I often thought back to the dream about the shell and its message. I occasionally asked, *Aren't I already broken enough? How could I be any more broken?* Then, about six months later, a woman at Bible study felt led by the Holy Spirit to pray that I would be broken. Slightly stunned, I thought, *Seriously? My goodness, what is it going to take for me to be broken??? Haven't I endured enough?!*

God was bringing me through a long season of refinement. It was not pleasant, but if I yielded to His Holy Spirit, I would come out of this having character more like Jesus. Even for Jesus, obeying was not easy, but He did it anyway—He resisted temptations and was willing to suffer harsh circumstances. I thought about the Scripture in Hebrews 5:8 which says about Jesus that, "Although He was a Son [who had never been disobedient to the Father], He learned [active, special] obedience through what He suffered" (AMP). That Scripture brought me encouragement because I saw difficult things can still happen even when someone is obedient to God. Trials can be used to strengthen and deepen one's character. Realizing that the anointing is best stewarded when the person who receives it has depth to his or her character, I knew I was being prepared for what God would entrust to me in the future.

The Broken Bracelet

One night when Jacob was on his laptop, I figured he was up to something. After making my way across the living room, I jerked the computer away from him. Sure enough, he'd been downloading a topless picture of Cammi into his secret file.

Using the little bit of lead-time I had, I quickly hid the computer under the bed. He demanded to know what I had done with it. I went to bed and didn't tell him.

My consequence? He told me he would not let me sleep—he *really* wanted his computer. Turning on the light, Jacob proceeded to take my clothes out of our closet. I watched as my shirts and skirts got thrown onto the floor. After emptying a majority of my clothing from our closet, he shifted his focus. Leaning over me, he grabbed onto the silver mustard seed bracelet hanging from my wrist and pulled me up from the bed. Snap! *Not my bracelet!* Deep disappointment set in. I loved that piece of jewelry and the paraphrased Scriptures that were etched in it: "Faith the size of a mustard seed can move mountains," (Matthew 17:20, NKJV) and "For with God nothing is impossible" (Luke 1:37, NKJV).

Even though that beautiful bracelet was broken, the promises they spoke of were not. I still knew with God nothing is impossible and that faith could be used to speak to issues in life, even if they seem like mountains. God was indeed trustworthy, even if Jacob's deliverance didn't come as quickly as I wanted.

My attempts at control only made things worse. I didn't know how to hold Jacob accountable for his actions, so I just did the best I could to try and prevent him from doing things he shouldn't. As he pursued Cammi, his interactions with me grew increasingly rough, and I knew it was possible to justify leaving him to stay somewhere else during this time—but to what end? To make it easier for Jacob and Cammi to hook up?

Desperate and emotionally drained, I often didn't know what I should do. I thought about how other women might react in my situation. Some women may leave, determined that they should not put up with the physical aggression or lack of commitment. Others would stay, afraid to be on their own or hesitant to leave what is familiar. Perhaps some would be dedicated to their man no matter what (even to their own detriment). Even though our relationship was not as it should be, I knew it was necessary to continue living with Jacob until God released me.

A Rude Awakening

One time, after confiding in my Bible study facilitator about the situation with Jacob, she told me, "You need to take authority over the atmosphere. If you don't take authority over the atmosphere, then you become subject to it." That night, I went home to my apartment and said aloud, "I take authority over anything in this place that's not from my God."

Oddly, the next morning, I woke up around 5 a.m. No alarm was set, and I did not normally wake up this early. Immediately upon waking, I heard a demon talking to me! Laying there in the dark, with my eyes wide open and fear tugging at me, I listened as the demon communicated through thoughts. I knew the source was coming from my right side, where Jacob was sleeping. This thing tried to instill fear in me as it spoke, "I'm a punitive spirit…I want to harm you…wait and see what I do to you." It continued with disdain in its tone to say something about 20th century virgins and wanting Jacob and me to end up like Nicholas and Alexandra.

While lying in bed, I listened to what the demon said and did not speak back. I wondered if Jacob would reach out to try and harm me. Instead, he lay there, sleeping soundly. I got out of bed a few minutes after waking. There was nothing to indicate that the demon was done talking. After hearing the part about Alexandra and Nicholas, I left the bedroom.

After this rude awakening, I sat on the couch, eating my cereal. My eyes stayed fixed on the hallway by our bedroom to see if Jacob emerged. *Will he come after me?* Jacob did not wake up, but I was still concerned. Quickly, I got ready for work and left. *Will it be safe to go back home after work? What should I do?*

Up to this point, I'd only had one other encounter with a demon so clearly speaking to me. During that instance, I'd awoken in the middle of the night to an evil presence in my apartment and knew in my spirit it was somehow associated with an old friend. In response to that freaky incident, I decided to invite some ladies over from church and spiritually cleanse my home; so we prayed, I repented for anything sinful I'd done during that friendship, and we asked God to fill the apartment with His presence.

As I considered the rude awakening at 5 a.m., by a supposedly punitive spirit, I was not sure how to respond. I was not very experienced at this kind of thing. Thankfully, I didn't have these experiences very often.

After I got to work that day, I took a few minutes to look up Alexandra and Nicholas online and saw they were the Russian czar and czarina assassinated in the early 20th century and they had several unmarried children who died with them. I pondered the demon's monologue from that morning and concluded the demon was basically saying that it wanted Jacob and me to die. I thought back to the words used, "I *want* to harm you…" *Hmmm. It didn't say that it could.*

I continued to reflect on its words. It made sense the spirit would be punitive because Jacob had opened doors, through the sin in his life, which gave the devil access. Since I'd not had many encounters with a demon talking to me in such an overt way, I had carefully listened to and dissected what it said. But in retrospect it does not matter what the demon said. The Bible says that the devil is "a liar and the father of lies" (John 8:44, NLT). Since demons serve the devil, who is a liar, who can trust a demon anyway? Chances are they are just lying!

As I thought about that rude awakening, I came to a firm conclusion. *If anything is going to make me not return home, it is going to be God and not the devil! What audacity that demon had!* I wasn't going to let it keep me in fear, but I did want to use wisdom in the choice I made. *Am I sure it will be okay to return home?* I wondered if I should get a motel room for either myself or Jacob.

I tracked down my coworker, Daniel, who loves the Lord and often hears from Him. Hoping he wasn't too busy, I asked, "Could you pray with me?" Daniel made himself available, and we pulled aside into an empty classroom. We shut the door and I said, "I don't want to tell you why it is that I am asking you to pray, I just want to start praying first." Immediately after we began to pray, he was prompted by the Holy Spirit and said, "Don't be afraid." After he spoke that phrase to me, I said, "That's it! That is exactly what I needed to know. Thank you."

Being told not to be afraid gave me the assurance I needed so I knew it would be okay to return home after work. Then, I explained to Daniel what happened earlier that morning. I never told Jacob about my experience—I figured there was no reason to tell him.

As I considered my experience, I realized the enemy was trying to scare me because it felt threatened—the night before is when I had started to exercise my authority. I didn't know exactly how to respond to each situation, but I tried to lean on good mentors. I understood I had authority and wanted to learn how to use it effectively.

Fortunately, Jesus is the ultimate authority and He is greater and more powerful than the enemy. As long as I make Jesus my refuge, I don't need to fear the devil or his minions. Daniel's words, "don't be afraid," aligned with the Lord's heart. It's possible there would have been danger and God would have told me not to return to my home, but even in that instance, I could have simply exercised caution rather than being afraid.

God does not want His people to shrink back in fear. Instead, the Lord wants to encourage, strengthen, and embolden people. He wants them to know His perfect love. An example of God's heart can be seen through Moses' admonition to the Israelites when he was leading them into the promised land. Moses' words were, "Be strong and of good courage, *do not fear* nor be afraid of them; for the Lord your God, He is the One who goes with you. He will not leave you nor forsake you" (Deuteronomy 31:6, NKJV). Like the Israelites, followers of Christ are not to fear the enemy. They are to move forward in what God has for them so they can experience the fullness of what He has in store for their lives.

The devil tries to usurp a person's authority through fear. If I'd let the devil keep me in fear, I wouldn't have moved forward in what God had for me, and the devil would have had victory in that area of my life. I have come to realize that fear is actually a sin, because it is the opposite of trusting God. The only kind of fear God wants someone to have is the fear of the Lord (a reverential respect for God). There could be a time when I choose not to do something because it is unwise or I discern danger, but *fear* should never keep me from moving forward in the things of God!

9. FAMILY VACATION

God was faithful to protect my family. He heard my prayers.

"But certainly God has heard me; He has given heed to the voice of my prayer."
(Psalm 66:19, AMPC)

Vacation Out East

Vacation was a priority in my busy life. Eagerly anticipating an outdoor vacation for Jacob and I to go hiking, I made sure to get the vacation time approved at work. *Hiking out east will be great.* It was July of 2009, a couple months after Jacob's travels out west. Our hiking trip was soon approaching and Jacob was going to make the arrangements. However, he was more distracted with drinking, playing videogames, and Cammi than planning our next adventure. As the departure date neared, I wondered what the plan was. Curious, I approached Jacob, "Is everything set for the vacation out east?"

Jacob was standing by our sliding glass door, looking out over the beautiful view of the nearby sand dunes. Instead of hearing about the trails he'd researched and where we would set camp, I received a gut-wrenching response. Turning his head to look me square in the eye, he said in a threatening, informative kind of way, "If we go out there, I am going to leave you to go be with Cammi."

The park we'd intended to visit was near where Jacob grew up. It had some great hiking trails that would have made for a great experience. Unfortunately, Cammi lived only a few hours from there. It hadn't occurred to me—until Jacob's firm warning—that Cammi's proximity to the park would be an issue.

Deep disappointment set in and various concerns whirled through my mind. *I was looking forward to this trip. I already have the vacation time approved at work. What will I do? I can't risk going out to the park and letting Jacob leave me for Cammi.* It seemed my only option was to go to work and ask if I could take my vacation days some other time. Thankfully, my boss didn't ask why but simply said it was fine. That was really hard. I felt humiliated.

Ohiopyle

Although we canceled our July hiking trip, an opportunity came soon afterward to travel to Ohiopyle, Pennsylvania. My family was planning to go whitewater rafting. Both of us loved that kind of thing and we jumped at the chance to join them. We loaded into two vehicles and began the lengthy commute. The men of the family rode in the purple van and the ladies were in another vehicle.

As we neared a busy section of highway, a white car lost control and smashed into the van where Jacob, my dad, and brothers were. The rest of us had been driving behind them and watched helplessly as the accident occurred. Immediately after impact, the car sped off. *I can't believe the driver just left!* Thankfully, no one was hurt! Although unsightly, the van still ran. So, we made a short stop to file a police report, then continued the trip with our van that we nicknamed, "The Indestructible Vehicle."

Following that incident, the Lord gave me a dream that my enemy was driving a white car. Upon pondering the dream, I realized God was showing me I had unforgiveness against the driver who had endangered my family. The Scripture the Lord put in my heart was Luke 6:27-28, "…love your enemies, do good to those who hate you, bless those who curse you, pray for those who mistreat you" (NASB). Clearly, I needed to forgive the driver of the white car and pray for him. I thanked God for showing me that. *Thank you Lord, for reminding me that no matter what someone does to me I am to do good toward them and pray for them—not harbor a grudge, even if I feel justified.*

The first morning after we arrived, Jacob went for a walk down the dirt road next to our campsite. After his walk, Jacob approached the campsite, and announced, "I have something I need to tell all of you." Upon hearing that I almost crawled under the table. My stomach sank. *Is he going to announce to my family that he is leaving me to be with Cammi?* He continued, "While I was coming up the road, I saw a bear." I let out a breath. *Whew.* He was making up a story to tease my mom, who was always concerned about things like that. A wave of relief passed over me, even though it still took a couple minutes for the nerves in my stomach to calm down.

That weekend in our tent, Jacob woke me up in the middle of the night. "Alexa, are you crying and praying in tongues and saying, 'Please God. Please God'?" His question awoke me from a sound sleep. I explained I had been sleeping. Propped up on one arm, he said, "I saw you crying and praying in tongues." He paused, then laid back down, "I just had the most incredible experience."

Jacob's Vision

Jacob then began to explain how, for the last hour or so, he had seen what he described as a cartoon-type image flash before his eyes. It had been kind of like he was watching a movie. He described what he saw and heard:

The universe first zoomed out, then zoomed in. The Lord then said, "I have created this." Then, he saw a naked woman, God said, "I have created this." He saw a woman being double penetrated by men. The Lord said, "Man has created this."

Basically, the Lord was showing Jacob that His creation was beautiful and mankind had perverted and tainted those things that should be pure.

"You and I were supposed to be doing home-work together."

Jacob explained that the Lord had been referring to "Home. Work." This included laundry, dishes, and the other tasks around the home that he'd been neglecting. I rejoiced on the inside! This sounded like progress.

People had colors around them—red, yellow or white, representing their walk with the Lord. Those with red had authority; they could have others, who were not red, minister under them. Those with yellow were more soulish (selfish)—focused on their own interests and desires. The other people he saw were surrounded with white—these were the ones surrendered to God. The yellows tried to take over the others, particularly the whites.

These colors were representing a sphere of authority each person had. A red could allow someone who was a yellow to come under their authority for a time. In the vision, both Jacob and Cammi were a yellow. They resented that when they got close to a white, the white would not let them take over his or her sphere of authority.

One of the take-aways I had as I listened to Jacob's experience, was that each person has a sphere of authority upon which others will encroach—if someone permits it. This is one of the reasons maintaining boundaries can be so important. Proper boundaries can keep people from yielding their authority to another person.

There are times when coming under the umbrella of another person's authority may be a good thing. For example, submitting to a person in a position of authority can help keep someone under God's protection. Choosing to submit to someone is different than letting a person take over one's sphere of influence and authority.

The Lord told Jacob during that movie-like experience that he had been lusting after His daughter, Cammi, and he was not to do that. During this experience, Jacob knew in his spirit that if Cammi got right with the Lord, God wanted to use her to minister to women who didn't respect their bodies, like prostitutes and strippers. The Lord also revealed that the reason Cammi kept wanting Jacob was because he was the first person she'd been intimate with, and he had wounded her. It was like she was subconsciously seeking healing from that emotional wound she'd obtained years ago.

The experience that night was very significant to Jacob.

Processing Jacob's Vision

As Jacob described his vision to me, I was *so* grateful for what God had shown him. Yet, at the same time, I'd been kind of disgusted to hear that God had referred to Cammi as His daughter. I didn't think of her as a child of God. I saw her as a manipulative, seductive home-wrecker who was not following the example of Christ at all. I had seen how manipulative she was. And the fact that she was married to a husband of her own but pursued Jacob—while I was still married to him—was certainly wrong! Despite her behavior, the Lord still loved her and longed for her to be in relationship with Him.

I tried to quiet my inner emotions and knew I needed to recognize that it was *while we were still sinners* that Jesus died for us…that included Cammi. Romans 5:8 says, "But God showed His great love for us by sending Christ to die for us *while we were still sinners*" (NLT). Jesus didn't die for a bunch of perfect people—He died for mankind because each person is morally imperfect and has a sin debt only He could pay.

A Turning Point

After recounting that movie-like experience, Jacob was ready to approach the Lord with new revelation and conviction. Tenderly, he asked, "Will you pray with me?" Both of us were familiar with the Sinner's Prayer as a prayer one can say when first deciding to follow the Lord. Our version of the Sinner's Prayer went something like this:

> *Lord Jesus, thank you for dying for me on the cross.*
> *Please forgive me of my sins.*
> *Lord come into my heart.*
> *Help me follow You.*
> *In Jesus' name, amen.*

Deeply grateful, I reflected on all the tears I'd poured out, and the numerous times I'd prayed, over the last two years of our marriage. I was delighted with this breakthrough. *Jacob has finally chosen to surrender his heart to the Lord. Awesome!* I could appreciate the words of Psalm 66:19, "But certainly God has heard me; He has given heed to the voice of my prayer" (AMPC).

As I thought about Jacob's description, that he had seen me crying and praying in tongues (also known as a prayer language), I wondered if my most powerful prayers had been those spoken in tongues. Perhaps what God revealed to Jacob was just a snap-shot of the times I'd pleaded with God to deal with him. Maybe it was in no way implying the prayers spoken in tongues were more significant than my other prayers. Either way, I was thankful God responded to my prayers and was working in Jacob's heart.

I'm convinced having my prayer language is one of the reasons I was able to maintain my faith and hear from the Lord the way I have, even during very difficult times. Using my prayer language allowed the Holy Spirit to pray through me for God's perfect will and built me up in the faith, like Jude 1:20 says, "But you, beloved, *building yourselves up* on your most holy faith, *praying in the Holy Spirit*" (NKJV).

Shutting the Door

The day after we prayed together in the tent, Jacob concluded he would have one final conversation with Cammi, then discontinue communication. But she didn't like that idea. Since Jacob did not firmly put his foot down, they remained in touch for another month.

Even though there had been times when he knew he needed to stop interacting with her, Jacob would not *completely* shut the door with Cammi. A door that is not securely shut opens with just a little push.

As I reflected on that situation, I wrote the following:

> *A door kept open*
> *Makes it hard for copin'*
> *When sin lurks at the door*
> *And the devil says, "You want more"*
> *Things slip through,*
> *Temptations accrue*
> *No barrier there to keep the devil at bay*
> *Makes it harder to walk in the Way*

Simply not putting oneself in the midst of temptation is an effective strategy for avoiding sin. Lingering in a place of temptation rather than turning away, greatly increases the likelihood of succumbing to it. The progression could look something like this: first walking, then standing, and eventually sitting in a place that's not morally good. The draw is usually gradual. Psalm 1:1 says, "Blessed is the man who *walks* not in the counsel of the ungodly, nor *stands* in the path of sinners, nor *sits* in the seat of the scornful" (NKJV).

Each decision a person makes, takes him or her in a certain direction. Often, when someone ends up in a very difficult predicament, it is because that individual took several small steps, which took him or her down the wrong path. It happens one decision at a time. If someone was to ask me, "How did Jacob go from being zealous for the Lord, to a man in bondage to addictions and on the verge of having an affair several years later?" My answer would be, "Gradually."

Communication with Cammi Ended

A month after Ohiopyle, Jacob came with me to the other side of the state for some work I was doing there. In our hotel room, the Lord spoke to me and basically said Cammi needed to disappear from Jacob's life. After receiving this insight from the Lord, I strongly believed if she remained a part of his life it would not be a good outcome for him. When I shared this with Jacob, he finally decided to end things with her.

During the infrequent and eventual absence of communication with Jacob, Cammi found another guy who gave her attention and began to focus solely on him. Within the year, she and her husband were divorced.

Conclusion

When I think of Cammi's pursuit of Jacob, it reminds me that the devil is like a lion on the hunt, looking for any opportunity to capture his prey. Wherever the enemy can find an open door, he sneaks in and tries to lure anyone willing to take his bait. His bait varies. The devil could use fear, pride, lust, insecurities, offense, bitterness, criticism, judgementalism or any number of negative or sensual tendencies to draw people away from the Lord. People have free will, so it is up to each individual to decide if he or she will choose to give in to sin or follow the ways of the Lord.

Prayer invites the Lord into people's lives and can create an opportunity for someone to have an encounter with Him. God wants to reveal Himself to each person, but there are many distractions that may keep people from pursuing Him. Sometimes people decide they will wait until later in life before surrendering to God. Unfortunately, no man is promised tomorrow. Each person chooses for themselves, everyday, which path to take in life, as well as which doors to open or close.

10. DISCOVERING THE TIME

Hardships happen in life.
It takes discernment to know how to respond to them.

"Trust in the Lord with all your heart, and
lean not on your own understanding; in all your ways
acknowledge Him, and He shall direct your paths."
(Proverbs 3:5-6, NKJV)

Must Stay, No Matter What

Even though Jacob recommitted his heart to the Lord during our camping trip, our relationship became more tumultuous. I continued to seek the Lord, confident that He would direct me in what I should do. Jacob had already become somewhat verbally abusive and physically aggressive before his motorcycle journey out west. After his return, the way he treated me didn't get any better.

Knowing God's warning should be heeded, I kept in mind the Helicopter Dream. Since that dream, I had purposed in my heart not to leave. I was steadfast in my conclusion. *I will not leave because God told me not to.* So even when things started to get out of hand with Jacob, I resolved that I must wait it out. Unless God clearly released me to leave, I would not depart, no matter what happened. If I needed to leave, God would let me know. His Word tells me that if I acknowledge Him is all my ways, He will direct my paths (Proverbs 3:6).

Difficult times could not be used as a justification for me to leave. No marriage is easy. God expects spouses to work through challenges. Familiar with the common saying, "When the going gets tough, the tough get going,"

I believed this concept should apply to marriage. However, after watching one marriage after another disintegrate, I've thought, *Instead, it seems when the going gets tough, most people leave.* Often, God is willing to work healing in the hearts of those involved and guide someone through reconciliation. However, it could be possible the Lord would want some people to remove themselves from their current situation. God is the best source of wisdom. He knows all the details of everyone's lives. Therefore, it's important to discern His heart on each situation and respond accordingly.

As Jacob and I went through various challenges, I was confident God would bring good things out of the hardships I was encountering. I thought about how Jesus learned obedience by the things He suffered (Hebrews 5:8). Jesus was obedient to the will of God the Father, even though it meant suffering and experiencing hardship. I've concluded that sometimes people come closer to the Lord and understand His heart better as a result of adversity. *Perhaps I, too, can learn more obedience to the Lord and be refined by what I experience.*

This Time, If He Rejects You in Christ, Depart

In October 2009, I attended a retreat with several people who loved the Lord. There, a woman who knew little about my situation shared what she believed the Holy Spirit was saying. With an authoritative tone she declared, *"This time* if he rejects you in Christ, depart." Quickly filtering that word through my knowledge of the Bible, it wasn't making the cut. I would need biblical justification before accepting that as a word from the Lord. A moment later, I asked, "How is that scriptural?" Responding to my question, she quoted part of a Scripture from 2 Corinthians 6:14, "How can light dwell with darkness?" *Hmmm. I am not convinced that prophetic word is scripturally supported.*

I did not readily accept her explanation because I knew the Bible is pretty clear about what happens if someone divorces for reasons other than marital infidelity. Matthew 5:32 says, "But I say to you that whoever divorces his wife for any reason except sexual immorality causes her to commit adultery; and whoever marries a woman who is divorced commits adultery" (NKJV). Based on my understanding of the Scriptures, I believed exactly what it said. Apart from sexual immorality, I would not have grounds to divorce my husband. Having a reverential fear of the Lord and knowing that His Word stands, I was determined that I would never divorce for reasons other than marital unfaithfulness—but I didn't expect that to be an issue. Even though Jacob and Cammi had been communicating in recent months, they never actually met up in person.

I mulled the word over that woman had given me. *'To depart' is not the same as 'to divorce.' Perhaps it is possible God might have me move out for a while.*

Although biblical grounds for divorce seem quite specific, in the case of physical abuse, a wife could justify departing from her husband for a while. This is found in 1 Peter 3:5-6, "For in this way in former times the holy women, who hoped in God, used to adorn themselves, being submissive to their own husbands and adapting themselves to them; just as Sarah obeyed Abraham [following him and having regard for him as head of their house], calling him lord. And you have become her daughters if you do what is right without being frightened by any fear [that is, *being respectful toward your husband but not giving in to intimidation, nor allowing yourself to led into sin, nor to be harmed*]" (AMP). The Scripture then goes on to say men should be gentle with their wives and show them honor and respect.

I kept in mind the word from the retreat and watched to see what would happen at home. *What will that look like if Jacob does reject me in Christ? I hope he doesn't do that! How will I recognize it, if he does?* I didn't have any preconceived notions for what exactly that would look like.

When I returned home following the week-long retreat, Jacob's language and behavior toward me was terrible. I continued to justify living in our apartment and would often think in response to the scuttles that occurred between us, *It could have been worse.*

Out of the blue one day, Jacob informed me that he reserved the right to not let me take our future children to church and to deny me the right to listen to worship music. I thought about the word I'd been given, *If he rejects you in Christ, depart.* But I wasn't sure if these odd threats were technically "rejecting me in Christ". I didn't know what it would look like to be "rejected in Christ," so I just hoped I would recognize it if it happened. The weird proclamations Jacob made about church and worship music seemed borderline. *Well, he hasn't actually done that, he just threatened to.* We had no children, so at the moment this was not an issue. However, the idea that someday he might deprive them the opportunity to learn about God was disturbing.

Occasionally, Jacob tried to exercise his power by coming up with some new threat. Me filling the role of primary provider in our relationship and making the decision to take control of the finances made him feel powerless. At times, I think Jacob simply wanted to test me and see how I would respond to him.

In general, I planned to submit to Jacob's decisions for our household because he was the head, and biblically, as the wife, I am directed to do that. However, that submission is conditional. It only applies when the decisions made or directions given by the husband are not contrary to God's Word. When someone in a position of authority directs someone to sin or do something clearly outside the bounds of Scripture, one should not submit in those instances.

Scripturally, I am told to worship God (Luke 4:8) and not forsake assembling together with believers (Hebrews 10:25). So it would not necessarily be biblical for me to give into Jacob's odd declarations—if he actually did try to enforce those restrictions. I also acknowledged I would need to use discernment; it could be possible that submitting to my husband's odd declarations for a season, would allow God to deal with my husband and bring him conviction. If that was the case, the Lord would provide scriptural support when telling me to submit. However, I don't think God would want anyone to stay in that position for long, if at all, since He doesn't want anyone to be in isolation.

Rough Times

One night, I dreamt I was walking on eggshells. That dream was not hard to interpret. I did feel like I was walking on eggshells around Jacob. Since his return from out west when he had been in contact with Cammi, it had become very easy to stir up Jacob's anger. Anything could set him off. He was almost always ready to be offended—he just waited for an opportunity. I was not usually scared of him or his reactions. Neither was I timid, but I often weighed my comments before verbalizing them. I wanted to be cautious.

Various elements of physical aggression occurred, such as when he pulled my hair, then threatened to smash my face into one of our wedding pictures that hung on the wall. The reason? I had taken a DVD rental and put it in his bag so it could be returned. Then, when he asked where it was, I decided not to tell him. I should have just told him where it was, but because I'd done something helpful I didn't feel like I should have to give an account to him.

Another physical altercation with Jacob is burned into my mind, but I do not remember what I did to upset him that time. Sitting on the kitchen floor, my back was arched and my head was forced into an upward position while Jacob knelt beside me, holding my hair in a firm grip. Noticing a sharp knife on the counter nearby, I hoped and prayed Jacob would not grab the knife and threaten me with it. Thankfully, his attention remained on a different area of the kitchen and he did not notice the knife nearby. I think it is doubtful Jacob would have actually used the knife to hurt or threaten me, but I never knew what to expect from him. The point had not yet come where my husband had outright hit me, but it would just be a matter of time before the physical aggression morphed into something more.

It seemed like Jacob couldn't release the rage he felt inside. He was always ready to fight. Usually, I did not shout back or keep feeding into whatever the quarrel was, and my lack of reaction angered him. In nature, a fire burns out when it is not fed with more wood. In my situation with Jacob, there were many times when it seemed like the coals from the fire stayed red-hot, just waiting for something that could spark another fight.

Thankfully, instances where Jacob got violent with me did not occur very often, but when they did, I had no choice but to give in to whatever his demand was. My husband was not in his right mind much of the time. I could see how true the Scripture was in James 1:8, which says, "he is a *double-minded man, unstable in all his ways*" (ESV). Jacob was double-minded because he knew the right thing to do but often didn't do it. Indeed, he was also unstable and unpredictable.

One day, while sitting in his recliner, Jacob quoted James 1:8 as he reflected on his behavior. He knew he was unstable. Then he told me that the Scriptures say when someone *knows* the Word of God but does not *do* it, he becomes deceived. I had not remembered that particular statement in the Scriptures. Weeks later, I found that reference in James 1:21-22, "Therefore lay aside all filthiness and overflow of wickedness, and receive with meekness the implanted word, which is able to save your souls. *But be doers of the word, and not hearers only, deceiving yourselves*" (NKJV).

Knowing something cerebrally is different than knowing something in the heart. Jacob knew intellectually, about God and His love because he was familiar with the Bible. However, Jacob's heart and emotions weren't always surrendered to the Lord. Over time, my husband had allowed discouragement, disappointment, anger, rebellion, and resentment to accumulate deep inside. Various experiences had been difficult for him to respond to—ending Bible college, not having a job for a long stretch of time, and other failures from his life. That combination was a recipe for destructive behavior.

Dwindling Funds

Lashing out financially was one way Jacob could prove he had a measure of power. I'd never removed Jacob's name from our bank account, I just made it clear verbally that I would be in charge of the expenditures and credit card payments. Taking advantage of his access to the account one day, Jacob made a large transaction. After transferring *all* the money from our checking account to pay off most of his credit card, Jacob called me while I was at work to gloat in what he had done. My mind began to race. Quickly, I tried to assess the situation. *There are bills I recently paid. What about those checks that have not cleared yet?*

Once again, I would need to figure out how I should respond. There was no question in my mind as to why he did it. *He did this to be vindictive.* Even though communications with Cammi had ended and she was now out of the picture, that experience left its mark on Jacob. His heart was hard toward me and he felt the need to rebel and demonstrate he had power of some kind.

Since Jacob did not consistently have a job of his own, my earnings were often applied to his credit card bill. I'd allowed him to keep a credit card to purchase gas, especially with his commute to school. I knew when he used it on occasion for other purchases because I could monitor the purchases online. The night before he emptied our checking account, I told him I was not going to keep making the minimum payments on his credit card because he had used it to purchase alcohol. Logically, it made sense to me that I shouldn't pay for it. Wouldn't I be supporting his destructive habits otherwise? Instead of reacting in the moment, though, I should have asked the Lord for a strategy on how to approach the situation. My reaction had repercussions.

I'd just gotten paid prior to the transfer. All the money in our account was applied as a payment to a credit card that I had decided I no longer wanted anything to do with.

Thankfully, there was a little bit of money in savings (around $100). Immediately, I transferred all of our savings into the empty checking account to cover some of the checks that had already been written. We had at least one overdraft fee that month as a result of the transfer Jacob made.

Without an official separation of our finances, Jacob still had access to our bank account. To me, "two becoming one" (as described in Genesis 2) meant we should be one in every area of our lives. However, there is a risk in not separating finances. It can be very wise for a couple to separate their finances, especially if there is a spouse who is an impulsive spender, has a gambling addiction, uses drugs, or is an alcoholic. One person's bad decisions can impact both parties.

Although the control I exercised was well-intentioned, it did not produce good results. Intentions don't always matter. The more I tried to control things, the more Jacob rebelled. The more he rebelled, the more I tried to get a handle on the situation and exercise control. The decisions we made and the actions we took in our marriage fed into a vicious cycle of control and rebellion. Jacob's frustration about our situation and the resentment he had toward me were a driving motivation for him to make detrimental decisions.

The Conflict Continued

Jacob was not the only one whose decisions were not beneficial to our marriage; mine were too. One night, I called to cancel our internet service. I then proceeded to tell the representative on the other end of the phone we were cancelling because my husband viewed porn online. Before I could complete the cancelation, Jacob had taken my cell phone and smashed it against the tile kitchen floor. *Not my cell phone!* Jacob was furious—I had disclosed to a stranger one of his shameful behaviors. That was an awful night. I was really scared of what my husband might do.

Although it was not right for Jacob to smash my cell phone, neither was it appropriate for me to make the comments I did. It is humbling for me to admit some of the things I said and did.

The Day He Hit Me

The day finally came when I made my husband very angry and I anticipated he was about to hit me. As he approached me, I was sitting on the couch and took a preemptive strike. Leaning back, I bent my knees and lifted my sock-covered feet to gently make contact with his chest. Then I straightened my legs and pushed his whole body away from me. As I pushed, he hit my leg. I am sure it was a pathetic-looking interaction, but a barrier had been crossed that night. I knew it was only a matter of time before things would get worse. Immediately afterward, I stormed into the bedroom and set my jaw to the idea that I would begin working out regularly. That way, I could strengthen myself physically and take him on when things escalated again.

The next day, while sitting on my bedroom floor, blow drying my hair, I said, "Lord, speak to me from Your Word." I took the Bible and randomly opened it. The first words I laid my eyes on were off center and about two thirds of the way down the page, "I will not stretch out my hand against my lord, for he is the Lord's anointed" (excerpt from 1 Samuel 24:10, NKJV). The Holy Spirit gripped my heart.

Familiar with the story surrounding this passage, I knew it was the history of David. This portion of Scripture specifically discussed David's interactions with King Saul. If *anyone* was justified in doing evil to Saul, it was David. Saul (king over Israel) had been jealous of David and tried to kill him. For years, Saul hunted him down, causing David to run for his life and hide in caves. Saul was horrible to David. Yet, David dared not raise his hand against him. I got the message. Similar to how Saul was in a key role in David's life, Jacob was in a key role in mine. I needed to refrain from physically assaulting him—even if I thought he deserved it.

After reading that passage in 1 Samuel, I vowed to the Lord that I would never hit Jacob. I announced this at a Bible study one evening, "I've made a commitment that I will never hit my husband." *That night*, I got home and did something to upset Jacob. Afterward, when I'd finished brushing my teeth in our tiny bathroom, my husband stood between me and the entrance way leading into our hallway. Without instigation, he smacked me across the face, looked me in the eye, and told me how good it felt. Thankfully, I did not react. I remained calm, stood there until he moved aside, then went to bed shortly after. It had been a wise decision to never hit Jacob. He was stronger than me, and it would not have ended well. I was grateful that I had already purposed in my heart to not hit him and could reason it was best not to react at all when a physical dispute arose.

His resentment toward me seemed to know no end. Even though his interactions with Cammi were now over, there was a deep-seated resentment toward me that continued to fester. It seemed the whole decision to recommit his life to Christ, in the tent three months prior, had quickly faded. He had returned to his old habits, as many people do.

The prayer Jacob said during our camping trip, although sincere at the time, had not guaranteed he would follow God and exhibit godly characteristics. The Sinner's Prayer is just how a person *begins* their walk with the Lord. Asking for Jesus' forgiveness made his spirit new. However, whether or not Jacob's soul (which comprises the emotions and intellect) would be changed, depended on whether or not he chose to submit to the Holy Spirit.

Even though things had gotten out of hand in many ways, I continued to justify staying with Jacob. *Well. This was not good—but it could have been worse!* Finally, I reflected on what had been happening. I needed to remove myself emotionally for a minute and try to look objectively at the situation. *If I were a mouse in the wall and had been watching these events take place, I would determine this is unacceptable.*

Although I realized the way I was being treated wasn't good, I needed to be certain I had God's approval to depart before making a decision to leave. Dealing with the various issues that arose was difficult, but I continued to put my trust in the Lord. Thankfully, God gives strength to those who bind themselves together with Him. "But those who wait for the Lord [who expect, look for, and hope in Him] will gain new strength and renew their power..." (Isaiah 40:31, AMP).

The Switch in My Spirit

On New Year's Day of 2010, Jacob and I were at the movie theater with my family. While there, I saw Jacob take a swig of whiskey from the flask in his jacket. Suddenly—in that instance—a switch went off in my spirit. I *knew* it was time to depart. After we returned home, I told my husband, "This is the week. I am leaving if something doesn't change." Nothing changed.

On January 8, 2010, when Jacob refused to leave our apartment, I left. He had nowhere to go and no way to support himself, so I was not terribly surprised when he would not leave. Yet it was still hard accepting that it would be *me* who had to leave. I didn't want to be the one to go because *I* paid the rent, *I* had a job 10 minutes down the road, *I* needed to get ready for work each day. My stuff was there. It would be convenient to stay in the apartment. I didn't want to go anywhere else. But neither did he. When I told Jacob he had to go and he sat there, I knew my attempt to get him to leave the apartment was in vain.

The day of my departure, I did something to upset Jacob and he took me down to the ground by twisting my arm. That just confirmed I needed to live apart from him for a while. Perhaps the time had come because my safety would soon be at stake and God was positioning me to keep me safe. Psalm 12:5 says, "For the oppression of the poor, for the sighing of the needy, now I will arise," says the Lord; *I will set him in the safety for which he yearns"* (NKJV). Who knows what would have happened if I'd stayed? Things may have gotten very out of hand. I was confident that because the Lord let me know it was time to go, Jacob was in a place in his life where he would not crash and burn after I moved out. Previously, I don't think he could have handled me leaving.

Distraught, I went into the kitchen and stood in the back corner, out of sight from Jacob. I prayed about the fact that I would have to leave. *Lord, what do I do now?* As I prayed, an image of my friend, Rebekah, came to mind. I assumed the Lord was showing me an image of this friend so I would call her. *I don't want to call Rebekah. I don't want to call anyone.* I simply wanted to sulk in that corner. But I needed to gather my things and get going. I couldn't stay another night in that apartment with Jacob.

Gathering some work clothes, a few pieces of silverware, a bowl, a box of instant oatmeal, and my shower supplies, I loaded the handful of possessions into the van. *This should be enough to get me through the week.* Then, I drove a few miles down the road and checked into a small, inexpensive motel.

After arriving at my room, I looked around at the small, safe dwelling place that would be all mine for the next several days. Each day, I poured my packet of instant oatmeal into my only bowl and used the microwave provided to warm up my water. The meals during my stay were fairly monotonous. With the tight living quarters, the stay felt nothing like home, but I was safe and didn't have a drunken husband around. Taking time to think and journal, I tried to make the most of it. I got caught up on some phone calls and found myself working extra hours that week.

My motel visit was planned to last from Sunday evening through the end of the work week. Jacob had been informed that he had until Friday to get himself together. Soon, Friday came. I called Jacob.

We had a short, but insightful conversation. The day after I left the apartment, he was offered a job that he'd applied to months earlier! God provided just enough for Jacob. But still, absolutely no progress with his drinking had been made.

What will I do after work today? I can't go back to the apartment. Jacob has not made any progress. He is still drinking every day. After work, I drove around, wondering what to do.

While I was out and about, my friend Belle called me. I told her what happened and she provided a beautiful, comfortable place for me to stay until Wednesday. While I was enjoying the comfortable place Belle provided for me, I called Rebekah whom the Lord had prompted me to contact the day I had left the apartment. As it turned out, Rebekah needed a house sitter starting Thursday! If I'd called Rebekah the night I left the apartment, she would have let me stay with her, but things worked out perfectly anyway. Conveniently, I house-sat from Thursday to the end of the month. That gave me ten days to find a place to rent. Everything seemed to be coming together for me to be on my own for a while.

11. MY NEW HOME

I needed a place of my own and found the perfect one.

*"And He has made from one man every nation of mankind
to live on all the face of the earth, having determined their appointed times
and the boundaries of their habitation."
(Acts 17:26, NASB)*

Moving Out

Where should I live? What should I rent—an apartment or a house? A friend suggested I contact a particular realtor in town. With the realtor's assistance, I found the perfect rental house right away. Feeling a self-imposed pressure to sign as soon as possible, I rushed over to sign the agreement immediately after work. Arrangements had already been made for my mom to stay with me at Rebekah's that weekend and help me move. I needed to relocate my things and settle in immediately.

When the contract was in front of me, I hesitated. *Hmmm. I don't think I should sign this.* I couldn't get over the idea of signing something with the word "covenant" in it. A little desperate, I asked "Is it possible to replace the word 'covenant' with another?" The agent told me that I could not change the wording. I felt very uncomfortable having a word with such deep meaning in a rental agreement. Scripturally, a covenant is a strong binding agreement. I intended to keep the terms of the rental agreement…but to *covenant*?

I tried to explain, "I really need to sign this *today*. Isn't there any way we could replace the word 'covenant'?" They said no because they would not be able to get a hold of the woman whose permission they needed to make such a change. About five minutes later, the woman in charge happened to call the office. I seized the opportunity and asked if they would please check with her. Thankfully, she had no problem with changing "covenant" to say "agreement," "commit," or "contract". I breathed a sigh of relief. *Whew, I can sign it now.* I penned the changes onto the rental contract and was grateful for what I assumed to be the Lord's intervention.

The Visit

Rebekah said my mom could sleep in any bedroom. My mom *insisted* on sleeping in Rebekah's bedroom. I tried reasoning with her, "Mom, why mess up her bed? You can sleep in this room—there is space for both of us." It was to no avail. Days later, I found out Rebekah and her friend had prayed that Rebekah's sheets would be anointed (touched with the Spirit of God). Either God knew my mom would insist on her bedroom and prompted the ladies to pray over it, or my mom felt drawn to God's presence in that particular bedroom.

After her good night's sleep, my mom read some of the book, *23 Minutes in Hell* by Bill Wiese. For her to have spent time reading on Saturday morning was unusual. My mom does not usually read books. Then, Sunday, she rededicated herself to the Lord at church. *Wow! What a blessing! Something good came out of this move already.*

The Move Out

During Mom's weekend visit we approached the move in two phases. Phase One was to gather my items together at the apartment, so they would be easy to retrieve the next day. We went to the apartment Friday and collected my items into a giant pile. Some things we were able to load immediately into my minivan.

Phase Two would consist of relocating my items from the apartment where I had lived for the last three years to my new rental home. Saturday morning, I rented a moving truck to move the bigger things, such as furniture. One of the guys from church, Jeff, had agreed to come help with the move. Jeff came, but his helper did not. We were one man short. So, I ended up hiring Jacob at the last minute to help with the move.

Admittedly, having Jacob help with the move was a little weird, especially because he really didn't want me to take the big couch—and moving it was a production. It was big, very heavy, and barely fit through the entryway, but they still managed to move it. I reasoned that since I was leaving a smaller couch and the TV behind, that taking the big couch was fair. Despite what was being left behind, Jacob felt a bit slighted.

Brotherly Love

Jeff did not know Jacob, but when I'd first asked Jeff to assist with the move, I briefed him on the situation regarding the alcoholism. Jeff came from a similar past and really ministered to Jacob during the move. As the guys lifted and loaded the selected items, Jeff shared some of his story with my husband and encouraged him.

Following the move, Jeff refused to take any money for his help and made a point to get together with Jacob. They set a date to go skiing. Jacob loved skiing and was glad to have someone to go with him. Seeing Jeff reach out to my husband was touching. Loneliness was definitely something Jacob faced, so Jeff's invitation meant a lot to him.

Jeff was a brother in Christ who understood the importance of coming alongside people and loving on them. He wanted to live out the direction provided in the Bible that we are to come alongside one another and share each other's burdens. Galatians 6:1-2 says, "Brethren, if a man is overtaken in any trespass, you who are spiritual restore such a one in a spirit of gentleness, considering yourself lest you also be tempted. Bear one another's burdens, and so fulfill the law of Christ" (NKJV). In other words, it's often God's heart to use people to help each other overcome their struggles.

How Much Do I Say?

Prior to coming into town to help me move, Mom asked me point blank if Jacob had ever been violent toward me. I truthfully responded, "He twisted my arm, and I left later that day." There was quite a bit of background information I intentionally omitted. To be honest, in this instance it was probably wise not to tell my mom about the various physical altercations that had occurred. I would not have put it past my mom (just over 5 feet tall) to have made a special trip across the state to go toe-to-toe with Jacob, who was much taller than her, and twist him into a pretzel. She easily could have reacted that way in response to any knowledge of her baby girl being harmed—even though I was in my late twenties.

I limited what I shared with most of my family because of how unfavorable the truth was. Early on, when issues in my marriage started to surface, I reasoned it was best not to say anything. *If anyone besides my siblings knew, they could hold onto resentment. They will try to tell me that I should leave him, especially if they knew about the physical aggression that's occurred. What good would it do if they knew? I am not going to leave Jacob. And I won't move out unless God releases me.* Later, after things escalated, I still didn't want to stir up contention. *I know Jacob will get over this. I made a covenant with Jacob by marrying him and I intend to keep that commitment. It is best if they don't know. After Jacob gets freed from his bondage, I can tell my parents what has happened. Perhaps I should wait a long time after, so they will be less likely to be upset.*

I didn't want to foster resentment or concern in my parents, or the rest of the family. I loved my husband and planned to stay with him. Even after arrangements were made for me to live elsewhere, I still didn't want to divulge any of our secrets to my mom. However, I think she gained a little insight from my neighbor. While we were gathering my things from the apartment, the neighbor told my mom about an extremely suggestive comment Jacob had made to her one day after they'd been drinking together.

Most people try to protect the ones they love. My intent in concealing the situation between my husband and me was to protect my parents and others from unforgiveness, as well as preserve Jacob's relationship with my family. There were many people I really cared about—who I knew also cared about us—that I tried to keep from knowing about the issues with Jacob. Keeping the secrecy I did hurt some of our close friends when they later found out. They wanted to be there for us, but were not aware of the situation until after I moved out.

The Right Place

When the weekend move was complete, I stood in my little rental house and reflected. The place was small, but it would be perfect. Compared to the apartment, this would be an upgrade. Despite the realtor's description that it was a one-man house, I knew this place would be big enough for Jacob and I to share. Completely confident that we would get back together within the next year or so, I pictured us both living in the rental house. For the time being, though, having a place of my own meant I would not have to be subjected to Jacob's crazy behavior. *This will be so peaceful.*

It seemed as though God's hand of blessing was on this place. I was grateful for how the Lord provided for me each step of the way. God's heart is to take care of His children. Ultimately, He wants people to encounter Him and seek Him—wherever they live, and whatever their circumstances (Acts 17:26-27). In His foreknowledge, God knew exactly where I would live and what my circumstances would be, and He met me there.

12. GOD'S COMFORT AND CORRECTION

Our souls may be stirred with angst,
but God is willing to comfort us
when we come and abide in His presence.
In the darkest moments, God's comfort is still within reach.

"I, yes I, am the One who comforts you" (excerpt from Isaiah 51:12, NLT)

Precious Gifts

Several weeks after being in my new place, the ladies from Bible study came over to bless my rental home. They brought some gifts with them. Thoughtfully, they gave me a boxed silverware set. *Yay! Now I would have more than one spoon to use.* I'd missed having multiple eating utensils to choose from. Since leaving the apartment, I'd been using the small handful of silverware I took with me when I left.

Next, the ladies presented me with a big, soft comforter and reminded me, "God is your Comforter." I knew that was true. God says in Isaiah 51:12, "I, yes I, am the One who comforts you..." (NLT).

Prior to coming to my home that night, the ladies prayed and asked the Lord to speak to them about my situation. Gathered together in my living room, the ladies shared the prophetic words the Lord had given them. One word was about me blooming in the desert, and came with a gift of a potted henna flower. Another woman received a word indicating that Isaiah 54 was a chapter of the Bible depicting this season of my life; she had the chapter printed and laminated for me. My heart was touched. I clung to the words presented to me that night.

In the months that followed, sometimes after work I would come home, wrap myself in the comforter, and cry. I reflected on the encouragement those ladies had provided me and knew I could reach out to God. Curled up on my couch, reading the words of Isaiah 54, I identified with that passage of Scripture. The words were so applicable, "...like a youthful wife when you were refused..." (Isaiah 54:6, NKJV). *That's me.* I did feel refused and rejected. Occasionally, I wondered who could want me. *What do I have to offer to a man?* But I knew that God *always* kept wanting me. I could trust *Him.*

Although I had been disappointed by Jacob, my husband in the flesh, God is the Husband of the Church and I knew He was still reliable. Despite the fact Jacob attended Bible college and had much of the Bible memorized, I understood he did not accurately represent the character of God the way Jesus did.

Followers of Jesus are supposed to be a reflection of God. Their interactions with others *should* demonstrate God's heart. However, like anyone, Christ-followers fall short. Some followers of Jesus are humble and imperfect, others are pompous and imperfect.

All the people in the Church are works in progress—many are in bondage to various things or immature in their spiritual walk—and do not always reflect God's characteristics well. In the first century, when Jesus walked the Earth, He hated the hypocrisy He saw and boldly rebuked the religious leaders for it. Today, the Lord still hates hypocrisy.

Restoring Perspective

Developing a perspective about God's qualities and His expectations can be misleading when it's based on interactions with imperfect people. It can be easy to confuse the characteristics of someone who *should* be representing God—husband, father, pastor, or another individual—with those of God Himself. This happened to me.

At one point during my marriage, I came to the Lord with tears and found myself saying, "God, I'm sorry I'm crying." I then thought, *I have never apologized to God before when I cried. Jacob gets mad when I cry. I am approaching God the way I would approach my husband. Jacob is not God!*

That instance helped me realize I was projecting the conditions of my relationship with my husband on my relationship with God. Thankfully however, I knew I could come to God anytime, in whatever emotional state I was, to present my heart to Him. The Lord always knows my heart. It's not necessary to put up a front or be tear-free with Him. Ultimately it's God's desire to wipe away our tears and remove our pain (Revelation 21:4).

A Friend Moves In

Since moving out of the apartment and living by myself, I had to search my soul for the strength and motivation to go to work each day. I continued to work out of obedience. I knew God had given me that job, and He hadn't released me from it yet. At times I asked myself, *What is the point of working if I have no one to provide for?* I was so accustomed to someone needing me that I'd become codependent. I felt like I was at a loss without the responsibility to provide for Jacob. I needed someone to need me. As a result of not having someone depend on me financially, my extrinsic motivation to work was gone. I felt like I needed to muster all my will power just to go into work. It was not that the job was terribly difficult or that I worked with unpleasant people, I just had no emotional energy to face the day.

Soon after getting my own place, a friend asked if she could stay with me. Instantly, I welcomed her with open arms. Jacob questioned whether it was appropriate for me to let her stay with me. Although I had not prayed about the decision, I was sure it was fine. She was leaving her husband and had nowhere else to go.

I charged no rent and loved having her there! She was very sweet and I enjoyed her company. Unprompted, she often did the dishes and that meant *so* much to me. Knowing someone could benefit from the fact that I was obligated to work gave me a renewed energy to face the day. *Someone needs me. Because I work and am able to pay for this home, my friend can benefit from it.* I felt like I had purpose again.

Saddened by her decision to leave her husband, I wondered, *Does she have biblical ground for making this decision?* Concerned, I asked her and she confessed that she did not think so and explained, "I can't take it anymore. You wouldn't believe the things I have done over the years. I was responsible for so much at home, while he went golfing every week." Now that her kids were grown, she didn't feel as obligated to tough out the marriage. She felt very justified leaving. During her stay I presented my opinion about the decision she was making, and hoped my friend would eventually be restored to her husband.

After she had been staying with me for a while, I talked with her brother on the phone one night. Both of us wanted to see restoration in her marriage. As we spoke, I heard the Holy Spirit say, "In a multitude of counselors, there is wisdom." I recognized this concept from the Scriptures (Proverbs 24:6). A few moments later, my friend's brother said, "I don't know if I should talk to her about this right now." I considered what the Lord had just spoken to my spirit and shared what I discerned, "Yes, you should speak with her. If enough people counsel her in the direction she should go, perhaps she will reconsider her decision."

My roommate spent long hours talking with someone she was close to who had been divorced and remarried. She discontinued contact with most of the people she used to interact with on a regular basis because she knew they would tell her not to leave her husband. Isolating herself as much as possible from the godly counsel of her friends, she asked me to keep quiet about the fact that she was living with me. I saw the verse from Proverbs 18:1 come to life, "A man who isolates himself seeks his own desire; he rages against all wise judgment" (NKJV). That passage from Proverbs 18 described what I was seeing in my roommate's life. Even though a decision may seem justified in one's own eyes, it is not necessarily the right decision.

Pierced With Conviction

One day at church, about two months after my friend began living with me, the Lord dealt with me. Suddenly, I realized I'd been enabling my friend. I felt a piercing conviction. I approached the pastor, who was one of the few people who knew my friend was staying with me. I started, "You know my situation. I don't believe she is making the right decision, but we are supposed to love the sinner and hate the sin. Right?" His response was logical, "She is a believer. What do the Scriptures say about dealing with a believer?" I gave it some thought then looked it up in the Bible. Scripturally, a believer is told to correct brethren in the faith (Matthew 18:15, Galatians 6:1).

I couldn't get home fast enough—eager to correct my mistake. Walking through the door, I found her at the dining room table and bluntly said, "You gotta go. I don't know if you need to pay rent or find a different place, but I have enabled you." She began considering her options. Coming to the realization it had been wrong for me to let my friend stay with me created in me a sense of urgency. I wanted to set things right *immediately*—I needed an answer right now. Eagerly I questioned, *Lord, what should I do?*

The next day at Bible study, I submitted a vague prayer request to my sisters in Christ, "I need an answer from God for something." We prayed as a group, then a gal who knew nothing about my situation said, "I am hearing '30 days.'" *Thank you Lord! I have my answer.* I charged rent from the day I felt convicted and told my roommate she had 30 days to find a new place to stay. Letting my friend move in taught me that it is possible to be well-intentioned when reaching out to others, but sometimes those actions can enable others to make a decision that is not God-honoring.

I learned I should pray about decisions like letting people live with me. In the months that followed, when I asked the Lord about other potential roommates, I sensed it was just to be me and Him for a season. As much as living by myself had been a difficult adjustment, there came a point where I began to embrace it.

Since my first (and only) roommate in my rental home, there were at least three people I knew who needed a place to stay long-term. Each time, I kept quiet instead of offering to let them stay with me. If approached, I explained that I felt like I shouldn't have a roommate. For a while, it needed to be just me and God. Relishing my personal time with the Lord, I understood having another person around would certainly change the dynamics of my home. Sometimes God wants to remove the distractions of the daily busyness and turn someone's focus to Him. In Hebrews 12:2, people are encouraged to be "[Looking away from all that will distract us and] focusing our eyes on Jesus, Who is the Author and Perfecter of faith" (AMP). Living on my own would reduce the distractions and help me to fix my eyes on Jesus.

God desires to minister to each person and shape them so they will become a perfect reflection of His image and demonstrate His character. In that season of living on my own, the Lord was shaping me.

13. EASTER WEEKEND

Upon hearing my friend's vision of what the future held, I was devastated. How could this be?

"'I am the Alpha and Omega, the Beginning and the End,' says the Lord, 'Who is and Who was and Who is to come, the Almighty.'"
(Revelation 1:8, NKJV)

Friend's Vision

After I'd settled into my new home for a while, my friend Belle came to visit. We prayed together, and afterward she mentioned that she'd seen a vision. I didn't ask what she saw, until I called her several days later. Her response stopped me in my tracks, "I haven't prayed about it yet. But what I saw was you with a man who was not Jacob and two little kids." Shocked, I began to process what she was implying. She continued, "I heard the word 'Transformation.' Then, while walking out to my car [after our visit], I heard 'Paraclete.'" Immediately, I recognized "paraclete" as a form for one of the Greek words used to describe the Holy Spirit in the Scriptures. Particularly, "parakletos" is used when referring to God as the "One Who comes alongside."[1] After explaining my familiarity of the Greek word to Belle, she said, "Well, I didn't know what it meant, so I had to look it up. It is only by the Holy Spirit that you will be able to accept what I am telling you." I agreed, "You're right. I need God to reveal this *directly to me.*"

I knew it was dangerous to assume all revelation is from God. Revelation (accurate or not) can come to people from various sources. Therefore, it is important to exercise discernment. Prior to embracing revelation such as a vision, prophetic word or other message that one thinks may be from the

Lord, it is extremely important to verify it actually is from God—even if the revelation came supernaturally.

It's possible this could be from God because He is the Alpha and Omega—He knows the end from the beginning. Perhaps He is revealing a glimpse of the future. If the vision Belle saw was from God, then there would be an example in the Bible where something similar was revealed. My study of the Scriptures took me to 2 Samuel 12:7-21, where a prophet of the Lord came to King David and told him his wives would be sexually defiled by another man. When the king's wives were defiled he would no longer have marital relations with them. Considering that passage of Scripture, it seemed possible to justify the vision indicating Jacob and I would not stay married was biblical; God could reveal that a marriage relationship would come to an end. However, biblical context is important, and the passage in 2 Samuel 12 was set in circumstances quite different from mine; therefore, it could be debated whether or not the vision shared with me was considered biblical. I needed God to reveal *directly to me* that my marriage to Jacob would end before I could accept my friend's vision to be a word from the Lord.

Even if God did reveal this vision to my friend, should I have been told about it? There are times when God may reveal something to a person that is not supposed to be shared openly. Sometimes revelation is given for the sole purpose of having someone pray for a situation. It's also possible when someone is shown something by the Lord that the person is intended to hold onto it for a while, rather than share it. Other times, the revelation should be shared right away.

When I moved into my own place it was because I believed the Lord had indicated it was time for me to move out. It was not because I planned to permanently leave my husband. On the contrary, I expected Jacob and I to get back together after a while and hoped my absence would motivate him to deal with some of his issues.

Prior to my friend sharing her vision, I was certain my marriage would be restored. Why wouldn't it be? With all my heart, I had invested in my marriage and still had big dreams about what our future would look like. The thought of us being permanently separated certainly hadn't been part of the picture! Was it really possible that things would not work out between us after all?

Instead of neutrally approaching the Lord about the vision and asking God to reveal His heart on this matter, when I prayed I assumed His answer would align with what Belle had shared with me. Even though God had not yet told *me* that my marriage was going to end, I accepted her vision as likely being true. Reflecting on the implications of the vision, I earnestly sought God. I needed Him to speak to me. Mourning over the probable dissolution of my marriage—going back and forth between sobbing and shouting—I cried out to the Lord. Occasionally I gave brief thought to what the neighbors might think. *Surely, with their house being about 10 feet away they must be able to hear me. I know I'm being very loud. But I don't care what they think.* I was distraught, perplexed, and completely devastated. Pouring out all my emotions, I came before the Lord. For weeks, each day the same scenario would repeat. Work, come home, cry. Work, come home, cry. It was only by God's grace and my resolve to stay committed to where the Lord had placed me that I did not call in every day or simply quit my job.

To accept the idea that my relationship with Jacob was over was like running downhill, very fast, then suddenly needing to come to a halt. I'd invested as much of myself as I could into my husband and our marriage. My dreams—how I had pictured my life to be, how bright our future was going to be—they were shattering.

More than anything, I wanted to submit to the Lord's will. In my emotions, I really wanted my relationship with Jacob to be restored, but I loved God more. The greatest desire in my heart was to love and serve the Lord. When asked what the greatest commandment was, Jesus said, "You shall love the Lord your God with all your heart, and with all your soul, and with all your mind" (Matthew 22:37, NASB). And I did love God. With a heavy but yielded heart and tears streaming down my face, I told the Lord, "Whatever is best for Your kingdom, Lord. Let Your perfect will be done. Do whatever will make the most impact for Your kingdom." Ultimately, He would know best. The Lord could be trusted, that much I knew.

Freed From Legalism

A couple weeks after hearing Belle's vision, I went to a church service with several friends. Jacob also came to church that night. This service was unique because there was a pastor visiting from the Philippines who ended up prophesying over some of the people in attendance. During that service the speaker ministered prophetically to Jacob and me. He had a word from the Lord for Jacob and one for me. The word for me concerned changes and flourishing. For Jacob the message was about going before the Lord as a son, knowing Him as "Daddy."

I pondered what the man of God had spoken over me. *Changes. That lines up with the vision Belle received of me with a different spouse.* Although "changes" was a very general description of my future, I interpreted it through the lens (right or wrong) of the vision that Belle had shared with me.

In addition to the word about changes, the Lord spoke through this prophetic man and said to me, "I am freeing you from legalism right now." *I didn't know I had legalism. But great!* The word I received intrigued Jacob, "So what do you think about that? That you had to be freed from legalism?" I didn't have much of a response, other than acknowledging that I knew the word was from the Lord and I was grateful.

Legalism is often associated with having a rule-based relationship with the

Lord, where someone lives more by rules than freedom. I think Jacob's perspective concerning the word I received went something like this, *"Finally, Alexa, who was always coming up with rules that I didn't want to be subject to, has to recognize there may have been times where she was legalistic. She was so focused on rules. I knew it! I knew she was legalistic!"*

After having legalism broken off me, I experienced a wonderful freedom where I no longer carry the burdens of other people's sins. If people I know are sinning against the Lord, I can now separate myself from the situation and say, "God, deal with them." I don't need to be in anguish over *their* issues. Prior to being set free, I would be in emotional turmoil frequently over the lifestyles of others and the decisions I saw them making. Now I praise God for breaking legalism off me—it has been *so* freeing!

Easter Weekend Trip

Days after receiving that prophetic word at church, I traveled for Easter Weekend (April, 2010) and went to see my sister, who was away at college. During the three hour drive to her school, I asked the Lord for the umpteenth time if Belle's vision of me with another man was really from Him. *How could that be?? I've always said I would never leave Jacob. Your Word [1 Corinthians 7] says a wife shouldn't leave her husband and that a husband can be sanctified by his wife.* In the midst of asking the Lord these things, my thoughts were interrupted with the surprising statement, *"You're not going to leave him. He is going to leave you."*

I was dumbfounded. *I never considered that!* I assumed it must have been the Holy Spirit that had spoken that sentence to me. As I pondered that statement, "He is going to leave you," I concluded that Jacob would choose to be with another woman. Unbelievably, that possibility had just never occurred to me.

Now that we were over the Cammi thing, I had not fathomed that Jacob would leave me for someone else. When he had been pursuing Cammi, I'd actually told him rather matter-of-factly, "If you did leave me to go be with Cammi, I wouldn't divorce you. I would wait for you to come back." I really did plan to never divorce Jacob. No matter what.

After hearing what I assumed to be the Lord's response to my inquiry about the future of my marriage, I believed Belle's vision was accurate. Appropriate or not, I determined her vision had been tested and the response I heard was my confirmation that Jacob and I would not stay together for the rest of our lives.

I understood if Jacob was intimate with another woman, I would have biblical grounds for divorce. My mentality of staying with him *no matter what* was being adjusted. It seemed that the Lord didn't want me to wait for Jacob if he wandered elsewhere. I believed this was either because I would have waited forever for his return or the Lord was going to somehow bring good out of the dissolution of our marriage.

In the weeks following that Easter Weekend, I kept feeling like I needed to let Jacob go. That was so hard. *Haven't I already done that in my heart? How will I know when I have truly let him go?* Jacob and I rarely talked to each other while we lived apart. My husband was still drinking and did not make much effort to reach out to me, and I figured it would not do much good for me to contact him. I wanted to give my husband space so he could deal with his issues.

Forgiveness: Seven Times Seventy

One weekend, I sat on the floor in my little living room and asked, "Lord, which service should I go to this weekend?" In response, *Saturday* came to mind. That was not normally when I attended, but I made a point to go to the Saturday service. That weekend, Andrew Ironside, from Australia, presented a message about how to forgive others. He described how when someone upsets him, he takes his dog for a walk. While he is walking his dog, he says over and over, "I forgive you. I release you. I bless you. I forgive you. I release you. I bless you."[2] He does that until he feels like he has truly released and forgiven the person who upset him.

I recognized that Ironside's approach was practical and powerful. When the offering plate came around during service, I asked the Lord as usual, "How much should I give tonight?" The number seven came to mind. So, I contributed $7. At the end of the service I went up for prayer and decreed forgiveness over my husband.

The next morning in my living room, I was talking with the Lord and felt a gentle prompt in my spirit to attend service. *Really?? I was just there last night. It is going to be the same message.* Obediently, I attended the Sunday morning service.

During the time of worship, the number seven just rose up in my spirit. The thought kept coming to me. *Seven. Seven.* I didn't understand. *What is it about the number seven?* I counted the people on stage. No, there were only five of them. There was something about the number seven, but I didn't know what the significance was.

I made my way toward the presenter, stationed in the front row. I planned to tell him simply that, "There is something about the number seven." About halfway down the aisle, I suddenly realized why the Lord kept speaking the number seven to me. *Oh. Seven times seventy.* In Matthew 18 when Jesus was asked by one of His disciples how often someone should forgive, Jesus said, "Seven times seventy." That is 490 times in a single day! I then thought about how I had been prompted to give $7 in the offering the night before and how the Lord had me attend this service twice. Apparently, this message of forgiveness needed to get into my heart. Soon after this, I told the Lord I wanted to call Jacob and ask him for forgiveness as well as let him know that I'd forgiven him.

I knew the real test of forgiveness is when you can bless someone. *How can I bless Jacob?* Taking a deep breath, I decided I would be willing to give Jacob the couch I'd taken when I moved out.

Lord when should I contact Jacob? The time frame that came to mind was several days—almost a week. *But I don't want to wait!* I knew forgiveness is an important key to being right with God. Matthew 6:15 says, "But if you don't forgive others, your Father in Heaven will not forgive your sins [transgressions, failings, trespasses]" (EXB). For me, this is one of the hardest truths of the Bible—the importance of forgiving others. The possibility of not being forgiven by God because I don't forgive those who have wronged me, moves me to action to make sure that I don't harbor unforgiveness.

Although I'd already released forgiveness over Jacob at the church service, I was eager to make the forgiveness more tangible. I wondered, *Has Jacob forgiven me?* To increase the likelihood that *he* was not holding onto unforgiveness, I wanted to formally offer Jacob the opportunity to release forgiveness by overtly asking him, "Will you forgive me?"

Within a day or two, I called Jacob and talked with him. It went alright. The conversation felt kind of flat. He was no longer interested in the couch and it was hard to tell if making the call actually accomplished anything. In retrospect, if it had really been the Lord prompting me to wait before calling Jacob, I should have waited. God would have had purpose in the delay; perhaps Jacob's heart would have been better prepared for my apology.

14. ONYX RING

Jesus is the Bridegroom of the Church.
He is a faithful husband.

"For Your Maker is your husband, the Lord of hosts is His name;
and your Redeemer is the Holy One of Israel;
He is called the God of the whole earth."
(Isaiah 54:5, NKJV)

Fourth Anniversary

In mid-June, Jacob called to wish me a happy fourth wedding anniversary. My gift? Six days of sobriety. I couldn't think of a better gift! Reflecting on our conversation and Jacob's attitude I thought, *If I didn't know that things were going to end between the two of us, I would think restoration was possible.* He had often been angry and filthy in his speech toward me, but Jacob was nice that evening.

Later that night, I had a dream of a once vibrant city that turned dark.

Dark City Dream:

Jacob and I were at this place that seemed like a fairly illuminated, prosperous city. There was a famous football player there. But then something happened and the football player had a great fall and broke his neck (and died, I think).

I walked through what was now a somewhat desolate city. I saw a few dark-skinned people around. There were cobwebs under the bleachers near the football field. As I looked at them, I thought about how the place could be spruced up. I said to myself, "I wonder if

Facilities will come clean this place up." I asked a dark-skinned guy, "Have you ever thought about calling Facilities to come out here and clean this place up?" He told me no. I thought, "What a difference it could make if I could get this cleaned up."

Dead bats lined the path where we walked. When I reached out and touched a rock, it stung me. In response to getting stung, I thought, "I could lay some carpet here so people won't get stung if they touch the rock." Then I saw a spider crawl from under an opening. Suddenly, I remembered that I'd better keep on the lookout for lions!

Everything about the dream was representing darkness and death. Bats symbolized darkness; they live in dark areas like caves. The stinging rocks caused pain; in real life, words can sting. The cobwebs and spiders represented uncleanness, darkness. The lions represented predation. Scripture in 1 Peter 5:8 says, "Stay alert! Watch out for your great enemy, the devil. He prowls around like a roaring lion, looking for someone to devour" (NLT).

In the dream, Jacob and I were surrounded by darkness and death in every direction. Although I was trying to make the most of the situation, nothing was really being changed. The rocks would still sting, the lions and spiders would still be there. I believed the Lord was showing me that if I made restoration happen in our relationship, Jacob would not get free from his bondage and—although I would continue trying to make the most of things—both Jacob and I would be surrounded in spiritual darkness as a result.

Sin and darkness go hand-in-hand. Sin happens as a result of man's fallen nature and brings death. "For the *wages of sin is death*, but the gift of God is eternal life in Christ Jesus our Lord" (Romans 6:23, NKJV). God's desire is for people to have freedom and life in Him, but sin takes people away from what God has for them. The rebellion in Jacob's life was resulting in sin and propelling him deeper into bondage. Jacob is certainly not the only person to whom this has happened. The Psalms describe the misfortune of some, "Those who sat in darkness and in the shadow of death, bound in affliction and irons—because they rebelled against the words of God, and despised the counsel of the Most High" (Psalm 107:10-11, NKJV). Rebelling against the Lord doesn't produce good things in anyone's life; this was obvious in Jacob's case.

If Jacob and I did stay together, God would not have loved us any less. However, we would have created an environment which would hinder God's presence in our lives. As a Christian, I believed that God can transform any marriage and that He often wants and expects spouses to have grace with each other. Yet, I also understood that the Lord knows the end from the beginning and I needed to be obedient to what I believed He was directing me to do, as long as it could be scripturally supported.

Jesus Christ is the light that can penetrate any darkness, but He only shines where hearts are seeking Him. Perhaps I would have been too distraught to seek the Lord, or too focused on Jacob, to walk in the freedom God wanted me to experience. Although freedom in Christ is not dependent on the circumstances outside of someone's sphere of control, sometimes people yield to their unhealthy environment instead of walking in the freedom that's available. Freedom is determined by three things: the state of one's heart, obedience to the Lord, and willingness to turn away from sin.

Following the Lord comes with a great cost because people must make sacrifices to fully surrender their hearts to Him. At times, a person may be asked to lay down things that he or she holds dear—this could be with regard to lifestyle, habits, or certain relationships—in order to draw closer to God and be rid of the hindrances to one's relationship with Him. In my case, it was Jacob. To not let go of Jacob would have been placing him as an idol in my life. God is clear that He wants to be my only God. In Exodus 20:3 He says, "You shall have no other gods before Me" (NKJV).

Settle All Accounts

About a month after my fourth anniversary, I attended a Christian conference. Afterward, a friend who'd been at the conference, called and told me her husband had received a word from the Lord for me, "Settle all accounts." She explained it had come in a firm tone. I pondered this. *I guess that means I have to finally file for legal separation.* However, the more thought I gave it, the more I knew divorce was the only way to truly settle all the financial accounts that Jacob and I shared, such as the credit card and bank account.

Months prior, I'd researched legal separation. Filing for legal separation appeared to be the only way to show Jacob I was serious about needing to see a change in his life. The biggest change I wanted was for Jacob to stop drinking, but I also wanted him to become fiscally responsible. Considering all the factors of our situation, I rationalized that I should remove my name from our joint accounts. It seemed logical this could be accomplished through a legal separation. To my dismay, however, I learned a separation would be of no legal advantage.

Only through a divorce would the bank allow my name to be removed from our joint credit. Otherwise, I would still be legally responsible for his bills. Settling all accounts seemed it could only be accomplished through filing for divorce. But that wasn't an option I would consider unless Jacob was unfaithful, and there was no evidence of infidelity at that time.

Even though God had begun dealing with me about needing to let go shortly after moving into my own place, I still struggled with how to let Jacob go and entrust him entirely to the Lord. *Doesn't he need me? Wasn't I supposed to be there to see him through the difficult times in his life? Surely, he could get over this alcoholism and be free from its bondage, and we could restore our marriage. How will either of us have God's blessing to marry in the future unless Jacob commits the physical act of adultery? That is the only way I will divorce him.*

A Quick Visit

Giving it much thought, I finally determined I should probably take some kind of action and begin steps toward legal separation. So, I stopped by Jacob's to talk with him about what terms for a separation could look like. After our visit, I was in his living room preparing to leave when suddenly an image of a police vehicle flashed across my mind. I knew it was a warning from the Holy Spirit and took it to mean that I needed to leave right away. That specific image was one the Lord had shown me on multiple occasions when He was warning me not to remain in a particular situation. I didn't understand why the Lord would be prompting me to go, but I'd learned it was important to follow the leading of the Holy Spirit.

The next day, I called Jacob and canceled the invitation I'd extended for him to attend my Bible study in the coming weeks. Upset, Jacob thought I was trying to be manipulative, but his logic was askew. If he'd thought it through, Jacob would have realized that if I was trying to manipulate him, and get him to agree to my suggested terms for separation, I would have retracted his invitation *after* he signed the documents. Instead, I wanted to let him know right away that spending time together was no longer an option. That might sound ridiculous—to cancel plans for a Bible study—but the warning from the night before really struck me. With a reverential fear of the Lord, I considered the situation and thought it best to wait before seeing Jacob again.

Delivery Time

A couple months after the visit to his apartment (when I sensed I should leave) is when Jacob confessed adultery and we experienced that awful, crazy night. Assessing the circumstances after his hallucination, I realized if I offered to be at Jacob's aid during his recovery, it could promote reconciliation in our marriage. I saw no choice but to file for divorce immediately. Coming to terms with that, though, was very difficult.

Two days after Jacob's awful hallucination incident, I drove to my lawyer's and tried to come to terms with the fact I should file for divorce. Hesitant and filled with angst, I sat for a long time in my van at the parking lot of the lawyer's office. Thoughts swirled through my mind as I reflected on what I believed the Lord had shown me in the previous months. Following the drive to my sister's place on Easter Weekend, I had assumed it would be *him* who filed; after all, I'd heard, "You're not going to leave him, he is going to leave you." Anxious, I again asked myself, *Am I sure I am supposed to do this? I don't want to be wrong about this. I don't want to do something out of haste, but if I have to be the one to do this, now is probably the time.*

Accepting the fact that my marriage was about to end was *so* hard. I didn't want my marriage to end. I'd chosen to love Jacob and had committed myself to him. A huge investment of time and emotional energy had been put into my marriage. Before moving out on my own, I had high hopes for our future together. In actuality, I would have stayed with Jacob no matter what, if God had not intervened. The only reason I moved out in the first place was because the Lord quickened my spirit and I *knew* I needed to be in different living quarters.

While I sat in the parking lot, I called two close friends and asked them to pray for me. One shared with me that she heard the Lord say, "Stop analyzing." The other friend prayed and said she saw an image which symbolized I was feeling trapped. Their input still did not provide a very clear answer. I wanted to hear a direct answer from the Lord such as "Yes, you have to do this." Or "No, don't file. He will file." I ended the phone call and took a deep breath. Nervous and very hesitant, I reasoned within myself. *I have biblical precedence for divorce. I can't let restoration happen. I'd better do this. But this is not how I'd imagined it would be.* Mustering whatever bits of strength I could, I walked into the building and headed upstairs to talk with the lawyer.

Later that week, while still in the hospital, Jacob was served papers. The sheriff didn't want to deliver the papers to someone in the hospital. Who could blame him? To someone unfamiliar with the situation, this seemed harsh. Jacob's family thought I was being heartless, but I knew I needed to cut the tie.

I'd really wanted *him* to file for divorce. After what had just happened, though, Jacob would need a place to stay. He would need someone to help care for him while he recovered. His parents were there now. They would be able to support him and provide for his physical needs in the coming weeks.

If it was the Lord's voice I heard during the Easter weekend drive telling me that Jacob would leave me, perhaps me filing for divorce was done prematurely. Maybe he would have filed eventually. But I was concerned if I didn't take action that I would be put in the awkward position of needing to care for him.

I knew with forgiveness anything was possible and there was no relationship between two people still living which could not be restored with God's help. However, I felt confident that God did not want me to restore my marriage. It was purely out of trying to be obedient, to what I believed the Lord directed me to do, that I was allowing my marriage to end.

The Onyx Ring

Believing there would be another husband in my future, I stood in my bedroom one day (months before filing for divorce), looked upward toward the ceiling, and declared, "Lord, I can see that my marriage is coming to an end. The next time I get married, I want a silver ring with an onyx stone because You told me I am like an onyx stone. And that would be very meaningful to me."

Now, a couple months after that conversation with the Lord, the divorce process had begun, and I was approached by Ruby after our Bible study session. In her dining room that night, she said, "The Lord spoke to me tonight, and He said you need to read Chapter 5 from *Seated in Heavenly Places*, that book you read last summer. Because of the turmoil you were going through, you missed the word God had for you when you read that chapter."

That is so specific! Indeed, *Seated in Heavenly Places* was a book I read the summer prior, when Jacob and Cammi had been in communication. Apparently, I needed to re-read part of it.

As I revisited Chapter 5, I saw Scriptures from Song of Solomon incorporated throughout the chapter.[1] Those Scriptures deeply touched my heart. As a whole, the Bible can be thought of as both a history book and a love letter to God's people, but the Song of Solomon especially has the tone of a love letter.

Song of Solomon is a representation of God's desire to have intimacy with His people. Since discovering that book early in my walk as a Christian, those verses had enticed me to want to be in close communion with the Lord. I particularly loved the Scripture, "He brought me to the banqueting house and His banner over me was love" (Song of Solomon 2:4, NKJV). What a picture! The thought of God loving me *that* much, to take notice of me and have a banner of love over me, had warmed my heart over the years. Another verse I treasured was Song of Solomon 2:6, "His left hand is under my head, and his right hand embraces me" (NKJV). There had even been times in my life when I would go to bed, turn to the side, and imagine Jesus embracing me while I lay there, knowing the Lord loved me like a husband.

As I read the assigned chapter of *Seated in Heavenly Places* and saw Scriptures from Song of Solomon, I could see the Lord clearly saying, "You're My beloved." Tears streamed down my face. How precious to be His beloved.

The next time I went to Bible study, Crystal came and sat on the couch beside me. She was a dear sister in Christ who in many ways was like a mother to me. Turning to face me in her sweet disposition, she began, "Alexa, I didn't know you'd filed for divorce until today! I have something I brought for you tonight. I got myself this ring a while ago. The Lord told me I was not to keep it, but I was to give this ring to you and tell you that *He* is your Husband. You are to wear this ring until it is replaced by another." Crystal had been holding onto that message from the Lord for several weeks. That particular day, the timing was right to release it.

She handed me a beautiful silver ring with tiny diamonds surrounding an onyx stone! My mouth dropped open in surprise. Looking at my precious gift, I reflected. I'd told the Lord that I wanted a silver ring with an onyx stone to be my next wedding ring!

Wow! It was a perfect fit. It fits even better than my other wedding ring. Only God could think of a way to bless me so deeply and seal the decision I'd made to file for divorce with a confirmation like this one.

Studying the beautiful onyx ring, I said in my heart, *Lord, your ultimate expression of love was dying on the cross for us. But You have so many other ways of making Your love tangible in our lives.*

In awe, I explained to Crystal and the other women there, "I told the Lord I wanted a ring just like this one, except it is more beautiful than I pictured! And I thought it would come from someone a little taller!" We laughed together, rejoicing at the encouragement God brought me through that meaningful gift.

After speaking with Crystal, I realized she had been told to give me the ring around the time when Jacob's infidelity had begun. That made sense because that was when my marriage covenant had been broken. I was glad she waited until she did to present the onyx ring to me. Receiving this ring and the associated word of encouragement when I did, served as confirmation that I'd made the right decision to follow through with the divorce.

Unless the Lord Builds the House

After filing for divorce, two married couples (good friends) from church wanted to meet with me. I knew it was because they didn't agree with my decision to divorce. *They don't know how God has faithfully walked me through this process and made it clear this divorce is necessary.*

As I came up from doing laundry in the basement and contemplated their request to meet with me, I inquired of the Lord. *What do I tell them, so they will know this is of You?* Immediately, what came to mind was, *Unless the Lord builds the house, they that build it labor in vain.* I didn't remember the last time I had read that Scripture, but I knew that response was from the Lord. I looked up the verse and found it in Psalm 127:1.

I am thankful the Holy Spirit can bring Scriptures to someone's remembrance. If I put the Scriptures in me—either by reading the Bible or listening to someone speak verses aloud—the Holy Spirit can draw it out when there's a need (even if it is years later). I know the Holy Spirit can do this because John 14:26 says, "But the Helper, the Holy Spirit, whom the Father will send in My name, He will teach you all things, and *bring to your remembrance all things that I said to you*" (NKJV).

Thankfully, when I told my friends the Lord gave me Psalm 127:1 and explained some background about the situation, they were not so opposed to my divorce. I showed them the ring I'd worn since Crystal had presented it to me. That ring served as a constant reminder of how tangible God's love is. It also symbolized how God loves the Church and wants to be intimately involved in people's lives. Throughout the Scriptures, God is referred to as the Husband of Israel and the Bridegroom of the Church, "For your Maker is your husband" (excerpt from Isaiah 54:5, NKJV).

Softening of the Heart

Before the divorce could be legally finalized, I would need to wait a couple months. Those were the rules in the state where we lived. Within a few weeks of beginning the divorce process, I met a coworker, Kirk, from out of town. As I spoke with Kirk, I felt the Lord prompting me that this was a divine appointment. *I am supposed to be talking with this particular person.* We chatted for a few minutes and I invited him and his brother to church.

After church that weekend, they came over for breakfast and visited for a couple hours. Shortly after their departure, I leaned back on my soft, beige couch and reflected for a moment. Somehow, I could feel the callousness that had been over my heart, dissolve. The passion I once had for people had grown dull during my time with Jacob, but God was touching that place in my heart. There wasn't anything profound someone said to melt away the hardness in my heart, but it was suddenly gone. I was so thankful. I could feel my love for people returning.

Something about being in Kirk's presence had softened my heart. I later learned that was the only reason we were to connect—so I could be in Kirk's presence long enough to have my heart softened—and this only took a couple hours. God is the ultimate heart surgeon. He doesn't want people to go through life with a hardened heart. In Ezekiel 36:26, the Lord says, "And I will give you a new heart, and I will put a new spirit in you. I will take out your stony, stubborn heart and give you a tender, responsive heart" (NLT).

Wrong Direction

Kirk began to show an interest in me and I was receptive to his attention. Immediately after we started spending time together, I spoke to Belle and a couple other sisters in the Lord about the situation. Each had strong hesitations about this relationship being fostered. Kirk was at least 20 years older than I was. None of the ladies whom I informed about my developing relationship had peace about the situation. I too felt a bit hesitant. But *maybe* this is the guy I should be with.

In many ways, he swept me off my feet. A couple days after we started spending time together I pulled into my driveway after work and prayed. *God, what do You say about this relationship?* In my spirit, I saw an image of Kirk with a rope that needed to be cut and believed the Lord was showing me that Kirk should be cut off (from me), and it would be best if he was removed from my life. I continued to seek the Lord about this relationship. *What should I do? Is this Your heart Lord, for us to be together?*

A couple days later, I dreamt I was going the wrong way down a one-way road, calling out Kirk's name, and there was a choking baby in the backseat. Upon waking, I reflected on this dream. I understood the Lord to be saying, "You have taken this a direction this was not supposed to go, and, as a result, you are choking out what I want to birth." The decisions people make can choke out what the Lord is wanting to birth in them. God wants to nourish those things that He births. Psalm 71:6 says, "Upon You have I leaned and relied from birth; You are He Who took me from my mother's womb and You have been my benefactor from that day" (excerpt from AMPC). God's heart is to nourish and grow people. He loves His children and wants what is ultimately best for them.

What people choose to focus on, and the mindsets they adopt, can be like weeds choking out those things God is trying to grow and develop. There is a parable which discusses how some truths are choked out. Matthew 13:22 says, "Now he who received seed among the thorns is he who hears the word, and the cares of this world and the deceitfulness of riches choke the word, and he becomes unfruitful" (NKJV). Sometimes, a person hears the word (God's heart on a matter) but due to various reasons—such as a negative environment, bad advice, misplaced values, or difficult life experiences—the truth doesn't take root. Without truth being rooted in someone's heart the changes that could take place in a person's heart do not come to fruition.

I didn't want to miss what God had in store for me. I knew I had to end the relationship with Kirk. Sitting on the floor in my living room, I cried at the thought of telling Kirk we could not be together anymore. We had only been hanging out together for a week, but already had a deep emotional connection because we were two hurting people who each wanted to fill a void in our lives. As I cried in my living room, I had an unusual experience. Although tears of disappointment streamed down my face, there was a peace in my spirit. For the first time, I was able to sense a very clear divide between emotion and my spirit.

There were a few sisters in Christ whom I'd asked to keep me accountable when Kirk and I started hanging out. These ladies were my accountability partners—people I could confide in, confess any faults to, and ultimately be a source for correction and encouragement. Their input helped me grow and encouraged me to make good decisions. As accountability partners they could ask me questions like, "Have you maintained appropriate boundaries? How have you done this week with that issue you have often struggled with?"

When I told one of these sisters I would be breaking things off with Kirk, she said, "When you said that, I felt complete peace." Her peace was confirmation to me that ending things with Kirk was indeed the correct decision. The other sisters in Christ were also thankful to hear my conclusion.

I invited Kirk over and explained that we could not be together—it was not what God had for us. As I prepared to share this hard news with Kirk, I wanted to speak life over him. *What better way to speak life over people than to say what God is speaking and to tell them who God says they are?* I asked the Lord to give me a word for Kirk. As I prayed, I heard the Lord say Kirk was like Joseph of Arimathea. I looked up what was said about this Joseph in the Scriptures. Keeping that biblical character in mind, I wrote out a letter to Kirk. I included the Scripture reference for Joseph of Arimathea and expounded on his characteristics, explaining that I believed the Lord saw similar traits in Kirk. The night I explained we couldn't be together, I presented the letter to him and prayed for him. It was very difficult. We both shed tears—and it had only been one week!

Each of us wanted companionship in our lives and tried to obtain that without using the caution or discernment we should have. Discernment refers to a keen awareness to determine right from wrong, good from bad, and includes the ability to know whether something is from God or not. Without discernment, someone may not make the best decision.

The week Kirk and I spent together took place after I'd *filed* for divorce, but before it was granted by the court. So I was still married to Jacob at that time. I humbly acknowledge it had been wrong to start another relationship when I did.

Court Day

To make the divorce official, it would be necessary to go to court. I absolutely dreaded the thought of attending a hearing. There were so many unknowns. *What if the judge determines that I should pay a monthly stipend for spousal support? I can't bear the thought of testifying against Jacob.* I wanted to avoid speaking in court because I didn't want to smear Jacob's name. When his lawyer presented the first offer, I accepted it. I did this for two reasons. Primarily, I wanted to preserve as much of Jacob's reputation as possible. Secondly, I didn't know what the outcome would be if I tried to make a case for keeping my assets.

Prior to the negotiation between the lawyers, I shared with my lawyer the highlights of what happened during our marriage. Jacob had been angry that I revealed certain things, like the martial unfaithfulness. However, he did not get money for spousal support because of the infidelity—I was *extremely* grateful I would not have to pay alimony.

The verdict, though, was far from ideal. The court's decision for me to give my ex-husband half of my retirement and pay off the entire balance on our shared credit card (that only he had used) did not feel fair. *This has already cost me money during the nine months we were apart. Now I need to give him the retirement money I've earned. And it will cost me thousands of dollars to pay off the credit card.*

In court, it doesn't matter who earned the money. A marriage is viewed like a business contract. This means things like retirement accounts usually get divided evenly. Adding to my disappointment was learning how Jacob would be filing for taxes—I would need to give the government significantly more money as a result. Despite the fiscal cost to me, I did not regret waiting until after his confession of infidelity to file. I dared not do something—especially as important as filing for divorce—without scriptural support.

Although I was very displeased with the court's decision, I wasn't going to let this become a point of bitterness in my heart. No part of me was excited to hand over my money to my ex-husband, or the government (for additional taxes). But I had a choice in how to respond. I could choose to sow the money by viewing this as an investment into Jacob and the government, then ask for God's blessing on those investments. Or, I could fork over the money in anger.

Sowing it seemed to be the better option. When I released the monies to Jacob and the government, I spoke in faith and said something to the effect of, "Lord please bring good out of this, I sow this money into them." I believed God to use it for His good. If *I had* to give up those monies, I wanted to do it with a heart that honored the Lord.

As long as I do not debase myself to being dishonest or sleazy—that is what matters. Even more important than a court ruling or allocation of monies is that I am right with the Lord, and don't do things which will hinder my relationship with God.

I understood that I needed to look to God for justice, not the court system. Even if I felt the court decision was unfair, I could leave it in God's hands. The Lord says vengeance is His (Romans 12:19). God is perfectly capable of implementing justice in one form or another. His throne is founded on righteousness and justice (Psalm 89:14).

15. CUTTING THE TIES

When things hold one back from pursuing the Lord, it's wise to lay those down—
this could include unforgiveness, certain relationships, or a variety of decisions
that keep someone from growing closer with the Lord.

"...let us run the race that is before us and never give up [with
endurance/perseverance]. We should [Let us] remove from our lives [get rid of;
cast aside] anything that would get in the way [impedes/hinders us] and the sin
that so easily holds us back [entangles/clings to us]."
(Hebrews 12:1, EXB)

Cleaning House

Gradually, I removed the pictures of Jacob and other items from my
house that reminded me too much of him or his family. Toward the end of
Bible study one evening, I clasped hands with one of my sisters in Christ and
we prayed. After we prayed together, she looked me in the eye and said, by
the Holy Spirit, "There is something in your house you need to get rid of.
You know what it is. It is in your bedroom." This sister in the Lord had never
been to my house, nor did she know what was tucked behind the dresser in
my bedroom. However, I knew exactly what she was referring to. The Lord
was putting His finger on something I had not yet parted with—the wedding
albums. Later that week, I dug out the wedding albums from behind the
dresser then deposited them into the trash.

Ridding my home of items that reminded me of Jacob was not out of
spite, but because I needed a new beginning and didn't want any remaining
ties to the past. That cleansing process was one of the reasons I had only one

AN UNEXPECTED END

bowl and a few pieces of silverware for so long after I moved into my new place. I also had some plates, but I'd considered them to be Jacob's. As soon as I got some dishes at a garage sale, I gave the plates away. Meanwhile, Jacob used another set that we'd received as a wedding gift from one of his family members. Getting rid of items from an ex does not in itself break any soul ties with that person—but it can help.

Jacob's Letters

In the year following the divorce, I only heard from Jacob twice. Both communications were with a letter. Upon receiving his first letter in July 2011, I had the briefest thought that I should wait to open the letter. Holding the envelope in my hand, it was hard not to be curious. *I wonder what it says.* Our divorce had been finalized several months earlier and I had not heard from him. I hesitated briefly, then dismissed the thought that I should wait and quickly opened the letter anyway. *Yay! Jacob said he started to get right with God.* I learned that Jacob moved out east after being discharged from the hospital (following the night of the hallucination). Being on that side of the country made sense. He was closer to his family, and there was a great treatment program he'd enrolled in where he could get the help he needed. I thanked God as I read the letter.

One excerpt stated:

"I was in a 4 month program for 6 months because God was going to keep me there until I was obedient. I have started to obey God not because I feel like it, but because it is what He has said to do."

The change of behavior penned in Jacob's letter was indeed revolutionary. *How wonderful!* Jacob had often done what he *felt* like instead of what he *should* and that undoubtedly created many difficult circumstances in his life and mine. This was the piece that had been missing from his walk with the Lord—submission to the Holy Spirit.

I noted how the timing aligned with what the Lord told me the previous July—that Jacob would start to get right with God in about a year. The letter was dated June 29. It had been about a year. Although I was excited to receive the update, I felt like Jacob and I weren't supposed to keep in touch and chose not to write him back.

A few weeks after receiving that letter from him, I spoke with a friend who discerned that God wanted to deal with my heart. I needed to put God first and let go of Jacob. As we talked, I felt convicted when I realized my fleeting thought, to wait before opening the letter, actually was from the Lord. However, instead of pausing and praying to see if that small prompting was

103

from God, I'd eagerly opened the letter. Taking to heart the correction that surfaced during that conversation, I asked God to forgive me for ignoring His prompting. Then, to show the Lord that Jacob did not mean more to me than He did, I disposed of the letter. By opening the letter immediately, despite God's prompt to wait, my actions indicated that Jacob was more important to me than God.

I was grateful for my friend's phone call and her discernment to share the words of wisdom and correction she did. My most simple, but powerful prayer has been, "Deal with me, God." King David prayed something similar in Psalm 109:21, "But You, O God the Lord, *deal with me for Your name's sake*" (excerpt from NKJV). I have often asked God to deal with me because I *want* His correction in my life—I don't want there to be any hindrances to my relationship with Him. Embracing the Lord's correction enables me to make necessary adjustments in my life. This allows me to move forward with the Lord and ultimately experience the next season God has for me.

Although it can be hard to hear correction or critiques, rather than ignoring or resisting those comments offered by friends or people in authority, I make an effort to consider their counsel. Often there is a point made which is applicable. If their suggestion is contrary to the Bible, or does not seem to align with God's heart, then I dismiss the advice.

A couple of months after Jacob's first letter, another one arrived. Normally when I get mail, I open it right away. The only time I'd had the random thought I should wait to open my mail was with that first letter from Jacob. Because of that experience, I figured I should take a different approach with his second letter. Instead of opening it right away, I prayed. *Father, what should I do with the letter?* Instantly, *Cupboard* came to mind. Obediently, I put the unopened letter in the cupboard.

Surprise Phone Call

A few months after the second letter arrived, I was busy in the office at work when I received an unexpected voicemail. Shocked, I listened to the message. *Jacob called! What do I do?*

I concluded, *The Lord has prepared me for this.* In the previous months, I'd had multiple dreams that I crossed paths with someone whom I was not supposed to be in contact and was overly friendly and warm toward that person.

Five minutes after hearing the voicemail, my phone rang. I gasped. *What if it's Jacob? It's probably not. He called 4 hours ago. He probably wouldn't call a second time. If so, I can't be overly warm.*

On many occasions I'd wished my phone contained a caller ID. This was one instance where it would have been especially helpful!

Taking a deep breath, I answered the phone, "Hello, Alexa speaking."

A familiar voice came on the other end of the line, "Hi Alexa, this is Jacob."

I was thankful that the Lord had prepared me for this. It was as though the Lord had trained me for this moment by using dreams (and my reflections of them) to make me aware of how I should *not* respond. Instead of saying, "How are you?! I hope you are doing well. What have you been up to?" I simply said, "Hello," and listened to his request.

He wanted to know if we could have a phone appointment to get closure. Things between us had certainly ended abruptly. I took down the number he gave me for his counselor and said I would pray about it. I was thankful I was able to keep my cool when talking with him.

Driving home from work that day, it felt like my heart had been ripped open. Just hearing the sound of Jacob's voice caused the pain to come flooding back. My emotions were deeply stirred. *I thought I dealt with this already. Why am I experiencing these emotions again?*

Between the emotional connection intimacy brings and investing in Jacob so much, my heart had been intertwined with his. During our marriage, despite the challenges we faced, I'd purposed in my heart to continue loving Jacob unconditionally as my husband. In many ways, love is a decision. Near the time of the divorce, however, I knew I could not keep viewing Jacob as my husband. So I'd made the decision to still care about him, but to stop loving him in a romantic kind of way. As far as I knew, that would be enough to begin healing—to forgive him and stop thinking about him like a spouse.

Throughout the drive, I tried to process how the hurt could come flooding back so easily. Suddenly, I remembered a time during our marriage when I cut a heart out of construction paper and gave it to Jacob. Upon presenting it to him, I said, "You have my heart." As I reflected on that, I became deeply distressed. *Lord, I gave him my heart!! What am I going to do? How can I get it back?!*

While in the shower the next morning, I inquired about Jacob's request, *God, what should I do?* In response, the thought came to me, *Serve him.*

I didn't understand. *Serve him? He is on the other side of the country, how can I serve him? I know Jesus served people. He even washed the disciples' feet. But how can I serve Jacob?*

A few days later, I was at Bible study in a time of extended worship and realized that when someone gets divorced, they are "served" papers. *Am I supposed to give Jacob another certificate of divorce?* That didn't seem to make sense. Then it hit me.

No! No, You can't mean You want me to send him his unopened letter! That would be so harsh. No, that can't be what You want.

I contemplated what He was asking of me.

Lord, what words would I put with that? Immediately the thought came, *It is finished.* I paused. *That sounds like something God would say.* Those words, "It is finished," were the words Jesus had spoken when He was on the cross and knew He had finished paying the penalty for the sins of mankind.

Taking a deep breath, I prepared myself to send Jacob's letter back to him. I had to be obedient to God. I couldn't believe He was asking me to do this. It seemed like such a reasonable thing Jacob requested—a phone appointment to provide closure. The Lord's response to this seemed so harsh. Deeply concerned, I wondered, *What will Jacob's reaction be?*

Reclaiming My Heart and Releasing the Blessing

The next weekend I played some worship music and took out a piece of construction paper. Eager to reclaim my heart, I cut out a new heart. Writing a simple dedication to the Lord, I wrote on one side, "To God. From Alexa. Every day. 12/10/11." On the other side, I wrote, "Alexa's heart belongs to God."

I planned to hang it on my wall as a reminder. Even though I was 28 years old, I was not above using arts and crafts to make sure God had my heart. I was extremely grateful to be able to reclaim my heart in a tangible manner and present it to the Lord.

Next, I needed to put the package together for Jacob. Taking Jacob's unopened letter, I wrote on the front side in red pen, "It is finished." The red represented the blood of Jesus Christ. On the other side, I penned, "The past is now under the blood of Christ. There is no reason to open it."

As a man familiar with the Scriptures, I was confident Jacob would understand that in the same way Jesus' blood removes sin from the past and creates a clean slate for people, our past now belonged to God. Our mistakes had been wiped clean and there was no reason to dwell on the past. However, I was not so confident Jacob wouldn't take offense at receiving his unopened letter. Oh, how I hoped this would be well-received by him!

The Blessing

While listening to the worship music, I took stationary paper that had green leaves printed in the background (symbolic of new life) and wrote the following blessing for Jacob:

Jacob,

I forgive you (and myself), I release you, and I bless you.
I bless you with peace, hope, and a good future.
I bless your family—both immediate and future.
I bless your children with hearts to follow Jesus all their lives.
I bless you with a life filled with love and encouragement.

I bless you with the fullness of God's plans for you.
I bless you with a heart like God's and the ability to sense His heart.
I bless you with ears to hear His voice.
I bless you with the Spirit upon you and the Spirit of wisdom, knowledge, understanding, counsel and might and fear of the Lord.
I bless you with faith that cannot be shaken.
I bless you with an established walk with Christ.
I bless your feet to always be on solid ground.
I bless your mouth, that through it words of life will flow.
I bless your eyes to see from God's perspective.
I bless your hands, that through them God's love and power be demonstrated.
I bless your body to experience God's supernatural touch each time sickness, disease or injury would be present.
I bless you with a long life.
I bless your finances.
I bless you with freedom and joy.
May all you put your hands, heart, and mind to prosper in Christ.
I release you with blessings on each area of your life.
I bless you. I bless you. I truly do bless you.

Sincerely In Christ,
-Alexa-

Alone in my living room that night, I listened to worship music playing in the background and read the blessing aloud, speaking those words over Jacob. Then I set the letter of blessing aside, to be mailed to Jacob the next day.

Ever since the Lord's instruction a few days before, to return the letter, I had frequently been praying God would put the phrase, "It is finished," in Jacob's spirit, over and over. That way, when he received his letter back, he would know it was by God's prompting. I really hoped Jacob would be receptive to this and not appalled.

I finished speaking the blessing, then asked the Lord if I was done. In response to my question, *20 minutes* came to mind. *Okay, Lord. I will worship for another 20 minutes.* Three songs later, the woman singing said, "I might have to give up some relationships but my soul says yes."[1] I came into agreement with those words as I sang along. Then, as my eyes were closed in worship, a picture came into my mind of a cord cut in two. As I processed what I was seeing, I believed the Lord was showing me that the soul tie had finally been cut. Two weeks after the Lord showed me the soul tie had been broken, I was reading *The Power of Blessing* by Kerry Kirkwood. I did a double take when I read that when a person forgives and blesses someone it breaks the soul ties between them.[2] *What?! That was not just my unique experience? It is a spiritual*

107

principle?!

In my circumstances, I believed a letter of written blessing had been needed for Jacob. Usually blessing consists of showing someone honor or providing encouragement. Since the Lord knows every person's heart and every circumstance, the best way to know how to bless someone is to ask the Lord for an idea. I was grateful for how He directed me that night to bless Jacob and break the soul tie from our marriage.

Since writing the blessing that night, I have thought about the wisdom provided in Matthew 5:44 where Jesus directs us to, "love your enemies, bless those who curse you, do good to those who hate you, and pray for those who spitefully use you and persecute you" (NKJV). Blessing people who have done wrong and caused hurt is contrary to one's human nature. However, there is power in this approach. Releasing forgiveness and blessing someone protects one's own heart from bitterness and catalyzes healing.

In addition to breaking soul ties, God was faithful to walk me through deliverance, encourage me in my identity, and guide me through a prolonged season of singleness.

16. GOING DEEPER

Everyone has purpose.
God longs to speak identity over each person.

"Before I formed you in the womb I knew you;
Before you were born I sanctified you"
(excerpt from Jeremiah 1:5, NKJV)

My True Identity

Several months after the divorce, I was getting ready to email a mutual friend of mine and Jacob's. Apprehensive, I wondered, *Do I include my last name? If I do, is that like advertising that my last name is not what it used to be? A last name carries identity.* Looking hesitantly at the computer screen, I then heard in my spirit, "There's identity in the blood." *Wow. Good point, Lord. Because I have been cleansed by the blood of Jesus, I have Jesus' identity.*

Similar to how the DNA in my blood makes up who I am physically and essentially gives me an identity, the blood of Jesus that cleanses me when I put my faith in Him also gives me an identity. In Jesus, I am made new. When I come to Him, transformation takes place in my spirit. New characteristics are developed, as I walk with the Lord and submit to the promptings of the Holy Spirit.

God longs to speak identity over me—and each person—as His child. Whoever believes in Jesus and chooses to follow Him has a new identity in Christ and will be equipped to fulfill their calling as they walk with the Lord. There is a calling and destiny from God on each person's life. Every single person is unique, designed with purpose, and given particular spiritual gifts. Coming together with others who have different giftings and abilities allows people to help each other experience all God has in store. Understanding my identity, and who God created me to be, is critical to understanding the fullness of God's call on my life.

Moving From the Head to the Heart

On my couch one weekend morning, I heard the Lord say, "You are who I say you are." *Wow.* I was slightly astounded. For a few moments, I sat, fixated on His statement.

I have often said about God, "He is Who He says He is. He can do what He says He can do." Now He was reversing my statement, telling me *I* am who *He* says I am. I had to ask myself, *Who does He say I am? What does that mean?* I knew that according to the Scriptures, I am: healed, set free, forgiven, redeemed, made whole, gifted, given a sound mind, endued with power from on high to preach to the captives and to bind up the broken-hearted, a child of the King, and a spouse to the Lord. Also, I knew that I am highly valued— each person is. Otherwise, Jesus wouldn't have sacrificed Himself for mankind.

Although I knew God loved me and I was familiar with the Bible, insecurities hindered me from embracing my identity in Christ. Cognitively, I understood that my identity is in Christ, but some truths still needed to make their way into my heart. Insecurities hindered both me and Jacob from experiencing all God had for each of us. Somehow I thought when I got married my insecurities would be loved away—what a misconception! Instead, after I married my insecurities surfaced and were magnified.

A Woman of God

For years, I compared myself to other women. *Am I like other women? Am I as beautiful as other women?* Comparing myself to others made me feel very inadequate and fostered insecurities in the area of identity, particularly as a woman. Body image was especially challenging for me; I felt subpar.

One day, I attended a church service where a team of people were ministering who have a gift to hear the Lord speak. Curious as to what the team would share with me, I went forward for prayer. The lady in the prophetic team looked at me and stated, "You are a woman." That might seem to many people like stating the obvious, but what she said spoke to my heart. Deep inside, especially when it came to being a woman, I needed affirmation. It had been difficult for me to call myself a woman. I could refer to myself with terms such as: girl, female, or gal, but not a *woman.*

This topic of identity is one the Lord would continue to work on in my life. Someone probably wouldn't have been able to tell I harbored the insecurities I did. I could appear confident in many different settings. During my marriage I had often wondered if I was good enough for Jacob. Following my marriage, I wondered if I was good enough for any other man.

Walking Out Identity

There came a day when the Lord challenged me to walk in my identity. While spending time with the Lord one morning, He prompted me with the thought, *I demonstrate My faith by My works.* The Lord was referring to Himself. Jesus always had something to show for His faith—it always produced change or had an associated action of some kind. I immediately associated the statement that morning with a passage from the book of James, which explains that faith without works is dead. In James 2:14-26, there is an explanation of how faith and works must go hand-in-hand. If someone has faith, it should be expressed in their actions. Every amazing and supernatural thing Jesus accomplished was evidence that Jesus had faith. By God speaking that phrase to me, He was challenging me to demonstrate *my* faith by *my* works. I responded, *This is a tough challenge, and a brilliant one!*

I needed to *walk* out my identity. Ephesians 5:8 directs me to walk in the light of the Lord, "For you were once darkness, but now you are light in the Lord. *Walk* as children of light" (NKJV). *How can I demonstrate, by my actions, that I am walking in my identity?* I decided that I could "tend to my feet." So, I got a pedicure. And although I do not enjoy shoe shopping, I made the trek to a large shoe store in a neighboring city and purchased a pair of new dress shoes to signify my identity as both a woman and a child of God.

Doing something tangible to symbolize what God is doing, or wants to do, in someone's life can be called a prophetic act. This can serve as a benchmark, as something to look back on and help build one's faith. To make a decree when performing a prophetic act can help root what God is doing in my heart (or the situation) and help catalyze change. For example, when wearing my new shoes I can say when putting them on, "From now on, I am walking in my identity as a child of God. As of this day forward, I am walking in my calling." There is power in words that are spoken. Making a decree, with or without a prophetic act, can help to release what God wants to do in a situation.

God continues to encourage me to walk in who I am as a woman and a follower of Christ. Occasionally I ask myself, *Am I truly embracing my identity?* I hope so. There are still times when the Lord calibrates my heart and adjusts my mindset. Embracing and understanding my identity is what determines whether or not I will walk in the fullness of what is intended for me.

17. THE BATTLE WITH LONELINESS

Loneliness was a struggle at times, but God was always with me.

"Teach these new disciples to obey all the commands I have given you.
And be sure of this: I am with you always, even to the end of the age."
(Matthew 28:20, NLT)

Patience Isn't Easy

Following the divorce, I wondered at times, *What man could love me? What do I have that I could offer a man?* I knew deep down regardless of whether or not Jacob had loved me, God has always loved me. What matters more than *anything* is that I have God's love. It's *His* love that ultimately fills me. The desire was still in my heart, though, to have a romantic relationship.

All Stirred Up

After I had moved out on my own, I began to adjust to living by myself. When I realized that Jacob and I weren't going to be together, I anticipated there would be another romantic relationship in my future. For the time being, though, I was doing ok without one. Then, when I dated my coworker, Kirk, for a week (before the divorce was finalized), something got stirred within me that made me long for a relationship and its accompanying physical affection.

Months after the brief relationship with my coworker ended, my friend Belle called and said, "I had a dream about you last night. You were holding onto a fallen electrical wire and being electrocuted. Then, a worm came up from the ground and began to wave back and forth and sizzle. I don't know what it means."

Instantly, her dream made sense to me. I responded, "I know what it means. Even though I am no longer in *contact* with Kirk, it is like I have opened *a can of worms* and need to *die to my flesh* all over again."

Her dream completely fit the situation. Months earlier, Belle had been prayerful and discouraged me to continue the relationship with Kirk. I was very grateful for her prayers and the insights the Lord often provided through her. My communication with Belle helped keep me accountable when I'd made the decision to end things with Kirk.

As a result of responding to Kirk's interest and entertaining the idea of a relationship with him, something in my flesh had been reawakened. Subsequently, I wanted very much to be in a relationship. I found myself trying to fight off the urge to constantly want attention from men. I wanted to have someone to cuddle with, not to mention it had been difficult being celibate since leaving my husband. Even though I was determined to wait until after I was married again before being physically intimate with another, the desire for physical intimacy had been stirred. This experience helped me understand the Scripture which says, "Do not stir up nor awaken love until it pleases" (Song of Solomon 2:7, NKJV). When someone stirs something up prematurely, it can awaken a hunger within that person which is difficult to ignore, particularly in matters such as love.

The dying to my flesh part was difficult. What does it mean to die to one's flesh? Ultimately, it is depriving oneself of certain pleasures or comforts; this may look a little different for each person. Dying to the flesh could refer to limiting a particular activity or avoiding something completely. Some examples of this could include: eating healthier, giving up a television show that provides questionable entertainment, waking up early to spend time with the Lord, or, in my case, not seeking attention from a man.

Dying to the Roots

Many weeks after having the discussion with Belle about needing to die to my flesh, the Lord showed me that He wanted to get to the root of the issue (of me wanting attention from a man). Thankfully, God does not just want to deal with surface level issues—He gets to the root of things. Matthew 3:10 says, "And even now *the ax is laid to the root* of the trees. Therefore every tree which does not bear good fruit is cut down and thrown into the fire" (NKJV). The Lord wants things that aren't beneficial to be removed. To do that effectively, He needs to get to the root.

The same day the Lord brought up the need to deal with the root of the issue, He spoke to me about lingering in a place of comfort. Instead, He wanted me to move forward at His direction. I needed to stop thinking about the comfort of the past, like having a man in my life. I also needed to be sure that I wasn't treating my male friendships like pseudo boyfriends.

Just A Friendship?

A couple years after living on my own, I was introduced to a male neighbor. We became good friends and began to spend a lot of time together. He was single, loved the Lord, and lived within walking distance. Because of the vulnerable place I was in emotionally, and realizing how much I missed the companionship of a spouse, I knew I needed to be careful with how much time I spent with male friends.

It was easy to justify hanging out often with my neighbor. We enjoyed fellowshipping together and agreed to be very upfront with one another so there would be no confusion as to the status of our friendship. Early on, he said, "If you want me to know something, just tell me. Don't expect me to figure it out." This concept struck me. *That is brilliant! If men and women did this, it would revolutionize their relationships!*

After spending time with him one day, a friend told me I was naïve when it came to relationships between men and women. Her statement was very direct. Even though it was hard to hear, I took some time to think about her comment and concluded it was true. Spending significant amounts of time together tends to build a connection. Without a concerted effort, a person may let the guard down that protects his or her heart—and it can become increasingly difficult to identify what is only a friendship and what is more. Sometimes one person perceives the relationship very differently than the other person does. Assumptions and lack of discussion with each other about the status of a friendship can create confusion.

Boundaries

A couple months after my neighbor and I had been hanging out, the Lord spoke to me one morning upon waking. Clearly, the thought came to mind, *Breakfast at Tiffany's.* I'd never seen that movie, nor did I know what it was about. Believing the Lord had brought that movie to mind, I made a point to rent it later that day. As I watched it, I noted a severe lack of boundaries between the main character and the men in her life. In particular, there was an extreme lack of boundaries between the woman and her neighbor, who was a good-looking single gentleman. *Lord, I couldn't be as bad as her with the lack of boundaries!* Nonetheless, I got the message. I needed to establish boundaries.

Spending so much time with this friend had started to penetrate my heart. When I prayed about this situation and brought it to the Lord, *Timewise* came to mind. I believed the Lord was saying that I needed to be wise about the frequency of our visits and how we spent time together. One change that resulted from this was that we stopped spending time together late at night.

To get wisdom, I could come to the source of wisdom, which is God. Scripture says, "With Him are wisdom and strength, He has counsel and understanding" (Job 12:13, NKJV). I knew I needed to apply wisdom to each area of my life, including this one. Spending so much time together put us both in a position where we needed to make a concerted effort to keep our friendship from advancing to the next level. When I prayed and asked God if this was the man He had for me, I believed God showed me that we were only to be friends. We both needed to keep our hearts guarded.

Reducing the amount of time we spent together was a tough adjustment. We'd grown accustomed to hanging out together and often ate together. One of the first nights after I decided we needed to spend less time together, I had to make an effort not to choke when I ate my dinner because I was crying at the same time. At first, it was hard to be by myself. Eventually, I got used to having more time alone.

Life's Seasons

Sometimes I've had a tendency to want to rush into the next season of my life rather than patiently wait for it. Since ending my relationship with Jacob, I had been eager for God to bring me the man He had for me. *God, could You please bring this next season (new marriage) about sooner than later?* Instead of giving me an instant answer to prayer and bringing me my future husband, the Lord was faithful to teach me the importance of patience. During my visit to California, about a year after my divorce was finalized, I had a dream that helped me understand the importance of waiting on God's timing. I refer to it as the "It's Too Early to Get Married Dream."

It's Too Early to Get Married Dream

There were two high schoolers getting married at 7 a.m.! I thought about how young they were—and it was so early in the morning.

Then I showed up with a man to a park, where we met a man and woman from a show called, "It's a Different World."

As I reflected on the dream, I was encouraged. I understood the dream to be the Lord saying, in response to my requests to please bring me my future husband, that it was *too early* for me to get married. When someone gets married *it's a different world.* That dream really helped me have peace about being single.

Fortunately, God is faithful to deal with me during the times I try to rush things or when I begin to step outside of what He intends for me. I trust God's timing is perfect. It is just often different than I would choose.

Another way I developed an appreciation for the season of singleness was when I asked the Lord one morning, *What do you want me to do today?* In response, the thought came, *Evaluate singleness.* That day, I made a list of things I could do as a single person that would be more difficult as a married person. Realizing there were things I can do as a single person more easily than when I was married, helped me embrace my season of singleness and make the most it. Flexibility of schedule and opportunity to travel were a couple items I saw as an advantage to the single life. I had already traveled a bit, and made a point to continue traveling after this realization.

The Scriptures address some differences between single life vs. married life in 1 Corinthians 7. One difference discussed is that a single person is able to be more focused on serving the Lord because there aren't the distractions of trying to please a spouse.

Although there are some advantages, singleness also has its challenges. One challenge is simply not having someone else around. Times where I have had a tendency to dwell on the fact I don't have a significant other is when: I've been sick and miss the comfort of having someone else around, traveling by myself, or there's a task with which I need assistance. Putting in the window air conditioner unit—and any other two-person job—can suddenly become monumental tasks when faced with doing them by myself. To not be able to take care of something on my own has been frustrating, and even disappointing. Many times, when those tasks arise, I've had no choice but to reach out to others and ask them for help, even though it may be an inconvenience (to them and me). Relying on others has reminded me how valuable friends and family are. It's also shown me how much people need each other.

Various Seasons of Life

Everyone finds themselves in different seasons throughout life. When Jacob and I were married, we sought out opportunities to get together with other young couples with whom we had something in common and could connect. We knew that who we spent time with could influence us and help us grow as a couple.

In each season of life, I can learn new things and grow in different ways. Therefore, every season has purpose. Ecclesiastes 3:1 says, "To everything there is a season, a time for every purpose under heaven" (NKJV). I once knew someone who said that he never wanted to rush whatever season God had him in because he didn't want to miss anything the Lord wanted to teach him. When he told me that, I was in awe. *That's so profound. What an awesome perspective. I don't want to miss anything God wants to teach me either, but I also don't want to linger in any season longer than necessary!* My obedience to the Lord can be a significant factor in how long I remain in a season of life. I have often prayed, "God help me to be teachable, so I can get everything you have for me [to learn and do] in this season, then advance without delay into the next one!"

Dissatisfaction with my present situation or seeing someone else in a season of life that *I* want to be in can catapult me into jealousy if I don't guard my heart. Maybe the timing is not right for me to be: in a relationship, a time of promotion, starting a new job, or being a parent. However, I should be happy for the people who are in those seasons of life! Focusing on what others have, and comparing their situation with what I don't have, is likely to lead me into a place of resentment. Often, comparison only produces pride, discouragement, or jealousy. Being jealous or resentful of where someone is in life is not God's heart. Romans 12:15 says, "Rejoice with those who rejoice, and weep with those who weep" (NKJV). In other words, I should mourn with others during their losses and rejoice with them in their successes.

Expecting

Gathered around the table with my family one Thanksgiving day, we celebrated the surprise announcement of my younger sister expecting her first baby. All the women had tears in their eyes after the announcement. We were all very happy for her and her husband. My sister would be an incredible mom and her husband would be a great dad. I was so happy for them! And I loved the idea of being an aunt.

Despite the excitement I had for them, I had to exercise self-restraint not to begin outright bawling. Why? Because *I* didn't have children, and she would. I knew it was selfish but couldn't really help it. The only one who picked up on this even a little bit was my dad. He gave me one of those smiles, as if to say, "I know," and gave me a hug.

Because I was at such a different place in life than I expected to be, there were occasions, like my sister's announcement, where I needed to make an effort to avoid self-pity. That mentality begins to surface if I let myself meditate on past (or present) disappointments. When self-pity is trying to settle in, it is easy for me to recognize because it feels so familiar. Immediately after detecting it, I need change my way of thinking, lest I fall victim to it again.

Avoiding the Pitfall

Worshiping the Lord one day, I clearly saw in my spirit an image of barbecue sauce with the word "Pit" on the label. The Lord was dealing with me. I understood Him to be saying if people entertain self-pity it keeps them in a pit. As I reflected on this, I could see how this was applicable. When I spend time feeling sorry myself, self-pity steals away my time and energy.

Although it can be easy to fall into the trap of focusing on mistakes and various disappointments, it is a pitfall that can be avoided when I choose not to dwell on certain thoughts.

It's only when I consistently spend time with the Lord and surrender to Him that I experience the contentment of which the Apostle Paul spoke of in Philippians 4:11-13, "for I have learned how to be content with whatever I have. I know how to live on almost nothing or with everything. I have learned the secret of living in every situation, whether it is with a full stomach or empty, with plenty or little. For I can do everything through Christ, who gives me strength" (excerpt from NLT). Paul was a dedicated follower of the Lord and knew contentment because of his connection to the Lord. He attributed being content to the fact Jesus gave him strength. If Paul can experience hardships like surviving multiple shipwrecks, beatings, imprisonment, and even being stoned, and still say it's possible to be content in Christ alone, then it must be possible. Yet, feeling satisfied with where I've been in life has still been a challenge at times.

Overall, I've tried to make a conscious effort to embrace whatever season of life I am currently in. Being single has its benefits. Living on my own permitted me to freely dance around the house while listening to worship music or simply enjoy times of solitude, which has made it easier to spend time uninterrupted with the Lord. While I've hoped to have a spouse with whom I can share my life, I have been thankful to know that I am never truly alone because I know the Lord is always with me. "…And be sure of this: I am with you always, even to the end of the age" (Matthew 28:20, NLT).

18. DELIVERANCE AND RESTORATION

In Jesus Christ people can be renewed.
People do not have to be a prisoner to their past.
God wants each person to experience freedom.

"Therefore, if anyone is in Christ, he is a new creation;
old things have passed away; behold, all things have become new."
(2 Corinthians 5:17, NKJV)

Transformation

Since shortly after leaving Jacob, I knew God wanted me to experience transformation, but I didn't know how to expedite the process of being transformed, other than spending time with Him and continuing to yield to His Holy Spirit. I often wondered, *God, how do I experience transformation? What must I do to be transformed?*

Finally, one day I was listening to a message about the Bible on the radio and heard the Scripture read: "Do not be conformed to this world, but be *transformed* by the renewing of your mind, that you may prove what is that good and acceptable and perfect will of God" (Romans 12:2, NKJV). Then it hit me! *Of course, be transformed by the renewing of my mind! To do that, I should read the Bible more.* Spending time in the Scriptures would help me to let go of an old mindset and embrace a new way of thinking.

Months later, my cousin visited and handed me a gift, "My dad made this for you." Before me was a beautiful, wooden butterfly with inlaid jewels. I was touched. *Oh, how perfect! What better way to represent transformation than a butterfly?* A butterfly starts as a caterpillar, and after time in its cocoon, emerges as a transformed, winged creature. My uncle did not know about the longing that had been in my heart for the last couple of years to undergo transformation. It was not my birthday or Christmas. He simply had the idea to make a butterfly for me and made one. I believed it was a gift idea inspired by the Lord. To me, this was a prophetic gift symbolizing what God was doing in my life, even though the giver did not realize it. In truth, God wants to bring each person through a transformation process. "Therefore, if anyone is in Christ, he is a new creation; old things have passed away, behold, all things have become new." (2 Corinthians 5:17 NASB). I'm forever grateful that when people put faith in Jesus and continually surrender their hearts to Him, they are made new and transformed.

Stepping Stones to Freedom

In addition to showing me the importance of being intentional to renew my mind, God also showed me that I needed deliverance. Deliverance can seem intimidating. The term "deliverance" makes me think of dealing with evil spirits, such as those described in Scriptures. That is exactly what I am referring to when I say God brought me through deliverance.

God's desire is to set people free. Taking people from one place in their walk with the Lord to the next—while growing, healing, transforming, and refining them—is the Lord's specialty. Since moving into a place of my own, God dealt with me about forgiveness, showed me how to break soul ties, softened my heart, and humbled me. To experience the level of healing and freedom that God intended for me, I needed to undergo deliverance.

For a long time, I'd known deliverance is sometimes necessary. I understood that sinful behavior or holding onto negative emotions for a long period of time, can open a door to the enemy (unclean spirit), giving him permission to enter a situation or come into a person's life. But I never considered that *I* probably had spirits to deal with in my own self. After reading a book written by Frank and Ida Mae Hammond, a couple who'd been part of a deliverance ministry for years, I realized that I likely had things in me that were unclean. [1] That night when I went to bed, I was uncomfortable at the thought of being alone.

I was confident my sins from the past were forgiven because I'd already accepted Jesus into my heart and asked Him for forgiveness. But was it possible God had a deeper layer of cleansing which could bring even more freedom into my life? I concluded the answer was yes. Eagerly, I anticipated the Christian conference I would soon be attending. *Lord, when I go to the conference, I want to be delivered, completely. Surely there will be a strong presence of the Lord there and many dedicated Christians—I want one of them to walk me through deliverance.*

There was no question that God's heart is to set people free. In the Scriptures, there are many examples of Jesus commanding unclean spirits to leave people. One such example is in Matthew 8:16, "When evening had come, they brought to Him many who were demon-possessed. And He cast out the spirits with a word, and healed all who were sick" (NKJV).

Although I knew that I had authority through the name of Jesus Christ, I was hesitant to command the unclean spirits to come out by myself. The idea of approaching deliverance by myself was a bit daunting. *What if a manifestation occurs—where a demon screams or tries to make a show to delay its departure? What if the demons put up a fuss?*

Instances are documented in the Scripture where demons did not come out quietly. For example, Luke 4:41 describes what happened when Jesus was casting demons out of people, "Demons also were coming out of many people, shouting, 'You are the Son of God!' But He rebuked them and would not allow them to speak, because they knew that He was the Christ (the Messiah, the Anointed)" (AMP).

On a few occasions, I had seen someone delivered. One time, I saw a woman who went to the altar during a church service and began to heave, and I knew she was being delivered. No one laid hands on that woman to induce that response. It seemed that simply being in the Lord's presence, and setting her heart before God, had been all that was needed to deliver her. Perhaps others had been praying for her deliverance over the years and it was finally taking place. Another time, I was with a friend who was being delivered and noticed she vomited as the unclean spirit exited her body. It was awesome to see the freedom my friend encountered afterward—there was an obvious change in her behavior! Reflecting on what I'd seen, read in the Scriptures, and the testimonies of the Hammonds, I was concerned as to what might happen if I began my own formal deliverance process.

As God would have it, my Bible study leader, Ruby, decided to attend the conference. We even ended up sharing a hotel room. While we were there I explained to her that I believed I needed deliverance, but I didn't know which unclean spirits were present. Ruby suggested we each pray and ask God to tell us what I needed deliverance from, then we could call out the unclean spirits one at a time. This sounded like a good approach. So, we each inquired of the Lord and made a list of the things He revealed. My list included: Travesty, Blasphemy, and Palmistry.

What did those three things on my list mean? Travesty refers to a tragic event; the difficult experience I went through during my marriage and the self-pity I wallowed in probably invited that spirit into my life. Blasphemy can consist of speaking against, or lacking respect toward, God.[2] I don't know when blasphemy was invited into my life—I'd not always been a Christ follower, so it could have been from before I gave my heart to the Lord in college. As for palmistry, I did spend time as a teenager researching how the markings in people's hands could be equated with one's characteristics or their future. Months after attending the conference with Ruby, I was cleaning my house and found "palmistry" written on a list of my goals from high school. Long ago, I'd learned that writing down goals increased the likelihood someone would accomplish them. Apparently, I took this to heart. It was not until I met the Lord in college that I understood insights about the future should only come from the Holy Spirit. Other sources lead away from Jesus Christ, not toward Him, which means they also lead to spiritual darkness, even if someone does not realize it.

The Lord spoke to Ruby and on her list of things from which I needed deliverance was Jealousy, Procrastination, Anger, and Rebellion. *Procrastination can be a spirit? I never would have guessed that. The others I can see, because it is clear those can cause people to sin. I trust Ruby has heard from the Lord. Procrastination must be a spirit I have.* Procrastination did run in my family. My mom was known for always putting things off to the last minute and that habit was always creating stress in her life. My brother won the award for "Biggest Procrastinator" in his high school. Unfortunately, I too had a tendency to wait until the last minute. I could see where it was an unfavorable habit to have, but never considered that there could be a spirit causing that tendency. Not everyone who puts things off to the last minute at some point in their lives has a spirit of procrastination. However, if someone *routinely* procrastinates, there could be a spiritual influence fostering that behavior. It makes sense that the enemy would want to delay people completing their tasks and responsibilities because waiting until the last minute can create chaos and disrupt a peaceful atmosphere.

Eager to be set free from any unclean spirits I might have, I sat down in the hotel room. We addressed them one at a time. After I repented of the sin associated with that spirit, by asking God's forgiveness and purposing in my heart to not behave that way anymore, Ruby would then call it out. The order in which we dealt with the unclean spirits did not matter to me. I trusted Ruby to discern which one to call out next. Her commands were quite simple: "Rebellion, come out in the name of Jesus…Procrastination, it's time to come out. Come out in Jesus' name." In agreement, I also told the spirits they needed to come out.

At one point Ruby told me to look her in the eye. After I made eye contact with her, she spoke to Blasphemy. I was in complete control of myself but noticed when she spoke to Blasphemy, I stopped breathing. *That's strange.* I then made a point to take a breath. My friend discerned, "This one will come out by blowing." Her statement made perfect sense to me. That explained why I found myself needing to intentionally take a breath. The spirit of blasphemy didn't want to come out! Unclean spirits will delay as much as they can. Afterward, I told Ruby about my experience when she was calling out Blasphemy so she would know that she had accurately discerned. How grateful I was to have a sister in the faith at that conference who had discernment and operated in the authority that Jesus gives believers! With

Ruby's assistance, I was confident the unclean spirits were no longer inside me.

After that experience, I did not feel differently, but I trusted I was delivered. Going forward, I would need to guard those areas of my life so as not to allow those spirits back in. If they were to come back, their influence would be even stronger. Matthew 12:43-45 says, "When an unclean spirit goes out of a man, he goes through dry places, seeking rest, and finds none. Then he says, 'I will return to my house from which I came.' And when he comes, he finds it empty, swept, and put in order. Then he goes and takes with him seven other spirits more wicked than himself, and they enter and dwell there; and the last state of that man is worse than the first..." (NKJV). Thankfully, this re-inhabitation of the unclean spirits can be prevented when people ask the Lord to fill themselves with the Holy Spirit after they are delivered. Because the Holy Spirit is able to prevent the unclean spirits from returning, asking the Lord to fill all those openings with the Holy Spirit is wise. Then, the people delivered must guard against sinning in those areas that originally allowed the unclean spirits in. "Therefore, submit to God. Resist the devil and he will flee from you" (James 4:7, NKJV). To not resist him, by habitually sinning, would give the enemy grounds to stick around in someone's life.

Crying out to the Lord by oneself may be enough to experience deliverance from a spirit causing oppression. Other times, it may be necessary to have a follower of Christ come alongside someone in a deliverance process and call out the unclean spirits; it is important for the people ministering deliverance to use discernment and to follow the Lord's guidance for the given situation.

Expelling Demons

Only if a person wants to be delivered and agrees to surrender to the Lord (which may include willingness to make changes to one's lifestyle) should demons be cast out. If someone is not willing to make a change in lifestyle and does not want deliverance, it would not be wise to cast anything out. Otherwise, the deliverance will do no good and could be a risky thing to attempt. If the person agrees to be delivered and repents, but then starts talking nonsense when the process begins, that nonsense talk is probably the demons delaying the process or trying to cause the folks doing deliverance to abandon the idea.

When Ruby walks people through deliverance, she has an effective approach. Before she begins the process of calling out the demons and delivering the person, she lets the person ask God's forgiveness and repent of their sin (otherwise, those demons have the right to stay). Then she gets the person's consent by asking them to verbally state they submit their will to the Holy Spirit and want to be delivered. The Holy Spirit does not transgress a person's will and the demons know that. She explains her reasoning: "Then I know that I, as the deliverance instrument, have confidence in my authority in Christ and am not violating the person's will as they have already submitted their will to the Holy Spirit's will and agreed to the process." That way, if the demons try to resist, the person getting delivered has already submitted to the work of the Holy Spirit and Ruby knows it is fine to continue anyway.

Followers of Jesus are called to deliver people. They also have a responsibility to share the gospel, the love of Christ, encouragement, and when necessary, correction. Part of helping people experience deliverance may include mentorship and coaching regarding lifestyle changes. Delivering people may also include casting out demons. Jesus appointed His disciples "to have authority and power to heal the sick and *to drive out demons*" (excerpt from Mark 3:15, AMPC). Disciples are people who are fully committed to Jesus—they obey the promptings of the Lord and are willing to pay the cost of following Him.

Barak

Immediately following the deliverance, Ruby prayed for me and shared the message she felt the Lord had given her when she prayed, "I am your Barak. The name for your outreaches will be Project Barak." She had no idea the impact those words would have on me.

Long before Jacob and I had gotten together, one of our friends told him that he was like Barak from the Bible—I did not learn this until a couple years into our marriage. Interestingly, a few years before we were married, the same friend told me I was like Deborah.

Since then, multiple people had spoken over me that I was a Deborah, and I'd come to identify with some of her characteristics. The story of Deborah and Barak is captured in Judges 4. Barak was a man called to do something great for Israel but lacked the courage to do it. Subsequently, Barak told Deborah (the prophetess who was judging Israel at the time) he would only go into battle if she accompanied him. So, she went with him. *Together* they obtained victory.

When Jacob had shared with me that he'd been told he was similar to Barak, I was struck. *It is so fitting that he is a Barak because I am a Deborah.* When we went through difficult times, I thought about the parallel between us— Barak and Deborah. *He needs me to help uphold him. It's okay that he hasn't obtained victory over his struggles yet. He will be victorious because I am by his side.*

When my marriage was ending, I was disturbed that things hadn't worked out. *If Jacob is like Barak, then doesn't he need me? I thought I was his Deborah. I thought I was going to be by his side—to see him through to victory.* However, things had not turned out the way I'd anticipated.

The word Ruby released, provided me with a sense of restoration. God said, "*He* is my 'Barak.'" This statement had double meaning. God, Himself, was replacing the Barak [Jacob] who had been in my life. *Barak* is also the Hebrew word for blessing.[3] I understood God to be saying *He* is my blessing, and the source of my blessing.

After receiving this word, I decided to call the outreach events I would be leading for my Bible study "Project Barak." Literally translated, it could also be "Project Blessing."

Being told that God is my Barak was very meaningful and brought me great encouragement!

Restoration and Letting Go

Several months later, another example of restoration came, this time with regard to my role as an aunt. During my marriage, I'd looked forward to an opportunity to pour into Jacob's little niece and nephew. However, when we divorced, I wasn't able to maintain contact with any of his family. Incredibly, my sister gave her daughter the same name as Jacob's niece! To now have a niece with the same name has been so meaningful. Only God could orchestrate something like that.

Giving up contact with Jacob's family when we divorced had not been easy for me. I liked his family but had to accept that we would no longer have contact. Similar to when someone is disowned, the relationship came to a sudden end. His family didn't want to hear from me. When the divorce process began, I wanted to talk to his younger brother one last time, and tell him what a bright future he had. But when I contemplated calling him, a picture of a yellow caution sign popped into my mind; I felt like the Lord was telling me to use caution. Realizing it would not be such a good idea, I decided not to contact him. I didn't want to create any more dissension than there already was.

Long after the divorce, while attending a play, one of the characters reminded me of Jacob's brother. *I liked Jacob's family. I wonder how they are doing.* My heart was stirred thinking about his family. So, I talked with the Lord about it and He clearly said, "Entrust them to Me." Taking that comment to heart, I again released his family to the Lord and asked God to provide for and encourage them. To help make this release more tangible, I wrote out my decision to entrust that family to God. I then posted the letter on the wall near my stairwell. This way, if I needed to remind myself not to be thinking about them, I could look at that letter as a reminder.

19. HUMBLING MYSELF

There are veils over the heart that can keep people from seeing clearly.
Thankfully, Jesus specializes in calibrating hearts and adjusting perspectives.

"And why do you look at the speck in your brother's eye,
but do not consider the plank in your own eye?"
(Matthew 7:3, NKJV)

Ruby Speaks the Truth

It was three years after my divorce when my trusted friend and mentor, Ruby, sat down with me at the coffee shop we frequented. Soon into our visit, she looked me in the eye and said, "I feel compelled to tell you that you came across during your marriage as critical, self-righteous and controlling." Trying to absorb her comment, I stared at her. As much as I didn't want her observation to be true, I could not dismiss her assessment.

Ruby knew me very well and accurately discerns God's heart on a lot of matters. For several years, she'd served as the facilitator for my Bible study and been a source of wisdom for me. I had given Ruby a platform to speak into my life and respected her too much not to give her comments serious consideration. More than I wanted to feel justified, I wanted to know the truth. Although I was a bit surprised at what she said, I didn't scoff at her stated observation. Trying to process her comment, I wondered how I could have responded differently to Jacob.

After a moment I concluded, *If she is telling me this, it must be true, even if I haven't thought that.* I hated being associated with those characteristics, but I was thankful Ruby was so honest with me. That entire weekend, I grappled with her comments. Wanting to be teachable, I realized that I must consider feedback even when it's unfavorable.

If Ruby had not mustered up the boldness to tell me I acted self-righteous, controlling, and critical during my marriage, I do not know if I would have ever realized it. A trusted friend pointing out my unfavorable traits served as catalyst for me to be able to take ownership for the things I had done wrong. It also prompted repentance.

Following that meeting with Ruby I wondered, *Would I have ever seen my contribution to the problems in my marriage if she had not been so honest with me? How many years would it have taken me to realize what I did wrong?*

I am far from all-knowing and need others to call me out when they see character flaws and help me realize when I've been wrong. That way, I can recognize the areas of my life that need change. Only one person was ever exempted from needing correction and that was Jesus. Everyone else is still a work in progress.

My new awareness of the mistakes I'd made during my marriage meant I would need to humble myself before the Lord. As I took time to reflect on what Ruby told me, I felt like scales were removed from my eyes. I'd been so blind. There is an adage that says, "Love is blind." My personal adage says, "Pride is blinding too." If both Jacob and I had made a point to be humble, that would have helped each of us take ownership for the mistakes we made. But unfortunately, neither of us were humble. Lack of humility in Jacob caused him to gradually withdraw and harden his heart. The affect it had on me was different. It propelled me to feel justified all the time. Because I didn't have a humble heart, I did not feel motivated to try to understand things from Jacob's perspective. I prayed for Jacob, but was not intentional to ask the Lord what *I* could do differently.

"Pride goes before destruction, and a haughty spirit before a fall" (Proverbs 16:18, NKJV). Indeed, we did fall, into a downward spiral that took our marriage into a dark place. Looking back, I see that I was prideful during my marriage. I could have quickly listed the repercussions of Jacob's decisions, but it took me a long time to recognize how *my* behavior contributed to the downfall of our marriage.

I wish God would have dealt with me about all my mistakes *during* my marriage instead of years afterward, but I think my heart was hardened. I didn't humble myself and invite Him to work in those areas of my heart. God will go only where He is invited. That is why He does not force salvation onto people. He waits until people recognize their need for Him. Often, followers of Christ discuss their faith with others, explaining who God is and how much He loves people, because they want to help others understand their need for Him.

When Veils Are Removed

Unfortunately, one's perception may often be skewed due to the veils over that person's heart. There can be veils of pride, intellect, insecurities, disappointment, and other mindsets which keep someone from having an accurate perspective. Self-righteousness had been one of the veils over me during much of my marriage. The veils over me influenced my behavior, such as trying to control everything rather than seeking godly counsel from others. Until God removes the veils—which often happens through humbling oneself before Him, repenting, and asking Him to calibrate one's heart—a person may not see clearly.

On the day Jesus was crucified, there was a veil (a thick curtain) which surrounded the Holy of Holies (in the Temple of Jerusalem) that was supernaturally torn. "And the curtain of the temple was torn in two, from top to bottom" (Mark 15:38, ESV). No person came and ripped it. So, why did it tear? Because the Spirit of God, which previously resided in the Holy of Holies and was separated from mankind by the veil, was being made accessible to people. As a result of Jesus' sacrificial death, the Holy Spirit would no longer be dwelling in a temple made by human hands. Instead, He now resides in the hearts of mankind—in each person who puts their faith in God and chooses to make Jesus Christ their Lord (Acts 17:24).

That tear in the veil indicated the release of God's Holy Spirit. In the same way that the veil separating mankind from God's presence was torn, God wants to tear and remove the veils over every person. That way everyone can have more access to God and experience what He wants for their lives.

The Apology Letter

After meeting with Ruby and realizing there had been veils over me during my marriage, I felt compelled to apologize to Jacob. I wanted him to know that I realized my mistakes. That weekend, I humbled myself before the Lord, confessing what I'd done and asking His forgiveness, then I wrote an apology to my ex-husband. We hadn't been in contact since I sent the letter of blessing a year and a half earlier.

After sending this apology letter to him, I learned the unopened letter I sent back to him (with the blessing) was his apology letter. Thankfully, releasing forgiveness to someone does not have to be contingent on receiving an apology. That's not to say I discount the power of an apology. On the contrary, apologizing allows someone to take ownership of a situation and accept responsibility for their actions. It shows initiative toward reconciliation and can often prompt mutual forgiveness.

Often, when I apologized during my marriage, I would follow my apology with "But if you hadn't..." Tagging that phrase onto my statements, even though they started with "I'm sorry," pretty much nullified any apology being offered. Unfortunately, this was my approach during our entire marriage. It was a way for me to justify myself and avoid taking ownership for conflict that arose. Since then, I have learned the importance of taking ownership and have appreciated an explanation offered by Dr. Emerson Eggrichs in his book, *Love and Respect*. With regard to taking ownership in a conflict or misunderstanding, Eggrichs says the first person to apologize should be "whoever thinks they are more mature."[1] After one person takes ownership, the other person will usually confess their fault in the situation. However, it is possible that an individual may not ever see what he or she did wrong. If each person waits for the other to take action, reconciliation may never take place. And from experience, I know that adding "But…" onto an apology has a minimal effect on promoting reconciliation.

To be sure I did not come across as accusatory or negative in my apology letter, I asked my siblings to read it. I wanted to verify that I came across as sincere, not self-righteous. The letter didn't come across to *me* as self-righteous, but neither had my decisions during our marriage. Thankfully, my siblings said it looked fine.

I wanted to let Jacob know that I was sorry and recognized I had not been faultless during our marriage. Writing the apology letter was a way for me to humble myself and give Jacob explicit permission to forgive me:

Jacob,

I want to give you my deepest apologies for so many things.

I realize that during our marriage, I came across as self-righteous, critical, and controlling. It does not matter how well-intended decisions such as taking control of the finances were. My actions of attempted control provoked rebellion and fed into the vicious cycle we found ourselves in—of control and rebellion. I wanted so much to see you set free. I tried to do everything in my power to set you free; however, my choices along the way did not help you.

Please forgive me for:
- *The numerous times I approached you to apologize but justified what I did, "I'm sorry, BUT…"*
- *Not effectively providing the support structure you needed.*
- *Allowing good intentions to be justification for my decisions that eventually became destructive to our marriage, like taking over the finances. I realize this was controlling and am sorry I deprived you the way I did. I realize this contributed to you feeling like you did not have any power in our relationship.*
- *Not responding the way you needed me to.*
- *For being critical.*
- *Behaving in a way that ultimately pushed you away.*
- *Enabling your struggles.*

- o *Not recognizing your need for mentorship, and therefore not encouraging you to find a godly man who could help you discover your identity. I know identity was something you were wanting to have a better grasp of and I should have somehow encouraged you in a direction that would have helped you find your identity.*
- o *Being so angry and disappointed during our marriage.*
- o *Not being balanced in my life with work. Work was a bit of an obsession to me, not because I wanted to be so focused on it, but because I didn't know how not to be. This was unfair to you.*
- o *Not dressing in a way that was attractive to you.*
- o *Not being balanced in the kind of time we spent time together.*
- o *Being resentful when things were not done the way I thought they should be.*

The next section I offer not as a justification for my actions, but simply as an explanation:

I loved you very, very much. During our time together, I felt like I did everything I could to honor you; this included not telling people about the drinking. However, trying to keep the drinking a secret from others turned out to be one of the many detrimental decisions I made. If I had not tried to hide that aspect of our lives, perhaps I would have positioned myself to receive advice that would have helped me make more beneficial decisions. With input from others, I may have been able to take actions that would have been supportive and uplifting, rather than take actions that deepened the rift between us. I am sorry I kept the struggles that came up during our marriage hidden from people who cared about us.

… I was wrong in many of my interactions with you.

Years ago, in early January of 2006 (New Year's Day), you called and left a message on my phone and said that the Lord had shown you, "We have so many veils over our hearts." I think, similar to deception, it is difficult for someone to see when a perspective is not accurate, due to the veils over that person's heart.

For me, during our marriage, there was a veil of self-righteousness and what I saw was filtered through that veil. I did not give you the space or support you needed. At the time, I had reasons for not pursuing counseling, but I now realize I should have encouraged counseling for both of us. This would have provided an objective view point of our situation and perhaps helped prevent me from feeding into the cycle of control the way I did.

I have never stopped believing in you. I still believe with all my heart that God has a great plan for your life and that He desires to do great things through you. I am truly sorry for any obstacles or delays in your walk with Him, or with others, that have been caused by me. I am sorry for the consternation I have caused you and your family.

If there are other things that I have done to hurt you that are not listed in this apology, but you want me to know so that I can ask your forgiveness, please let me know what they are.

If you choose not to reply, please know that I wish you only the best.

Sincerely,
-Alexa-

Moving Forward

Following this apology letter, Jacob and I were in contact via email for a while. Eventually, we decided to no longer keep in touch—not out of bitterness, but because keeping in contact had the potential to complicate things and imply that perhaps our relationship could be restored.

Jacob and I went our separate directions after the divorce, and lived in different areas of the country. Thankfully, God continued to work in each of our hearts.

I am still trying to work out different aspects of my life, such as my desire to be a wife and mother. I continue to press into the Scriptures and wise counsel to live my life well. No matter what my marital status or stage of life is, life has just as much purpose and I can continue to serve the Lord. I understand now the importance of being humble and teachable, and I will be intentional to use the gifts and talents I've been given.

Over time, God has continued to humble me. I now recognize how detrimental criticism as well as harsh or rash responses can be, even though it may seem easy to justify. Prayerfully and humbly approaching a situation with gentleness and humility is a much better response. The former can create coercion and possibly produce rebellion and resentment. The latter approach can inspire and intrinsically motivate someone toward change.

I am grateful for the time I had with Jacob, and for how much I learned from our relationship. Although he had struggles, there were many favorable qualities he exhibited too. Over the years, many people grew in their faith because of what Jacob shared with them from the Scriptures.

One morning, to my complete surprise, I received a message that Jacob passed away. It was two weeks after this book was finished. The irony of the book's title hit me. It was indeed an unexpected ending.

It's been difficult to accept that Jacob is now gone. He was 33. I hoped he would live a long, fulfilled life, but it ended sooner than expected. No man is promised tomorrow—which is why no one should delay cultivating a relationship with the Lord. For this same reason, it's also important to prioritize making amends, reconciling, and forgiving.

POST SCRIPT:
THE ULTIMATE RELATIONSHIP

The love God has for each person is overwhelming.
Out of His love for us, He made a way for us to be in
relationship with Him. That is the ultimate relationship!

"We love Him because He first loved us."
(1 John 4:19, NKJV)

Without question, the Maker of the Universe wants a relationship with His creation. All people are created by God and born with purpose. He made people to be in relationship with Him. Knowing Him is the ultimate relationship—and it is a relationship anyone can have. What's even more incredible is that God wants that relationship to last into eternity!

The reality of eternity can be seen not only in the accounts recorded in the Bible, but also in the present day. Each person has an eternal spirit. How can we be sure? Accounts of near-death experiences are one way the reality of eternal life has been confirmed. Many instances have been recorded where people knew details about what went on while they were "dead", which is only possible if their spirit was alive and able to see what was happening.

Especially compelling are the situations where a person can describe things after dying and being resuscitated that they could not have otherwise known. John Burke (a pastor in Texas) studied this topic and wrote a book called *Imagine Heaven*, where he consolidates research involving at least 1,000 interviews with people who've had a near death experience. Vicky, who was born blind, was one story Burke recounts. She was able to describe things she *saw* during a near-death experience. Those details could not have been conjured up in her memory because she had never *seen* anything before that day.[1]

Another compelling example was a man who told the medical staff where his lost dentures could be found. The dentures had been taken out while the man was in deep comatose. There was no way he could have seen with his physical eyes which drawer they were put into. A week after they were lost, he said he'd seen a staff member put them into the crash cart drawer.[1] When they checked that location, that was exactly where the dentures were! How could the man have known that? He was watching them while they worked on his body. The man's body was shut down, but his spirit was fully alive, outside his body. Spirits don't die.

We are eternal beings. God has "planted eternity [a sense of divine purpose] in the human heart [a mysterious longing which nothing under the sun can satisfy, except God]" (Ecclesiastes 3:11, AMP). That's why mankind has always believed there is something more when we die—we know it in our hearts. This life is temporary, but a person's spirit lives on even after this life is over.

The Decision That Affects Eternity

During this lifetime, the most important decision someone can make is whether to accept Jesus as his or her Lord and Savior. It's that decision that determines where someone spends their eternity. Why does that decision affect someone's eternity? Because without Jesus paying for sin, each person is held accountable for their own sins. It is only through accepting the payment of Jesus' redeeming blood that someone can be forgiven and have their sins removed, permitting them access to Heaven.

Jesus was the Son of God and He *never* sinned. He lived a life of moral excellence but was put to death like a criminal. His innocent death paid mankind's sin debt, which could not be paid any other way. Each person sins at some point during their lives and therefore is in need of redemption. "For *everyone has sinned*; we all fall short of God's glorious standard" (Romans 3:23, NLT).

Prior to Jesus coming into the world, an animal such as a lamb was sacrificed to God as the way for people to pay for their sins. This was necessary because when the first man and woman, Adam and Eve, disobeyed the Creator, sin entered the world and became a barrier between mankind and God. Subsequently, there needed to be a way to reconcile with the Creator. Otherwise, there would remain a distance between mankind and God. Shedding the blood of an innocent animal is how God chose to pay for sin until Jesus came. When Jesus died on the cross and shed His own innocent blood, He paid the full price for the sin of mankind. When Jesus paid for sin, He made a way for that sin barrier between mankind and God to be removed.

Cleansing Power

The shedding of Jesus' blood removes the film of moral filth and cleanses us. God's desire is to cleanse each person and give them His righteousness. This cleansing is similar to taking away someone's dirty clothes and replacing them with a clean, pure white robe. "And all who have been united with Christ in baptism have put on Christ, like putting on new clothes" (Galatians 3:27, NLT).

The times when someone has lied, stolen, cheated, fornicated, had a poor attitude, been prideful, been bitter, or done any other wrongs can be forgiven if that person is willing to confess his or her sins to God and repent. Jesus paid for all sin when He was on the cross. There may still be consequences in the physical world around us as a result of our sinful actions, but we can be washed clean in God's eyes and ask Him for healing and restoration.

Jesus

Jesus is the Messiah, the One who saves mankind from their sins and eternal death. He has been referred to as "the Lamb of God" because He was the final sacrifice—the Ultimate Lamb—who would make the payment once and for all for the sin of mankind (John 1:29). His role as Messiah was validated in three ways: Jesus fulfilled the biblical prophecies about the Messiah, He performed miracles, and—the most astounding proof—He rose from the dead after saying He would!

After dying on the cross, Jesus rose from the grave three days later. By rising from the grave, Jesus proved that He conquered death and has eternal life. He now lives with God the Father in Heaven.

There is ample evidence, both experiential and historical, that prove the resurrection of Jesus Christ. Some of these historical findings—such as the multiple eye witness accounts of the resurrection and the validity of the historical records documenting it—are captured in Lee Strobel's book, *The Case for the Resurrection*.[2]

The belief that Jesus Christ was only a good person is one of the greatest deceptions—and it is not a logical option when one looks at His life. This was pointed out by C.S. Lewis when he said, Jesus was either a liar, a lunatic, or the Lord.[3] Jesus did incredible things and made incredible claims—like being the Son of God. Either He was lying, crazy, or really was the Lord. Fulfilling prophecies, performing miracles, and coming back from the dead after saying He would, validated that Jesus really is the Son of God and what He said is true.

Jesus Dies For Us

Jesus is completely righteous. Those who trust and follow Jesus receive *His* righteousness, which enables them to come into relationship with God. "Righteousness" could be described as "right standing" with God.

When Jesus died on the cross about 2,000 years ago (between the year 26 and 36 A.D.),[4] He provided a way for you and me to have a personal relationship with God. Jesus' sacrificial death paid for sin and purchased redemption for anyone who chooses to receive it. The same God who created us, redeemed us. "For God so [greatly] loved and dearly prized the world, that He [even] gave His [One and] only begotten Son, so that whoever believes and trusts in Him [as Savior] shall not perish, but have eternal life" (John 3:16, AMP).

Is there a greater expression of love than laying down one's life for another? I cannot think of a great measure of love than that—this is how much God loves you and me. God the Father sent His Son, Jesus Christ, to die for us so we could have eternal life.

Making Him Lord and Savior

Having eternal life with God and walking with Him in this life is indeed possible. In fact, that is why each person was born. God eagerly anticipates the invitation to be actively involved in a person's life.

To have this relationship with God, it is necessary to believe Jesus died for your sin and rose from the dead. Romans 10:9 says, "Because if you acknowledge and *confess with your mouth that Jesus is Lord* [recognizing His power, authority, and majesty as God], and *believe in your heart that God raised Him from the dead, you will be saved"* (AMP).

What does it mean to have Jesus as Lord? It means following Him and submitting to the promptings of the Holy Spirit; this also includes turning from sin. Thankfully, we don't need to be perfect to come to Him! In fact, it is in the midst of our imperfections as we seek God that He works in our hearts. No one is perfect; God knows this. Only Jesus was perfect.

If there is a lifestyle choice that you don't think you can give up, but you know it doesn't align with Jesus' heart, you can ask Him to help you. Not asking God into one's life for fear of not being able to live up to God's standard would be the enemy's great deception. It is precisely because no one is perfect that we need Jesus. Struggles with decisions and lifestyles should motivate someone even more to invite Him into one's life versus serving as a deterrent to come to Him. God meets each person where they are. He merely waits for the invitation to come into one's life.

Making Jesus Christ your Lord and Savior is simple. To do this, there are two things you must understand—the need for God's forgiveness and the importance of repenting of sin.

Need For God's Forgiveness

Because everyone has sinned, everyone needs God's forgiveness. Sin includes sexual impurity, lying, stealing, murder, and any other behaviors contrary to the Ten Commandments or God's law. Some sins may seem much worse than others. However, the Bible says in James 2:10, "For the person who keeps all of the laws except one is as guilty as a person who has broken all of God's laws" (NLT). So, regardless of how many times a person has sinned or which sins they have committed, everyone needs God's forgiveness. Thankfully, forgiveness is available through Jesus Christ.

To be forgiven, a person needs to ask God for forgiveness, acknowledging that Jesus paid for sin and rose from the dead. It is faith in Jesus and accepting what He has done that allows a person to be seen as righteous when they die and go before God.

Repentance

Sin creates a barrier between mankind and God because He is holy. It's repentance that removes the sin barrier. To be in right standing with God repentance is necessary.

How does someone repent? A person repents of sin by asking God to forgive him or her for the sin committed, then turning away from it and changing that behavior. When someone sins or does something wrong, then he or she repeats the process: ask God for forgiveness and try to refrain from committing that sin again. It is important for a person to ask God for forgiveness each time he or she sins, asking only once does not forgive every instance that will ever occur.

Asking for God's forgiveness and being cleansed by Jesus' blood is similar to how taking one bath in a lifetime does not keep a person clean for the rest of his or her life. A person must bathe routinely to stay clean, so should believers in Jesus routinely ask God for His forgiveness and cleansing. "If we confess our sins, He is faithful and just to forgive us our sins and to cleanse us from all unrighteousness" (1 John 1:9, NKJV).

God as Our Judge

Each of us will die someday and stand before God who is the Judge. Hebrews 9:27-28 says, "And as it is appointed for men to die once, but after this is the judgment, so Christ was offered once to bear the sins of many" (excerpt from NKJV). The Bible is clear that there are only two possible verdicts from that judgment. Either a person's sin is forgiven or it's not.

God's desire is that each person would be forgiven of sin, but if someone doesn't put his or her faith in Jesus and ask for forgiveness, then that person retains the guilt of their sin. As a just God, the Lord judges each person after death. "For we must all stand before Christ to be judged. We will each receive whatever we deserve for the good or evil we have done in this earthly body" (2 Corinthians 5:10, NLT).

Verdict 1: God's Forgiveness Granted

Often people assume that to go to Heaven someone simply needs to be a good person. Do good people go to Heaven? No. Forgiven people go to Heaven.[5] Why? Because no one is good enough, no one (except Jesus) is morally perfect. That is why everyone needs Jesus! God's forgiveness is granted when someone has been washed clean by the blood of Jesus. Being cleansed of sin is what allows someone entrance into Heaven.

Heaven is a place in God's presence where there is love and joy for all of eternity. Anyone is forgiven if he or she confesses Jesus Christ as Lord, believes He rose from the dead, and asks God to forgive their sins. To be forgiven by God is what permits someone into Heaven after they die—meaning they dwell with God for all of eternity. Heaven is a place that has no sin; otherwise, there would be the same chaos in Heaven that we see on the Earth (which includes pain, suffering, and all kinds of bad things).

Verdict 2: God's Forgiveness Not Granted

Those who are not forgiven by God are held responsible for each sin they have ever committed. Sin is not allowed in Heaven, so unforgiven people are not permitted into Heaven. Instead, they are cast away from the Lord's presence.

The place absent of God's presence is Hell. Hell is a horrible place that was never intended for mankind; it was created for the devil (who rebelled against God long ago) and the angels who chose to follow the devil (called demons). However, a person's eternal spirit is sent there when that individual is not cleansed by the blood of Jesus. People will go to Hell for not putting their faith in Jesus Christ and not asking Him to forgive their sins while they were still alive. It is not God's heart that anyone should go there! That is why He sent Jesus—to give people a way out.

The Great Exchange

In a great act of love, Jesus died to make the great exchange—His life for ours. However, God leaves the choice up to us, whether or not we choose to accept Jesus. He gives man free will, letting each person make their own decisions—even when those choices are contrary to what God wants.

Following Jesus does come with a cost because God wants us to turn from sin. God won't force anyone to follow Him. If someone chooses not to follow Him, then he or she will not be with God in Heaven when this life is over. A follower of Jesus should be quick to repent when they sin and make an effort to make God-pleasing choices.

To Begin a Life with God

If you want to begin a life of following Jesus, you can commit yourself to God. Praying something like the following is a great way to start your journey

(I encourage you to pray aloud):

I believe Jesus died for my sins and He rose from the grave.
Jesus, please come into my heart and be Lord over my life.
Forgive me God for sinning against You.
Help me love like You love.
Teach me Your ways.
Fill me completely with Your Holy Spirit.
In Jesus' name, amen.

If you made Jesus your Lord and Savior, welcome to the Kingdom!

Making Jesus Christ Lord and Savior does not mean all of someone's life circumstances will get better or that there will be no more hardship. What it does mean, is that Jesus is with you, and the Holy Spirit comes to live in your heart, providing guidance and conviction.

Growing in Relationship with God
Helpful steps in fostering your relationship with God include:
o Reading the Bible
o Praying
o Attending a church or Bible study
o Receiving Mentorship
o Getting baptized
o Forgiving others

The Bible
The Bible is the Word of God and has the answer to any of life's issues—it is an instruction manual from God, the Creator of Heaven and Earth. This sacred book provides the guidance that God has given to His people and describes what He wants for each person. It also serves as a historical record of what God has done and includes His laws, prophecies, and promises.

Reading the Bible is an important way to get to know the Lord and to hear from Him! When I began to read the Bible it brought God to life in a way I'd never experienced before. Becoming familiar with the Bible allowed me to encounter the promises of the living God.

We need the Holy Spirit to help us understand and apply the truths from the Bible. If you read a passage of Scripture and don't understand, it can be helpful to ask God what it means: "How does this apply?" "What do You mean?" "I don't get it. Lord, open my understanding."

One should keep in mind that the Bible also records the history of His people—the good and the bad of what people have done. So, just because someone's actions are recorded in the Bible doesn't mean those actions are a good idea. For example, in Genesis 19, a man named Lot offered his two virgin daughters to a crowd of angry, perverse men, so they could have their way with them. Lot's absurd response to offer up his daughters is not a reflection of God's heart in that situation—it is an account of what happened. The highlights of the history of God's people are captured in the Scriptures. There are accounts of brilliant strategies, good intentions by key historical figures, leaps of faith, as well as a record of the mistakes and selfish decisions made along the way.

*Note: Not all Bible translations are reliable:
Please see *Recommended Bible Translations* in the back of this book.

Praying

Praying is a very important way to get to know God because it is how someone speaks to God and grows a relationship with Him. It is through prayer and the surrendering of heart that God is given access to a person's life.

Often, people ask God for guidance such as, "What should I say to…?" or "What should I do about…?" The Lord wants people to come to Him with whatever concerns they have—both big and small. People can talk with Him about anything. When people tell God what is in their heart and ask Him for input or guidance, that is praying. Prayer is intended to be a two-way conversation where it is not just someone speaking to God, but also a time where He responds.[6]

Prayers can be presented to God in various ways—they can be spoken aloud, said silently in a person's heart, written, or sung to the Lord. This is something that can be done individually or with another person.

A good way to begin prayer is by starting with praise and adoration, telling God how wonderful or faithful He is, before making various requests. This approach is beneficial because it invites God's presence into our hearts and helps us focus on who He is. This approach to prayer can increase one's faith because it reminds us who God is before we begin to ask Him for things in prayer. For example, if I am going to pray for someone who is sick, it would be wise to begin my prayer with something like "God, thank you that You are the Healer, You are holy, with You all things are possible…please bring healing to…"

Worship

God wants our hearts. He wants us to love Him with our whole being, and to love others. One way we express our love to God is through worship. Worship essentially refers to having God at the center of one's life and letting Him know.

There are lots of ways to worship. Some examples could include:

surrendering one's heart to the Lord, having a lifestyle of obedience to God, serving others with a glad heart, financial giving such as tithe and offerings, and singing or playing music for the Lord. Many church services take time for worship music because it has a special way of helping someone get connected to the Spirit of God. Worship music helps people to focus on God and His goodness, as well as make an emotional connection. Worship music can usher in God's presence and help people to encounter God.

Attending Church or Bible Study

No matter where you are in your spiritual walk, I encourage you to consider getting involved with a Bible study or a Bible-believing Church. This will provide a place where you can learn about the Bible, grow in your faith, be in community, and mature as a believer. Hearing the testimonies of others and examples of God's faithfulness, builds one's faith and creates a deeper understanding of Who God is and how He works. Since not all churches are scripturally-based, it's important to be at a church where the Bible serves as the basis for all their teachings and practices. Especially if the church being attended is very large, to grow in the faith and have a good sense of community, it can be very important to participate in a Bible study.

Mentorship

In new situations or times of uncertainty guidance from others can be very helpful. Mentorship can be pivotal in helping a person grow in the faith and work through life's challenges.

The value of having people speak into each other's is presented in Proverbs 27:17, "Iron sharpens iron, and one man sharpens another" (ESV). People need one another to help sharpen each other's understanding of the Word, and to point out things in people's character that should be addressed. Encouraging each other and praying for each other is also very important. Having a mentor—whether it's a friend or someone from a Bible study or church—who is mature in the faith, can be very beneficial.

Walking With the Lord

The closer a person draws to the Lord and the more he or she lets go of the filth that comes from the world—which consists of things like negative thinking, criticism, bitterness, pride, immoral behavior, or any other sin—the more that person experiences the Kingdom of God. Partnering with Jesus in this life provides access to God's Kingdom—which includes righteousness, peace, and joy. It also means walking in love.

God's heart for His followers to love others and reach out to them is made apparent throughout the Scriptures. When a man asked Jesus what the greatest commandment was, "Jesus said to him, 'You shall love the Lord your God with all your heart, with all your soul, and with all your mind. This is the first and greatest commandment. And the second is like it: You shall love your neighbor as yourself.'" (Matthew 22:38-39, NKJV)

As people surrender their hearts to God, He helps them become more like Him (loving, kind, holy, just). The more someone pursues the Lord, spends time with Him, learns about the Bible, intentionally applies the teachings of God's Word, and yields to the Holy Spirit, the more transformation they will experience.

Baptism

The physical act of being baptized is important in a believer's walk with the Lord. It is an outward expression of an internal decision someone makes to follow Christ and repent of their sins. The Baptism of Repentance was first performed when John the Baptist stood in the Jordan River and had those who wanted to repent of their sins come into the river. (Matthew 3)

Being baptized consists of getting briefly submerged in water, then coming back up, symbolic of being cleansed of one's sin and having newness of life. Baptism is considered a public declaration of one's faith. This is done in front of witnesses such as other believers, friends, or family.

Baptism of Repentance (also known as water baptism) is only done once after someone chooses to follow Jesus, meaning the baptism process is not repeated every time a believer makes a mistake and sins (Ephesians 4:5). Because baptism is a step of obedience to the Lord, doing this can strengthen one's walk with the Lord and help them walk in the newness of life they have in Christ.

Forgiving Others

It's very important for each person to extend forgiveness to others so there is not a hindrance to one's relationship with the Lord. "But if you don't forgive others, your Father in Heaven will not forgive your sins [transgressions; failings; trespasses]" (Matthew 6:15, EXB). We *need* to extend forgiveness to others because God forgives us. Forgiving can be difficult, but as one enters into a relationship with the Lord, He is able to help someone learn how to forgive.

God Lights Our Path

As a person seeks God for direction and listens for His response, He directs each person's path and provides wisdom for decisions. His Holy Spirit will show people how to live for Him. Throughout my life, I have needed the Lord's direction many times! I am thankful for the guidance of the Holy Spirit and the Bible. I agree with what the psalmist David says, "Your Word is like a lamp for my feet and a light for my path [it shows how life should be lived]" (Psalm 119:105, EXB).

Conclusion

Having a personal relationship with God in this life is amazing! Walking with God can be difficult at times, but also very exciting. Each person is created by God with a purpose. Everyone has unique gifts, talents, and backgrounds. People who come to the Lord may find that He places different burdens (passions) on people's hearts. One person may have a passion in their heart for children, while another feels compelled to fight human trafficking, another mentors young married couples, and another has a different group of people on his or her heart. As one continues his or her walk with the Lord, new burdens or passions may arise along the way.

All those who know Christ are expected to present His love to those around them and to share the good news—about forgiveness and eternal life available through Jesus—so others can enter into a relationship with God. The Lord longs to be in relationship with each person.

PART 2:
THE LESSONS LEARNED

More depth on selected topics:

A. **Marriage Reflections**:
   Lessons learned from my marriage, and a deeper look at topics related to relationships.

B. **Faith Insights**:
   Explanation on topics related to foundational principles for walking with and hearing from God.

PART 2A:
MARRIAGE REFLECTIONS

Love and Respect
Criticism
Control
Repercussions of Resentment
Power of Confession (and Accountability)
Responding to the Confessions of Others
Pornography
Seeking Wise Counsel
Considering Input from Others
Forgiveness
Blessing
Codependency
Enabling
Loneliness
Seeking Value
Perception and Self-Esteem
Brokenness
Direct Your Thoughts
Is Divorce Permissible?
Marriage Covenant

LOVE AND RESPECT: TWO ESSENTIAL INGREDIENTS

Dr. Emerson Eggerichs, who wrote *Love and Respect* (2004), addresses the Scripture, Ephesians 5:33, "Nevertheless let each one of you in particular so love his own wife as himself, and let the wife see that she respects her husband" (NKJV). He points out that, naturally, men tend to focus more on respect in a relationship whereas women have a tendency to focus more on love.[1]

While attending a marriage conference with a small group for married couples, it became clear that most men, if they had to choose between being loved or respected, would choose to be respected. Although I had come to understand that respecting my husband was very important, I still did not realize when my actions or voicing criticisms were perceived by Jacob as disrespectful.

For women, love tends to be something they naturally think about and try to foster, whereas men may need to make an intentional effort to demonstrate love. The inverse is also true: men are naturally mindful of respect, whereas most women need to make an effort to demonstrate respect. To a man, getting respect from his wife is like oxygen—it is something he desperately needs.[1] I do not mean to suggest women don't need respect and men don't need love! There should be mutual love and mutual respect in a marriage. However, since there are different things most important to each gender, both husbands and wives need to make an intentional effort to meet their spouse's primary need. Natural wiring, as well as life experiences, create a personal lens which influences people's perceptions and shapes how they respond to others.

Collecting wisdom for how I could have responded differently to Jacob, could have been as simple as asking him questions like:
o   What do I do that makes you feel respected?
o   Is there anything I have done that makes you feel disrespected?
Likewise, Jacob could have asked me:
o   What can I do to help you feel loved?
Those kinds of questions could have surfaced discussion about the interactions between us that had been damaging and helped me realize how to better show Jacob respect. Otherwise, how would I know his perspective? There may have been small things in our everyday interactions, that I was unaware of, which also made my husband feel disrespected. Respecting Jacob the way *I* thought he should be, did not mean that he actually *felt* respected. I should have asked him how I could have shown him respect.

Through the research of Shaunti Feldhahn, I learned men's primary concerns are different than women's. She surveyed thousands of men and women when conducting her research, and found that men constantly ask themselves questions like, *Am I adequate? Do I measure up?* [2]

A wife should be able to discuss concerns with her husband, but the way it is done can make the difference between working through an issue and chipping away at his self-esteem. If concerns are not voiced in the right way, then each time they are mentioned, a feeling of disrespect and inadequacy can be fostered. Realizing how harmful it was to Jacob's self-esteem to be criticized and deprived power in our relationship would have shaped how I approached Jacob with my concerns. One way I made Jacob feel inadequate was by taking control of the finances; it implied to Jacob he didn't measure up. Verbalizing my concerns multiple times was likely perceived as nagging and bred not only resentment and discouragement, but also a feeling of inadequacy.

CRITICISM

A wife has the opportunity to empower her husband in amazing ways that can give him the inspiration to accomplish his goals and produce positive changes in his life. Displaying patience, grace, and *intentional encouragement* certainly helps empower others, and so does a sincere statement of, "I believe in you." When a husband knows his wife believes in him, it can increase his confidence and self-worth dramatically.

If a set of spouses each painted a portrait symbolizing the type of cheerleader the other person is, what would be written on the pom-poms in that portrait? Encouraging words in one hand, with supportive statements and actions in the other? Or would there be criticism and bitterness in one of those hands? Unfortunately, criticism, resentment, anger, and bitterness are often the pom-poms frustrated spouses pick up. Being a cheerleader for someone who disappoints on occasion or seems unappreciative is not easy, but it is an opportunity to influence in a powerful and positive way. Even outside of a marriage context, people still need a cheerleader. Cheerleaders could be anyone within a person's sphere of influence—friends, family, coworkers, neighbors, or others.

It was not until long after the divorce that I realized criticism was perceived by Jacob as disrespectful. If someone had asked me at the time, I would have said it was necessary for me to bring up the things I did—because I was desperate for change in my husband's life. *Maybe if I say it one more time there will be breakthrough.* In reality, breakthrough doesn't usually come from pointing out faults again and again while describing what needs to be changed. Breakthrough comes when someone realizes for oneself what needs to change and has the power of the Holy Spirit. Then, along with encouragement from others, change is fostered and transformation takes place.

Instead of trying to control everything, I should have sought to understand the root of the issue, then helped Jacob work through that. Nagging and trying to control someone does not produce change. It only produces resentment or a feeling of belittlement. Thinking that criticisms and sharp comments would convict my husband instead of simply anger him was twisted and immature on my part.

I could see when Jacob did something wrong or inappropriate. But I seldom recognized when I was stepping outside of bounds with what was appropriate or fair—because I felt justified. Justification prevented me from humbling myself. I didn't often feel it was necessary to ask my husband for forgiveness or change my approach.

The wall of defensiveness Jacob instantly built whenever someone close to him broached certain topics is a natural response many people have. People who are hurting are sometimes just not able to process and respond to criticism in a productive way. Rarely are hurting people willing to have a mature conversation with someone, admit fault, and apologize. Anything implying inadequacy or fault is often more than they can handle. If a heart is full of hurt and emotional pain that has accrued over the years, there is sometimes no room for correction; it gets converted into hurt and the person simply isn't able to process it in a constructive way.

For anyone, criticism should be given in small doses, and with love. It can be incredibly destructive to an individual's self-esteem or to a relationship if a person is constantly being told how he or she falls short. Even *constructive* criticism should be presented in moderation. Eventually, after there are enough negative comments from a loved one, friend, or coworker, a person may dismiss the feedback or shut down emotionally.

Usually, the criticisms and hurtful things spoken by someone are unnecessary. However, there are times when it may be necessary to share a difficult truth with someone. In those instances, it is imperative for the person offering the correction or insights to check the motive of his or her own heart. God's desire is for His followers to be rooted, grounded, and established in love (Ephesians 3:17). If the person is operating in love and the heart motive is right then the observation or correction can be shared.

The way correction is offered (including the timing) will often determine how it is received. In the end, the way the recipient responds to the correction will depend on the state of his or her own heart. It's possible a person may not be open to correction, even if the perfect approach is taken.

Having a neutral third party or trusted individual offer input may be wise. Sometimes people hear comments differently—even if they are the same statements one's spouse has made—from people who are perceived as non-threatening. Particularly when people have felt rejected, criticized, or unsupported, feedback from certain individuals may be quickly dismissed.

A friend once shared her mother's filter for whether or not something should be spoken. That filter could be called the "Love Test." It included three questions to help someone determine if a comment should be made:[1]

The Love Test

1. Is it true?
2. Is it necessary?
3. Is it kind?

She attested that if a comment didn't pass the "Love Test" then it probably wasn't worth sharing. I am confident many people would talk a whole lot less if they asked themselves those three questions!

CONTROL

Eventually, I came to realize that I cannot force my values and convictions on another person. Each person is responsible for their own decisions. Communicating with the other person and deciding *together* how to approach a situation is much more effective than trying to force a change in behavior—especially when dealing with adults. Although coercion may produce a temporary, outward change, it won't produce the inward change that brings true transformation.

Rather than trying to control Jacob's behavior, it would have been much better to discuss what appropriate expectations would be, and come up together with approaches we should take if those expectations weren't met. This would have given him ownership over his decisions and treated him like an adult. Additionally, if I would have come alongside Jacob to address the deeper issue of *why* he drank, that could have been life-changing for us. Although well-meaning, the control I exercised in trying to stop Jacob's excessive drinking turned out to be more damaging than helpful.

What if, when Jacob told me about the drinking, we had taken a few days to develop an effective strategy together for how to help him? Doing so may have meant taking time to pray, gathering wisdom from others, and talking with Jacob about various approaches. Deciding *together* on a best response would have presented me as someone on his side, supporting him, versus someone he was competing against. However, in my haste and zeal to help, I went for an immediate, "nip-it-in-the-bud" approach.

I *thought* I was doing everything right. When people see a situation through their own perspective and use their own rationale, it is possible to justify anything. Rather than immediately reacting, I should have been more intentional to invite the Lord's input when making decisions; He always knows what is right and what is best for each situation.

Years after the divorce, I was reminded of my rash response to take control of the money during my marriage, while attending a speaking engagement called *The Justice Event*. One of the keynote speakers, Rob Morris, the founder of Love 146, shared a story that resonated within me.

While he was in Cambodia, a leader of a human rights organization came to him and asked, "You know what your problem is as Americans?" Rob gave her his attention and she said, "You don't think. You react. You see some gross human rights abuse…instead of taking the time to be strategic and come up with solutions that are going to be useful, that could be effective and really work. Sometimes your reaction causes more harm than good later on down the road."[1]

Had the intervention of the Americans seemed justifiable when they responded to whatever issues or injustices they saw? Did they think they were doing the right thing? To both of those questions, I would answer, "Probably."

Even though a response may be well-intentioned, it can still end up being detrimental. Governments as well as individuals may be tempted to *react* rather than *thoughtfully respond* in a way that will be beneficial to whatever situations arise.

Scripturally, people are encouraged to get understanding and to search for wisdom like it is a hidden treasure (Proverbs 2:4). I need to make a point to seek out wisdom and understanding—it is not automatically going to hit me over the head.

I now realize that instead of trying to exercise control, there is a great approach described in James 5:16 for how to handle situations where someone confesses a wrong-doing, "Confess your trespasses to one another, and pray for one another, that you may be healed…" (NKJV). There are a couple things to be noted here. First, confessing out loud to another person. Jacob did this when he confessed to me. Second, praying for one another—this helps initiate healing. After hearing Jacob's confession, my response was not to pray with him and ask God for his healing. Taking an approach filled with grace, instead of merely reacting, would have been contrary to my natural response of wanting to immediately fix the problem.

How *should* I have responded when Jacob confessed his drinking to me? The perfect Christian response would have been for me to thank Jacob for letting me know, tell him I still loved him, and pray with him. I could have prayed something like, *Thank you God for Jacob's confession. Please heal any inner wounds driving this addiction. Encourage and strengthen us. Give us wisdom to know what to do next.* Then, I should have suggested we seek wise counsel. However, I did not do any of that. I was ignorant, felt betrayed, and really wanted to see a change in behavior. Subsequently, Jacob felt very unsupported.

I truly believe God is able to deliver people from their bondages and realize that while I wait for someone's deliverance there are approaches I can take that will be constructive for the person, rather than destructive. Ensuring someone feels supported is extremely important. Focusing on the positive can be a great way to do that. I've also come to understand the importance of taking a prayerful approach versus reacting.

Before pointing out the areas where change is needed, it's also important to ensure I am not being hypocritical in any way. If I do need to point something out which is also a weakness or tendency for me, I need to be humble and acknowledge that I have to work on that area of my life too. Someone need not be completely perfect in order to help others identify areas for improvement in their lives, but it's wise to deal with one's own issues, or at least acknowledge them during the conversation. Matthew 7:3-5 says, "And why do you look at the speck in your brother's eye, but do not consider the plank in your own eye?...First remove the plank from your own eye, then you will see clearly to remove the speck from your brother's eye" (NKJV). This means I should deal with my own issues in order to effectively help others address areas in their lives where change is needed.

REPERCUSSIONS OF RESENTMENT

Anger robs a person of peace. Eventually, anger and frustration give birth to resentment, bitterness, and criticism—all of which are poisonous to any relationship. When I do something wrong and get angry with myself, I hate the guilty feeling that often surfaces. How I feel about myself can affect the way I treat others. Anger can cause me to lash out at others if I don't practice self-control and deal with that emotion in a healthy way.

There can be lots of reasons to embrace anger such as failure, being mistreated, past hurts, frustration, fear, unmet expectations, and perceived inadequacy.

The anger Jacob carried was the result of hurts, feelings of inadequacy, and knowing his lifestyle choices were not right. He carried a lot of anger and, therefore, often reacted immaturely to conflict and various situations. Saying things that are mean, making accusative statements, yelling, or things of that nature are not a mature approach to conflict. Yet, those kinds of responses tend to be the approach an angry person takes—unless they exercise self-control and remove oneself from the situation long enough to cool down.

An effective approach I have found to deal with anger is to:

o   Take a deep breath
o   Remove myself from the situation for a moment
o   Make a decision not to harbor that emotion

Unmet expectations caused me to have a lot of frustration, and I allowed that to morph into resentment. There were many things Jacob did which disheartened, disappointed, and upset me, and I did not always respond in ways I should have. Responding out of the flesh is not only very easy to do, but can also be very harmful. The control I exercised and disrespect I unintentionally displayed triggered resentment and rebellion inside Jacob.

Jacob's addictions and the deterioration of our marriage was like the erosion that occurs in nature. In nature, over time, bits of rock or soil get removed when wind or water pass through an area. Entire patches of ground that once seemed sturdy, move. Without a strong root system in place, large chunks of soil may break away. Subsequently, whatever was built on that ground gradually falls away. Each event that disappointed Jacob and his response to those, as well as my reactions to various situations (making poor decisions and focusing on the negative things), were the wind and water that eroded our marriage.

The foundation of a marriage is laid through a series of experiences and the decisions of each spouse. Decisions that build trust, such as demonstrating love and commitment, provide the strongest foundation. Incorporating Christ into the relationship is very beneficial because if both spouses are actively pursuing the Lord, they will become rooted and grounded in love and experience conviction when they are treating each other in a way that is not right.

Over time—no matter what comprises the foundation of a marriage—if there are enough bad decisions, the foundation will erode. Practices of deception, criticism, sharp comments, and lack of intimacy can erode the ties of trust, honesty, and closeness into their opposites—suspicion, defensiveness, and distance.

If the foundation erodes, it must be rebuilt or it will crumble. To properly rebuild the foundation of my marriage, it would have been necessary for both Jacob and I to make changes. Changes were needed to each of our personal lives as well as how we treated one another. We were both stuck in a turmoil of emotions—Jacob with a feeling of inadequacy and anger, me with a feeling of frustration and disappointment. Eventually, this produced resentment in both of us. Continuing the marriage relationship in such unfavorable circumstances was very difficult.

I needed not only a humble heart, but also wisdom, to approach my marriage differently. Proverbs 8:9 says concerning words of wisdom, "They are all plain to him who understands [and opens his heart], and right to those who find knowledge [and live by it]" (AMPC). In other words, if people do not harden their hearts, but seek to understand and apply the knowledge they gain, they are able to operate in wisdom. If I'd had more wisdom, perhaps I would have known how to show my husband more respect and responded differently to the obstacles in my marriage. Even if the end result of my marriage was the same, at least I would have taken the best approach.

POWER OF CONFESSION
(AND ACCOUNTABILITY)

Jacob understood the power of confession and its importance. He did the right thing by confessing to me about his drinking. Unfortunately, my response was not what it should have been and Jacob did not have an older male that he could relate with and be held accountable by. Without a consistent, effective source of accountability in his life, change was not likely to occur.

When something is confessed to another person such as a confidant or accountability partner, it is exposed to the light. When someone brings his or her wrong thoughts or decisions out into the open, the devil has a harder time holding those over someone's head. Transparency brings freedom. The lies spoken by the devil such as, "If only someone knew what you've done…" no longer hold as much weight.

Conversely, keeping bad decisions or struggles a secret will produce a sense of shame—guilt that takes someone away from God. In turn, shame causes people to feel lonely, isolated, rejected, or have a sense of low self-worth. Shame is from the enemy and keeps people from experiencing the healing and freedom that God has in store for them. Trying to hide one's unfavorable choices can also create other problems—like lying to try to cover it up.

Power of Confession

Bringing things to light that have been hidden can be incredibly difficult. But it is freeing. Confessing wrong decisions, mistakes, or even unfavorable thoughts and feelings is almost always the first step toward healing the soul. When people have a traumatic experience or sin in various ways, their souls get wounded. Thankfully, those wounds can be healed.

There are two components to receiving healing found in James 5:16—confession and prayer. "Therefore, *confess your sins to one another* [your false steps, your offenses], and *pray for one another, that you may be healed* and restored. The heartfelt and persistent prayer of a righteous man (believer) can accomplish much [when put into action and made effective by God—it is dynamic and can have tremendous power]" (James 5:16, AMP).

After confessing one's sin to God and asking for His forgiveness, a person is forgiven. But it's helpful to also confess the sin to a trusted person who will pray, because that promotes healing and restoration of the soul.

If someone is not sure who to confess to, it would be wise to ask the Lord who it should be. Sometimes it may be necessary to confess (and apologize) to the person who was wronged or affected by the action. Other times, confession could consist of telling one's mistakes to a trusted person like a confidant or accountability partner.

Confession catalyzes healing because it removes the *secrecy* of sin. The devil effectively uses what is hidden and kept in darkness to make someone feel isolated or ashamed.

Accountability

Another advantage to confessing a sin or struggle to a confidant—whether it be a friend, parent, sibling, counselor, pastor, or other trusted individual—is the opportunity for accountability.

For example, let's say Yvonne has a tendency to cheat on exams at school and knows her behavior is wrong; she confesses this to Sally, her sister. Sally is then able to hold Yvonne accountable (assuming she wants to do the right thing and stop cheating on exams). As exam time approaches, Sally can pose a question such as "Are you studying for the exam this time? What strategy do you have to keep your eyes on only your paper?" Or after the exam, Sally can ask, "Did you cheat on this exam?" Knowing someone will be asking her about the exam makes Yvonne more likely to refrain from cheating.

With accountability, real change is more likely to be sustained in a person's life.[1]

Avoiding Secrecy

When trying to determine if it was okay for me to share what was happening with Jacob, I considered the possibility that telling others would betray his confidence. There were things Jacob didn't want me telling anyone. If he found out I told someone, he would be very upset with me. He did not want his bad decisions made known to others. However, the sin or poor choices of one person can greatly impact another. Therefore, it is probably appropriate, and even necessary, for the affected person to confide in a counselor, mentor, or trusted friend about what has been happening. Thankfully, I had people in my life I could confide in, and I did share with them some of what was going on in my marriage. I should have taken it a step further and sought counsel for what to do about the situations that arose; that was one of many lessons learned along the way.

There are some situations where discretion must be used and confiding in only one or two people is appropriate. It is inappropriate to *broadcast* someone's failures or imperfections. However, it is often wise to share with someone like a confidant or an accountability partner what is happening in a person's own life, which may include a description of another person's decisions (like a spouse, sibling, parent, friend, or acquaintance) and the impact of those decisions. Choosing to confess, repent, and forgive others is very important in order to move toward healing.

If someone is in a situation like mine, my advice would be to seek the counsel of God—this would be done through prayer, reading the Scriptures and consulting true followers of Jesus (who are prayerful in the advice they offer). To not share with *anyone* about what is going on is probably not wise.

Unless God Himself says not to tell anyone (and there's confirmation it was really God saying that, with biblical text to support it), I recommend confiding in at least one person who can be trusted, ideally someone who knows the Lord. It is also very helpful to choose someone who has some life experience and can provide helpful insights rather than just sympathize.

Abuse

Keeping any kind of abuse a secret could prolong an unsafe situation, as well as put others at risk of becoming a victim of the abuse. Confiding in someone about what has occurred may be necessary to protect oneself or others. It may also begin the process of the abuser getting needed help. Concern about the people involved getting into trouble, or the possibility of being viewed differently by others, may make someone hesitant to share about what's happened. However, if individuals who've undergone abuse don't talk to a person they can trust (and the authorities if necessary) he or she may never experience the freedom or healing God has in store.

Unfortunately, many people don't think they can share their situation with someone. Particularly, in the case of sexual abuse, individuals often keep what's happened a secret. Because of the extremely personal nature of traumatic experiences like that, many people have a hard time confiding in someone. I've seen statistics on the number of people who have been sexually abused range from 1 in 6 to as many as 1 in 3 people! Either end of that range is staggering. There is so much perversion in this world because of the devil. One of the enemy's best tactics is to make people feel shame or fear, and to feed them lies—like saying they should not tell anyone what has happened.

Whether someone has been a victim or a willing participant in the scenario being confessed, it is imperative to tell someone who can be trusted about what's happened. Regardless of when it occurred, be it a long time ago or an on-going issue, talking about it will help someone take the first step toward getting free and beginning healing.

My advice to someone who has been a victim of sexual assault or sexual abuse would be to tell an individual who is compassionate and trustworthy, regardless of who was involved. Of the many sexual abuse victims I have met, only one experienced healing before confiding in someone what happened. For her, healing came when she attended a church service and was given a prophetic word that brought her healing. It is almost always necessary to talk with another person to experience the healing God wants each person to have. Whether it is sexual abuse or any shameful experience a person goes through, telling a confidant is important because it is a step toward freedom.

RESPONDING TO THE CONFESSIONS
OF OTHERS

Ideally, a person should be able to have a safe conversation with one's spouse or loved one. This means not feeling judged and criticized when confessing or revealing a fault. It is never necessary to condone bad behavior, but letting the person know he or she is still loved is foundational to responding in a way that reflects God's heart. Sometimes a stern tone may be needed, particularly if the person does not plan to change their behavior, but often someone confesses because there is a feeling of shame and that person already knows he or she has done something wrong.

Showing someone grace is important, but it's also necessary to share truth. Discussing difficult truths with a person should not be dependent on emotion, or it may never get done. It may be uncomfortable to address particular topics, or encourage someone to surrender an area of one's life to God, but it can be life-changing. That said, discerning God's timing and direction for how to broach certain topics can make a big difference in how someone responds.

As someone spends time with God and invites Him into his or her life, He becomes actively involved and provides the guidance one needs to make the best decision. Rather than assume I knew what was best, I should have sought God's guidance. Often, when I came before the Lord, I cried, prayed, expressed how frustrated I was, and asked Him to change my husband and set him free. But complaining to the Lord is different than asking Him for His input. Instead of being consumed by frustration, I should have humbled myself before the Lord on a consistent basis.

Sincerely asking for the Lord's input and guidance may have looked something like this:

God, what do you want me to do in this situation? How can I better love and respect my husband? It's You that brings transformation to people's hearts and lives. Please transform Jacob's heart. What can I do to encourage and empower my husband to walk in the freedom You have for him?

At times, I used only my logic and emotion to address the situations that arose with Jacob. Humans are designed to have emotion and logic, and the Lord expects us to reason. God even said through the prophet Isaiah, "Come now, and let us reason together" (Isaiah 1:18, NKJV). The Lord wants to help us understand and reason through scenarios. He wants to put into perspective who He is and what He will do. So, although reasoning and logic are good things, there are many occasions where the best course of action is determined when someone takes the time to listen to what the Holy Spirit is saying. Using only one's own logic and cutting God out of the conversation is not the best approach.

As I reflect on my relationship with Jacob, it seems undeniably clear that the guidance of the Holy Spirit is very important when making decisions, especially when a person is contending with hurt or disappointment. Otherwise, someone may react by trying to control the situation or make decisions based on one's own insecurities and hurt.

Responding to situations where someone feels vulnerable, like confessing a shameful behavior or a bad decision, can be very challenging. Emotions can be difficult to control and may cloud one's rational thinking.

Helpful Tips For Responding to Others:

- o Don't interrupt.
    - o Being interrupted can prevent a person from being able to share everything that was on his or her heart.
    - o Commenting on the situation or verbalizing correction, if the individual doesn't seem to realize their behavior is wrong, can wait until the person is finished sharing.
- o Don't act like the issue causing concern is trivial.
    - o Coming across as though a concern is trivial can show a lack of compassion.
- o Offer encouragement and prayer.
    - o This may be deeply appreciated—especially when someone is feeling vulnerable.
- o Let the person know that he or she can be forgiven by God and is still loved.
    - o Reinforcing forgiveness and love can be very important.
- o Stance matters.
    - o If the person confessing is sitting, sit instead of stand. This gives a sense of being on the same level, not "above" or "more powerful" than the other person.
    - o Positioning yourself next to someone can give the sense you are on that person's side—not against him or her. Facing the person can give the impression of "you vs. me".

PORNOGRAPHY

Viewing pornography fosters a twisted perception about intimacy and can spawn a lust that drives some people to do things with kids, women, and men that are perverse and clearly outside of God's heart for those relationships. That behavior also creates distance between spouses. A pastor who counseled many couples over the years said that often when a husband distances himself from his wife for no apparent reason, it is probably because he is viewing pornography. That secret habit serves as a wedge between him and his wife.

For those who struggle with viewing pornography, confessing this sin to a trusted person and asking him or her to provide accountability is a great step toward breaking free from its control. Participating in a program like *CovenantEyes*, where alerts are sent to selected individuals (such as a spouse and accountability partners) when visiting websites with explicit material, can be helpful to those who want accountability.

It *is* possible to be set free from the bondage of pornography. I have a friend who was addicted to porn since before the age of 8 years old and was delivered in his twenties. One day, my friend saw that something wasn't right spiritually, so he and his wife asked a trusted Christian mentor to come over. After confessing the pornography addiction to his wife and the mentor, he was led through the process of repentance and deliverance. He asked God's forgiveness and made a decision to be done viewing pornography. Afterward, when facing temptation, he was able to resist. Freedom from the bondage of pornography was a whole new experience for him! This deliverance experience took place after my friend had a relationship with the Lord and began tithing, giving 10% of his earnings to the Lord. My friend's wife attributed tithing to be what catalyzed his deliverance and attests to the verses from Malachi 3:10-11, which say that when people tithe, the Lord rebukes the devourer for their sake.

Each person may have a different kind of experience for how they get set free from bondage. Asking the Lord for guidance and following His direction is always wise. Self-control is also a factor that determines how much freedom someone experiences.

Viewing pornography and the self-pleasure often associated with it creates a chemical release in the brain that makes someone feel good. For those who view pornography, over time, it becomes more difficult to attain the same level of chemical release. There needs to be a longer, or more intense, exposure to explicit material in order to get the same release as before. Pornography can become an all-consuming power in someone's life. As with any addiction, avoiding triggers is very helpful. Triggers are circumstances that tend to prompt the addictive behavior.

Being intentional to develop a different response when triggers arise can help someone form new neural pathways. For example, instead of coming home after a stressful day at work and sitting down to view pornography, a person could hit the gym before going home. That is a different, healthy way to deal with the stress. Eventually, when they feel stressed, their reaction will (hopefully) become "I should go to the gym" instead of "I will view porn."

Lack of Understanding

There's no question that pornography is a major issue throughout the world. It's the number one source of human trafficking and generates lots of problems in society. Some estimates say the U.S. is responsible for at least $10 billion annually of the nearly $100 billion global porn market.[1] How many damaged marriages does that translate into? My heart hurts to think about it.

Early in my marriage, my sister gave me a book she thought would be insightful. Unfortunately, I spent very little time reading that book before dismissing it because of a poor attitude in my heart. After randomly opening it and reading a couple paragraphs, I was frustrated. I assumed the following text would continue on to say it was okay for men to have images of women pop up in their mind because that's just the way it is. Rather than reading on to see an explanation about how men are wired biologically to be visual, I set the book down in disgust. *This is implying that it is okay for my husband to be drawn to pornography. Well it is not! That is unacceptable.*

Instead of trying to understand Jacob's struggles, I dismissed articles and research that seemed to indicate it was normal for someone to struggle with pornography and alcohol. Simply put, I did not think Jacob *should* have some of the issues he did. Rather than trying to learn about Jacob's struggles and what fed into those, I was just plain resentful.

Dismissing the fact that a temptation is real is not fair. If I'd taken the time to understand that the struggle with pornography is prevalent because men are designed to be visually stimulated, perhaps I could have responded differently to Jacob. With only a superficial understanding that men are visual,

I dismissed the "wiring to be visual" as something that Jacob would have to reign in or resign from.

It was not until long after things had gone south in my marriage that I realized my husband cared about how I dressed. One day, out of the blue, with a disdainful tone and slightly narrowed eyes, Jacob said, "That [baggy] red sweater and those striped [over] shirts you always wear..." I didn't have either of those items on, but from the tone in his statement, I suddenly realized what I wore mattered to Jacob and it bothered him when I concealed my figure. Until that moment, I'd had *no* idea! Reflecting on his comment I thought, *I wish I would have known how much my clothes mattered to him at the beginning of our marriage, instead of years later.*

I'd heard men were wired to be visual but hadn't really thought about what that meant. Understanding how sensitive men are to visual stimuli might have helped me give Jacob grace when he was fighting visual temptation from outside sources.

One of my many shortfalls was not understanding how I could capitalize on the fact my husband was visually wired. If I had realized men respond to visual stimulus the way women respond to touch, it would have changed my approach to how I met some of his needs.

SEEKING WISE COUNSEL

People draw conclusions based on the information they have. Yet, every individual's knowledge is limited. That means there is always room to make mistakes.

God's design is for people to be in community—which provides the opportunity to obtain input from others and be an inspiration to each other. These relationships help people realize things about themselves and share helpful insights with others. Consulting others to get additional information and perspective often helps someone make more sound decisions.

Who someone seeks counsel from should be carefully considered. Some counselors or mentors may have a skewed perspective or share things that are not true. Therefore, it's wise to bring any advice one receives to the Lord and ask for His input.

Questions to ask the Lord when considering feedback could include:

o   Lord, what do You say about this?

o   Is it true?

o   Are they saying this because they have been misguided or hurt?

Hindrances to Seeking Counsel

At times, someone such as a spouse or family member may forbid a person to reveal or discuss a situation which affects them. To deprive a person the option of discussing an issue that impacts him or her is not a loving decision. To do so in a marriage is like saying one's own pride is more important than his or her mate getting support and counsel. Married couples may try to hide many things. A handful of examples for what people may try to hide include: addictions, anger problems, abuse, excessive control, health problems, and poor stewardship (through gambling, compulsive shopping, or other poor spending habits).

No spouse should be told to keep something a secret when that behavior or issue impacts the partner, kids, or even other people. Forbidding a person to share with others about a struggle or situation by which he or she is impacted is selfish and unfair. Spouses need support from others too! It is probably unwise to submit to the direction to keep a problematic behavior of a spouse or loved one a secret.

A spouse feeling forbidden to share what's going on may feel isolated and not receive the support or counsel he or she needs. Ephesians 5:11 says, "And have no fellowship with the unfruitful works of darkness, *but rather expose them*" (NKJV). When things are exposed through confessing—especially to a trusted Christian who can pray with the individual impacted, or a knowledgeable individual who can offer wisdom—the situation is better able to be dealt with.

Pride hides things, and pride comes before a fall (Proverbs 16:18). Transparency brings breakthrough. Secrecy and hiding bring shame—and can keep both, the spouse and the person with the struggle, from obtaining victory over the struggle.

Talking with someone about personal struggles is a first step toward getting healing. Being able to discuss the hurts, habits, and hang-ups impacting a couple may be very important in obtaining much needed encouragement and emotional support. Details that are otherwise kept confidential are usually appropriate to be presented when seeking counsel. It could be detrimental to withhold pertinent information.

Not seeking insight or counsel from people who have experience with addiction caused me to come up with my own approach to the situation. Obviously, that did not work. Responding to Jacob the way I did drove him deeper into bondage, instead of helping pull him out of it. Not having input from others was detrimental for both Jacob and me.

In addition to seeking input from others, I should have been more diligent to seek God over how I addressed Jacob's issues. I cried at the Lord's feet a lot. But I didn't necessarily ask God what *I* should do to help Jacob. If I had, I believe the Lord would have directed me to approach things in a way that could have brought edification and encouragement. If that approach didn't bring change, I may have still felt God prompt me to move out, but there's a chance taking another approach could have yielded positive changes in our marriage.

CONSIDERING INPUT FROM OTHERS

A great friend is the person who will speak both encouragement and the hard truths. Without question, I have benefitted from the feedback of others—I especially came to appreciate the importance of considering input from people in my Bible study, as well as various work settings. I should have applied the concept of seeking feedback to identify areas for improvement in my marriage also.

Some people have difficulty voicing various concerns or facing conflict. Regardless of personality differences, no one is exempted from the need to have uncomfortable conversations periodically. Since people may be hesitant to provide feedback or to share a difficult truth—even if someone needs to hear it—it's wise to actively ask for input. When asked, people may be much more likely to provide feedback, give insights, and share their observations.

There are times when I am nervous or even cringe on the inside at the thought of receiving feedback, but I know it has the potential to help me better myself if I am willing to consider the insights of others.

Some input is very uplifting and helpful. Other times it can be difficult to hear what someone has to say. There are also times when—even though I knew it already—I needed to have someone state a truth for me. Hearing a person say it, moved me to action.

Over the years, many of my shortcomings have been pointed out by spouse, family, friends, or coworkers. I wish I could say I have worked out all the kinks and am perfect now! Instead, I will be the first to admit this is not the case.

All people are a work in progress and have things about themselves that can be improved. Therefore, everyone can benefit when someone is real with them and is willing to point out areas of their personality or lifestyle that may need to be adjusted.

The way feedback is presented usually impacts how well it is received. It's still possible, though, that even when the perfect approach is taken to provide feedback, some people may not be willing to consider it. They might feel justified in their behavior and be unwilling to acknowledge what should be done differently.

If a person humbly considers feedback and correction from others, it can catalyze change. To avoid feedback could mean that issues never get dealt with. Some people may need to be told a certain behavior is unacceptable before they realize it. It's also possible that people may not even be aware they have some of the tendencies or unfavorable traits they do, until another person points it out.

Although correction is uncomfortable sometimes, I still try to consider it. How I respond to feedback or correction—even when it is delivered unfavorably—can determine what the Lord is willing to entrust to me. I want to be teachable, and have a tender, responsive heart so the Lord can trust me to respond well to whatever situations arise.

To determine how teachable I am, I can ask myself questions like:

o   Am I quick to consider feedback from others?
o   Do I have a bad attitude in response to feedback I receive?
o   Do I humble myself and come to God in prayer right away?

If my response is to immediately try and assess if there is truth in the correction, and I humble myself to come before the Lord, then I am probably allowing God to mold me and being teachable. Responding to correction can be a catalyst for making adjustments where needed, thus strengthening my walk with the Lord.

Especially if I determine that the Lord is correcting me and wanting to deal with my heart, I am careful not to dismiss it. Habakkuk was a prophet in the Bible who understood the importance of responding to correction. Habakkuk 2:1 says, "I will stand my watch…and watch to see what He will say to me, *and what I will answer when I am corrected*" (NKJV).

Not every piece of feedback or correction someone gives is necessarily accurate, but I should check with the Lord just in case there is truth in it. Input from others should be *considered*, not necessarily applied. The person who offers a comment may not have an accurate perspective. People's frame of reference varies. No matter who provides insight or feedback, it is always wise to run their input through the filter of the Bible, asking if the comments align with God's heart.

FORGIVENESS

Forgiving sets us free! I have learned that people forgive *for their own benefit,* not because the offender deserves it. What exactly is forgiveness? Forgiveness is choosing not to hold something against another person—even though one may feel justified. Releasing forgiveness over someone prevents bitterness and resentment from taking root in the heart.

In *Life's Healing Choices,* there is a statement that bore witness with what I have seen and experienced, "Nothing drains you emotionally like bitterness and resentment."[1] Choosing not to forgive, can makes one's own life miserable.

In the prayer Jesus taught the disciples, He said, "Forgive us our sins as we forgive those who sin against us" (Matthew 6:12, NLT). Receiving forgiveness from God and releasing forgiveness to others, go hand-in-hand. Forgiveness is a big deal to God. He says in Matthew 6:15, "But if you don't forgive others, your Father in Heaven will not forgive your sins [transgressions, failings, trespasses]" (EXB). I interpret this to mean exactly what it says. No matter how justified someone may feel holding onto bitterness and resentment, *nothing* is worth forfeiting God's forgiveness. People don't need to wait until they *feel* like it—otherwise they may not ever forgive. Forgiveness is a decision.

When people have been used, abused, or hurt, they may feel very justified harboring bitterness and resentment, instead of choosing to forgive. Atrocities and hardships take place sometimes in life that so hurt our hearts, and the Lord's. People may be wronged as a result of many evils—perversion such as molestation or rape, violence, someone taking the life of a loved one, betrayal, or any number of other bad things—causing deep hurt and devastating those impacted. These kinds of instances can create an emotional turmoil that hinders someone for the rest of their lives if they do not make a choice to forgive their offender.

If a wrong-doer apologizes, it may be easier to forgive, but even when the wrong-doer is unremorseful and continues to do wrong, it is still necessary to forgive. Some people don't think they can ever forgive a particular person. I would be so bold as to say it is possible to forgive, even when there's been terrible offenses. I know people who've forgiven others for things many would say are unforgivable (such as sexual abuse).

One funeral I attended for a hit-and-run victim was especially memorable when the victim's boyfriend made a point to tell each person he spoke with at the funeral how important it was to forgive the driver who'd hit and killed her. That kind of response is *not* in our human nature, but it is in God's nature. Through Jesus Christ, we have access to the Holy Spirit who wants to build the character of Christ in us.

Forgiving Doesn't Mean Letting Someone Repeatedly Hurt You

Forgiving doesn't mean letting people continually do wrong. Neither does it mean keeping oneself in a vulnerable position. In some situations, it may be necessary to cut ties with someone and end a relationship—be it romantic, a friendship, or a business relationship. Ending a relationship does not mean someone is spiteful, it could simply mean that it is not healthy or wise to maintain the relationship. It is especially necessary to have boundaries with those who tend to take advantage or hurt others.

Releasing Forgiveness

One test I could use to see if I have forgiven someone is to determine if the thought "that person owes me" pops up when thinking about the person who wronged me.[2] If I have the perspective that he or she owes me, then it is likely, if not guaranteed, that I have not truly forgiven that person. I want to be a forgiving person. So, if the thought arises, "he or she owes me because of this and that," I must refrain from embracing that thought.

Instead, I need to take my thoughts captive. There is wisdom in 2 Corinthians 10:5, which says people should be, "Casting down arguments and every high thing that exalts itself against the knowledge of God, *bringing every thought into captivity to the obedience of Christ*" (NKJV). That means when my thoughts begin to wander in a negative way, I should redirect them. For example, it is up to me not to think "That person owes me." Instead, I can say aloud, "I'm not going there. I will not hold that [whatever the incident may be] against him. I forgive him. I release him. I bless him. I forgive him. I release him. I bless him…"

The confession of one's mouth is a powerful thing, be it for good or bad. Confessing forgiveness over a person who absolutely doesn't deserve it— even though one's emotions don't want to forgive—can still be done when there's a *decision* to forgive.

It's possible to release the hurts, deep-seated anger, and resentment one has, regardless of how justified one has felt carrying those things. There is no benefit to holding onto those negative emotions. It only hurts the person who carries them. Thankfully, giving them to God is always an option. 1 Peter 5:7 says, "Casting all your cares [all your anxieties, all your worries, and all your concerns, once and for all] on Him, for He cares about you [with deepest affection, watches over you very carefully]" (AMP). The Lord wants us to give Him our anxieties and concerns.

Jesus was sacrificed so people could be set free from sin, and so they could be made whole. God wants to work in each person's heart and bring healing. When someone partners together with God, it's possible to forgive.

BLESSING

Forgiving and blessing others helps to guard one's heart from bitterness. A friend once asked me what it means to bless. I described it as speaking well of someone. When a person blesses another, he or she releases divine favor over another person.[1] Blessing can encompass a broad range of things—ultimately, it is wishing someone well. There are a lot of different ways to bless someone.

Some examples could include:
- o Giving someone honor
- o Serving others
- o Talking about someone in a positive manner
- o Presenting a gift

Ultimately, the best way to bless a person is to ask God for an idea. Perhaps the Holy Spirit will answer with, "Call him tomorrow" or "Invite him over for dinner" or "Sing him a silly song" or "Wash his feet for him and tell him how much he means to you." Sometimes blessing looks a lot like encouragement.

God may prompt a person to bless anyone—it could be a family member one rarely speaks with, an enemy at the office, a neighbor, a coworker, or even a stranger—without revealing the reason why. Blessing others can release favor into the lives of everyone involved and bring God's touch where it is needed. Thankfully, God is a personal God and knows what each person most needs. The Lord may direct a person to bless someone who has not treated others well; blessing another person should not be solely dependent on feeling. Blessing someone could simply be an act of kindness or it could consist of a unique idea from the Lord to do something that would be very meaningful.

CODEPENDENCY

Looking back, I realize that needing to have a relationship dynamic where someone relies on me is indicative of being codependent. I should not need to have a certain type of relationship in order to fully function. Codependency refers to what happens when unhealthy characteristics develop as a result of trying to meet someone else's needs in a relationship. Instead of functioning as an independent, healthy adult, someone feels like they need another person to rely on them, or doesn't know how to function without them. It's like the whole world revolves around that person.

Often, when boundaries are not appropriately set between individuals, people become codependent. Not having boundaries in place can eventually create an inability for people to separate themselves from those with whom they are in close relationship. Subsequently, one's own identity can become blurred as a result of being so focused on the other person in the relationship.

People who are codependent may:
- o Begin to constantly seek validation from the person they are in a relationship with (or other outside sources)
- o Look to others for their own happiness or peace, instead of having it of their own accord
- o Ignore inner promptings which indicate they should not be in relationship with a particular individual
- o Have a tendency to describe reality as they *want* it to be, instead of how it actually is

Codependency can cause people to lose a sense of who they are—this may include losing sight of their own personal interests, passions, and other unique traits. Unfortunately, this can easily happen in relationships, especially where someone has an addiction.

It is fine to make sacrifices for another person. In essence, love is sacrificial. However, when there is not balance or appropriate boundaries, someone can become codependent. In my case, I developed a dependency on being needed by another person to fuel me emotionally. I noticed this happened with my motivation for working. I became used to being the provider, and when I was no longer providing I felt a void. Part of my struggle may have been a natural transition, but my role in my relationship with Jacob was out of balance for so long that I did not know how to adjust to being normal and independent.

During my marriage I did not often do the things I enjoyed, like swimming, going for walks, or getting together with friends because I was always concerned about Jacob and tended to isolate myself. Instead of doing things I enjoyed and fostering my own personal interests, I was obsessed with how much I wanted to see my husband set free from his lifestyle choices. Being so focused on his behavior was emotionally draining for both of us and did not foster a healthy balance in my life. Healthy relationships must have boundaries, and there must be a standard for what's considered acceptable.

The Lord taught me about having a standard for how I let others treat me. One day after I'd moved into my rental home, the thought came out of the blue, *James and the Giant Peach*. Since seeing the previews for that movie when I was young, I'd never had any interest in watching it. But this was the second time that movie title had randomly come to mind—it had come to mind a year or two earlier when I'd been with Jacob. I realized the Lord had something to show me in that movie. So, I made a point to watch it.

The scene from the movie that stood out to me was where James finally stands up for himself. After being treated terribly by people who were supposed to love and protect him, he refused to go back to the way things used to be. It seemed that God wanted me to make the decision James did, and choose not to return to a place where I would be treated poorly.

Even though I would have been willing to return to the chaotic environment with Jacob, I believed God did not want me to return to an environment where there would be anger and scorn constantly present. Proverbs 29:9 says, "A sage trying to work things out with a fool gets only scorn and sarcasm for his trouble" (MSG). The Lord helped me understand that I needed to have a standard for how I let people treat me. I needed to resolve not to let people treat me however they want. It was *up to me* to set and maintain boundaries; otherwise people encroach on those boundaries as much as I let them.

ENABLING

What does it mean to enable someone? Enabling is when someone promotes a poor behavior in another person by assisting them to continue in it or not intervening in an appropriate way to curb that behavior. This often occurs in relationships where someone is bound to an addiction of some kind. However, enabling is not limited to addiction. Any bad behavior could be enabled in a relationship, whether it is cheating on a spouse, poor spending habits, irresponsibility, or a host of other possibilities.

Examples of enabling could include:
- o Giving money to someone (funding destructive habits or keeping people dependent on handouts from others, instead of allowing them to become responsible)
- o Isolating oneself and trying to hide (or keep secret) the behavior from others

Especially if those practices are done repeatedly over time, this could be an indication of being an enabler. Other indicators of someone who may be enabling poor behavior could include things like: isolating oneself; not facing reality; not calling the behavior what it is; and rewriting the story of what really happened (skewing or denying the facts).

Seeking out counseling and doing research on enabling, abuse, addiction, or whatever other issues are applicable for a person's circumstances could be very helpful for anyone who may be in that position. The more knowledge and awareness people have about their situation, the more effectively they can respond. Developing a strategy with the input of wise counsel is a much more effective approach than turning a blind eye or waiting for things to suddenly change. Simply hoping that an issue will go away does not produce change.

LONELINESS

Feelings of loneliness or hardships can tempt people to go into isolation and self-pity. Shutting out others or constantly thinking about how one longs for different circumstances and feeling sorry for oneself won't produce anything good; it just leads someone into depression.

People may feel lonely, even when surrounded by others, if they don't believe there is anyone they can trust or have a meaningful conversation with. People from all walks of life—married or single, from a big family or not, employed or not—may feel lonely, but people don't have to continue feeling that way.

There are ways to bring about change. Choosing to do something such as participating in an enjoyable activity, joining a group, intentionally connecting with other people, and actively avoiding negative thinking can make a difference.

Asking basic questions can be helpful, like:

o   What interests or passions stir excitement or bring contentment?

o   Which hobbies are especially enjoyable?

Those answers can help generate ideas for how to minimize loneliness.

Below are some ideas for how to connect with others:

o   Join a group of people that have common interests

o   Connect with old friends or make new ones

o   Attend church and join a small group

o   Practice meeting people [simple connections could turn into friendships]

o   Serve someone

o   Offer to use various talents or skills to help others

o   Reach out to others

o   Invite someone to have a meal or to go for a walk

People have been created to live in community and do life together, so it's important to have a good support system in place and be connected with others. Those who are lonely may be vulnerable or shy and it can mean the world to them to have others reach out. Making a point to encourage those struggling with loneliness and helping to get them connected with good people who will care about them, is a great opportunity to make a difference in those individual's lives. How each person responds will vary; sometimes people isolate themselves for multiple reasons.

One's life circumstances, such as the death of a loved one or the end of a romantic relationship can generate a feeling of loneliness. Some single people feel like they need to be in a romantic relationship to be happy; otherwise, they feel lonely. As a single person, loneliness is something I struggled with on occasion. It was not until I read a book called *Imagine Heaven* and gained a deeper understanding of eternity that I could honestly say I felt content with being single. Finding fulfillment in Jesus Christ alone really is possible.

God wants to be the ultimate source people come to for fulfillment, but He also wants us to be connected to other people. Being intentional to be in community not only provides a source of social interaction and encouragement along the way, it also allows people to use their gifts and talents to help and encourage others.

SEEKING VALUE

Have you ever felt a void on the inside of you? I have. Cammi has. Cammi and the Woman at the Well (described in John 4) are not the only women who have turned to a source other than God for fulfillment. Many women go from one broken relationship to another, seeking to fill a void. For most women, if not all, there is a deep desire on the inside to be loved and to be seen as beautiful.

There is a common misconception that giving oneself to a sexual relationship is equivalent to being sincerely loved by the person with whom one is intimate. Physical intimacy is meant to be an expression of love, not a means to obtain it. If bringing someone pleasure is the only grounds on which love is based, then the relationship will likely be shallow and the people involved won't truly appreciate the personality or character of the other person. Many women give themselves to sexual relationships because they think that will win the heart of their lover and, finally, they will truly be loved. In reality, this is a poor means of trying to establish value. True value is intrinsic. I believe the Lord would say to women of this mindset, "Daughter you are highly valued. Otherwise, I would not have sent My Son, Jesus, to die for you." When people (both men and women) realize they are valued, their decisions reflect that awareness.

At times, I have needed to affirm myself in God's love. One day in particular, I remember settling onto the couch and saying, "Lord, tell me how much You love me." I then opened the Bible and laid eyes on Zechariah 2:8, "For thus says the Lord of hosts: 'He sent Me after glory, to the nations which plunder you; for *he who touches you touches the apple of His eye*'" (NKJV). I felt like the Lord was speaking directly to me, letting me know I was precious to Him. In reality, His eye is not just on me, but on all His children. Each person has a purpose and is extremely valuable because God loves *each* man, *each* woman, and *each* child.

Something is considered valuable when someone is willing to pay a great cost for it. Since God sent His Son to die for you and me and paid a price so great, we must be pretty valuable! Each of us is created with a purpose and has a destiny. To seek fulfillment in places other than the Lord will not fill the God-shaped void inside of a person.

PERCEPTION AND SELF-ESTEEM

My educational psychology professor in college had a saying, "I am who *you* think I am." This statement captures the mentality of most people. Examples of negative thoughts that might go through some people's minds, as a result of how they think others view them, could include:

o *They think I am dumb, so I must be.*
o *Because that person said I will never amount to anything, I must be worthless.*
o *I messed up and failed when I tried that task. Probably nobody thinks I can be successful if I tried again. I don't think I can do it either.*
o *I didn't do what I should have, and people know it. I am not able to do the right thing.*

Each of the above statements captures a person's perception about himself or herself that is based on what someone else supposedly says or thinks. A person's perception does not change true reality. For example, each person has worth and is highly valued, even when someone doesn't think so.

Perception is important, though, because it influences a person's conclusions, actions, and abilities. If someone thinks he or she is not good enough, that mentality is often reflected in that person's decisions and actions. The weight perception has—and the power of influence comments can have—was seen in research conducted by Jane Elliott in the 1970s.

Experiment: Brown Eyed vs. Blue Eyed
Elliott was a teacher who divided her class of third grade students into two groups—the blue eyed and brown eyed. The first day of the experiment, she told one group they were better than the other students, and even allotted special privileges to the said superior group. Switching which group was superior the second day, Elliot again made comments about how capable, or inferior, a particular group of students was. Each day, the performance improved for the kids who'd been told they were superior while the

179

performance waned in the group told they were not as good.

For both groups, there was a notable difference in performance. The group treated as inferior had slower response times in solving math problems, struggled more with spelling, and felt like outcasts.[1]

The students' perception of what someone else thought of them lowered their self-esteem and impacted their ability to perform. They embraced the lies they had been told—as though it was the truth about who they were and what they could do. That perception kept them from experiencing their full potential. Afterward, the class discussed their experience, and developed a deeper understanding of how no one person is better than another.

Throughout life, people encounter harsh comments or criticism. If those lies are not addressed—and consciously rejected—they can take root in someone's heart and have lasting effects. Comments from others do not dictate truth, but it can impact how people feel about themselves and shape their perspective. Often, people live up to, or down to, the expectations of others.

There is a scene from *Facing the Giants* where a player goes out to kick the football for a field goal, but he misses. Afterward, someone comments that he acted like he was going to miss it even before he attempted the kick. The player explains, "I knew I was going to miss it before I even tried." He is then told, "Your actions will always follow your beliefs..."[2] Perception can indeed impact a person's actions and performance.

If people know they have a strong support structure where family or friends believe in them, that can make an incredible difference. Those who know someone believes in them are more likely to be confident and overcome life's challenges, believing it's possible to be successful.

Ultimately, it is God's opinion that dictates real truth—what He says is the *true* reality. Focusing on what the Lord says, is one way to build self-esteem and gain a more accurate perspective about oneself.

BROKENNESS

Brokenness can be used to transform and strengthen people. It can also increase one's dependence on God.

One of Jesus' most dedicated followers, Paul, viewed suffering in a positive light because he saw it as a way he could be closer with Jesus (Philippians 3:10). Even in difficult circumstances, one can grow closer to and be transformed by the Lord.

How could being broken bring someone to a deeper place in God's presence? Times of brokenness are often when people are the most willing to surrender to the Lord and allow Him to do a deep work in their hearts.

I have learned that God has big arms, and no burden or depth of pain I bring to Him is too much for Him to bear. He wants each person to be honest with Him and discuss their hurts and struggles. Coming to the Lord with hurts allows Him to address those soul wounds.

Responses Vary

Not all people respond to a difficult situation the same way. Some withdraw and try to distance themselves—either because of shame or as a way to protect themselves. Others may be especially open to connecting with people and want their input. A person may be very vulnerable during a time of brokenness and could be easily influenced. Therefore, it is important to be selective about who is speaking into one's life.

Some advice may not be beneficial. Input from the wrong people could lead a person away from what God wants to do in and through that person. For example, how many hurting people turn to drugs or alcohol when they are going through a difficult time because of the influence of other people?

Obtaining input from godly people and prioritizing time with the Lord is wise because God wants to minister to all people and walk with them through their struggles, providing guidance and support. Whether there are concerns over something small or extremely important, He is always there, ready for anyone to bring whatever burdens they are carrying.

When someone draws close to God during a time of hardship, He is able to establish that person in His truth. It's God's heart to bring people strength and encouragement. Drawing one's attention to Scriptures from the Bible could be one way the Lord strengthens and encourages someone. Another way could be when the Holy Spirit speaks to a person during prayer or worship. The Lord could also use people to bring each other encouragement. Encouragement can come to someone in many different ways.

Nothing is in Vain

Thinking back to a friend's vision about how God can use everything someone experiences in life to reach others has brought me encouragement over the years. While we were praying one day, my friend saw her arm covered in gold bracelets. Not understanding why she was shown that image, she asked the Lord, "What are you doing? Dressing me in jewels?" The Lord then showed her that each band symbolized an experience she had. And with each band, her arm got longer. Those longer arms would enable her to reach that many more people and pull them out of the darkness. Each hardship she went through increased the number of people she was able to relate to and therefore reach. No hardship she experienced would be in vain. This picture ties in well with Romans 8:28, which says, "And we know that *all things work together for good to those who love God*, to those who are called according to His purpose" (NKJV). God can bring good out of anything that is given to Him. People may experience many things contrary to the Lord's heart; it could be the result of someone's mistakes or for other reasons. Many of the hurts and hardships in life are not from Him, but God can still use them and bring *something* good out of them.

The Choice is Ours

It has been said, "Trials (adversity) can make you better or bitter. The choice is yours."[1] Upon hearing that, I agreed. When people go through hardship, they can become better when they choose to: forgive, love others, trust God, learn from their mistakes, continue moving forward, resolve themselves to be people of integrity, and extend grace to others. Whereas living with unforgiveness and anger can create a breeding ground for bitterness. It profits no one to continually focus on what happened in the past, refuse to let something go, or hold out for revenge.

Although I would love to erase my many mistakes and dumb moments, I can't. I just have to learn from my mistakes and try not to repeat them. Dwelling on past mistakes, disappointments, and lingering in a place where negative emotions stir can be tempting.

Because there can be a tendency to focus on the things that have gone wrong or to hold onto unhealthy emotions, I remind myself of these four things:

1. If I give any situation to God, He can bring good out of it.
2. I need to make an intentional effort to give my cares to God.
3. It is up to *me* whether I hold onto negativity.
4. I need to *choose* joy.

DIRECT YOUR THOUGHTS

Thoughts lead to actions. Actions determine one's character. Character determines what decisions one makes in life. One of the most important practices a person can have is to take captive any thoughts that are not God-honoring.

What Someone Focuses On Matters

When people focus on themselves, their short-comings, and what they don't have, they are more likely to get into the rut of loneliness, self-pity, or depression. The Bible directs one to meditate on things that are noble, true, praiseworthy, honorable, pure, and of good report (Philippians 4:8). People are to focus on things that are uplifting and to fix their eyes on Jesus (Hebrews 12:2). At times, I need to remind myself of those Bible verses. It is easy to fall into a rut if do not take my thoughts captive and redirect them. What a person meditates on can greatly influence his or her perception. This also has a significant impact on one's emotional and spiritual state and can ultimately determine which decisions a person makes.

Familiar Habit

One time, I spoke with a friend about how people tend to revert to feelings that are familiar, "When people are accustomed to experiencing a certain negative emotion that is familiar to them, their bodies produce endorphins that bring a sense of comfort." This struck a chord with her. She responded, "That makes sense. I have struggled with depression, and when I go back [into that depressive state], it's like I am going home." There is a tendency to return to what is familiar. This can be one reason people who've struggled with an emotional issue might not want to break free from it. People may also seek out chaotic, dysfunctional environments when that is what they have been accustomed to experiencing. How many people go from one abusive relationship to another? Or, how many people hold onto negative emotions? A part of them desperately wants a change, but there is often another part that wants to stay in that place of emotional turmoil. There is a draw to revert to those familiar feelings because it has become habit. Habits can be hard to break!

Even though it may be a natural tendency to let bad feelings linger, people can choose not to stay in that emotional state. Often, there must be an *intentional effort* to get out of that familiar place—of loneliness, depression, self-pity, or any other negative emotion. One way to do this is by actively choosing to not focus on things that foster those particular emotions.

If letting go of bad thoughts and emotions is a struggle, one can always ask God for help. Reading the Bible and praying are a couple ways to allow God to help redirect one's thoughts.

Especially when a marriage gets tough one might ask, "What is the Lord's heart on divorce?" Scripture is clear. God *hates* divorce (Malachi 2:16). Divorce is contrary to God's original design for marriage, but that does not necessarily mean He never permits it.

It is possible that God could direct a couple to divorce because of their situation. However, I believe it is generally God's heart to restore a broken marriage. According to the Bible, it seems that divorce is permitted in two circumstances. These are listed below, along with the two Scriptures upon which I base my opinion:

1. One of the people in the marriage is an unbeliever (does not follow Christ) and chooses to depart.
    o 1 Corinthians 7:15 says, "But if those who are not believers decide to leave [or divorce], let them leave [or divorce]. When this happens, the Christian man [brother] or woman [sister] is free [not bound to the marriage covenant]…" (EXB).
2. In the case of adultery (sexual immorality), a couple is not *required* to divorce, but they seem to have that option.
    o Matthew 19:9 says, "And I say to you, whoever divorces his wife, except for sexual immorality, and marries another, commits adultery; and whoever marries her who is divorced commits adultery" (NKJV).

When considering historical context surrounding the Scriptures in 1 Corinthians and Matthew, some people conclude that divorce is never permitted in God's eyes and remarriage following any divorce is sin. I don't want to do anything that opposes God, so I researched this possibility. In my studies, I found reasons vary for why biblical scholars draw different conclusions. One explanation could be because the betrothal process in the

Jewish culture (the context for much of the Bible) was different than today. In the Jewish culture, a couple was considered married, during betrothal (engagement). However, they didn't consummate the marriage until the wedding night. During the betrothal process, divorcing someone would have been more like breaking off a commitment to marry a fiancé, rather than ending an already established covenant of marriage.

Despite my research, I could not draw the same conclusion as some biblical scholars, that divorce should never be permitted in the case of marital unfaithfulness. Perhaps my perspective is wrong and God never permits remarriage when someone divorces after a marriage has been consummated. I wanted to be open about other perspectives, but after much angst and trying to gain clarity on this topic, I was left at the same place I started, taking the Scripture, "…except for sexual immorality…" (Matthew 19:9, NKJV) at face value.

Sometimes, even in the case of sexual immorality, God would have a couple to keep their commitment to one another. When considering God's heart for a marriage where adultery has occurred, I think of an instance recorded in the Book of Hosea (found in the Old Testament of the Bible). Amazingly, the prophet named Hosea was told by the Lord to marry a prostitute. He obeyed. Even when his wife went after other lovers, Hosea continued to pursue his wife and show her unconditional love. Hosea's marriage was a picture of God's relationship with Israel. It was symbolic for how Israel kept committing adultery against God (by worshiping other gods) but the Lord longed for Israel to come back to Him.

MARRIAGE COVENANT

Marriage is a way God provides companionship. It is intended to be a blessing, "He who finds a wife finds a good thing" (excerpt from Proverbs 18:22, NKJV). Because men and women are designed differently, they often complement each other when they partner together. When God established the covenant of marriage, it was with the intention for spouses to make a commitment to one another and stay together.

The marriage covenant between a man and woman is supposed to reflect the covenant God has with His followers (the Church). Analogously, Jesus Christ is the Husband and the Church is the Bride (Ephesians 5:23-27). In the covenant the Church has with Jesus Christ, the Groom (Jesus) is always willing to keep His commitment. If someone leaves their covenant with Jesus by renouncing their faith or ending their walk of faith, they can re-enter it by repenting and recommitting their lives to Him.

People enter into covenant with Jesus when they ask Him to forgive them of their sin and invite Him into their lives. To maintain the covenant with Jesus, it is necessary to repent of sin and draw near to God. The Lord longs for intimacy with people—where they share their hearts and souls with Him. Similar to marriage, there is sacrifice involved, a commitment to be maintained, and the need to be in close communion in order to foster the relationship.

Sadly, many people in a marriage covenant do not realize the permanence intended for that covenant. Instead, they forsake it by filing for divorce for various reasons—"we fell out of love," "we don't have anything in common anymore," "irreconcilable differences," or many other unfortunate scenarios. Oftentimes in reality, that covenant may still be in place in God's eyes. In my opinion, unless there has been a divorce for reasons of sexual immorality or someone divorces because one spouse became a believer in Jesus Christ and the other decided to end the marriage, biblically, the divorce cannot be granted. Scripturally, it seems black and white that when someone divorces without biblical precedent, they are never truly released from their marriage in the Lord's eyes. Scripture says if they remarry then that is adultery. I do not profess to know everything or to know every circumstance of people's marriages—surely, I do not.

After much research, I have yet to find the scriptural support for divorce other than the two reasons listed in 1 Corinthians 7:15 and Matthew 19:9. If someone has divorced under different circumstances, I would encourage him or her to talk with the Lord about it and He will provide guidance for that specific situation.

MARRIAGE REFLECTIONS:
KEY POINTS

- *Wives can empower their husbands.*
- *Nagging and criticism strips a husband of dignity and creates frustration in marriage.*
- *Trying to take control doesn't work.*
- *Respond with grace and compassion.*
- *Considering input from others can catalyze change.*
- *Welcoming accountability can help make change sustainable.*
- *People can go to the Lord anytime, including in times of brokenness.*
- *Healthy relationships have boundaries.*
- *It's important to perceive oneself the way God does.*
- *Each person is created with purpose.*
- *When a situation is given to God, He can bring something good out of it.*
- *Intentionally directing one's thoughts helps a person let go of unhealthy emotions.*
- *Divorce seems permissible in certain circumstances, per two Scriptures in the Bible.*
- *A marriage covenant is a big deal. It's intended to be for a lifetime.*

PART 2B:
FAITH INSIGHTS

Surrender
Carrying God's Presence
Fruit of the Holy Spirit
Identity
What Does God Require of Us?
Legalism
Are All Promises For Everyone?
Obedience
Filled with the Holy Spirit
Gaining Supernatural Insight
Ways God Speaks: Thoughts
Ways God Speaks: Dreams
Spiritual Warfare
Closing the Door to the Enemy
The Enemy's Tactics
Testing a Word
What If Someone Is Wrong About Hearing From the Lord?
How Do You Recover From Failure?
Confirmation
Collective Summary
Hope

SURRENDER

Recognizing how great the Lord's love is—along with His mercy, holiness, and overall goodness—causes people to *want* to experience the Lord. "We love Him because He first loved us" (1 John 4:19, NKJV). When the Lord asks people to surrender something, it is because He has their best interest in mind, wants to redirect their focus, or simply wants to be a priority in that person's heart.

Often, there is a surge of excitement and emotion people experience after first giving their lives to Christ. Over time, that emotion may wane, which can test a person's faith. God wants people to make decisions based on what they know to be right versus always yielding on their emotions. Simply following emotions can entice someone to make poor choices or go a direction contrary to how the Lord wants the person to respond. Choosing to yield to the guidance of the Holy Spirit and the Word of God, instead of following one's emotions, is a form of surrender.

When someone chooses to let God direct life's path, it may be necessary to give something up—it could be a relationship, lifestyle habit, or something else. As a living sacrifice, it's always possible to go back to the altar where something has already been laid down and pick it back up; this can easily happen if someone does not keep his or her heart guarded. Those issues could be: unforgiveness, hurt, letting go of a past relationship, or any number of things. Part of being a living sacrifice is continually surrendering to the Lord.

A couple of years after the divorce, I asked the Lord how Jacob was doing. Immediately, I heard in my spirit the words to a worship song, "I surrender all."[1] I took a breath, then said in my heart, *Okay, Lord. I surrender him to you.* Over time, I'd begun to think about him again. There had been many good times during our years together. Not everything had been bad. Letting myself begin to meditate on what we once had made me start to miss him and stirred a longing in my heart.

One day, I even began to call a male friend by the name of Jacob, even though that wasn't his name. I realized, *Since I have been thinking about Jacob a lot, he has gotten into my heart again. That's why I keep calling my friend, "Jacob," because he is in my heart.* I knew this was the case because Matthew 12:34 says, "…[For] The mouth speaks the things that are in [overflow from] the heart" (EXB). Apparently I had my ex-husband in my heart. What a person meditates on usually gets into the heart. I needed to make a decision to let go of Jacob *again*, and keep myself from thinking about him all the time.

In the movie *Fireproof* there is a great line that provides practical advice, "Don't just follow your heart man, because your heart can be deceived. You need to *lead* your heart."[2] People can lead their heart by taking their thoughts captive and not focusing on things they shouldn't. In other words, it's important to intentionally direct one's thoughts.

Proverbs 4:23 says, "Guard your heart above all else, for it determines the course of your life" (NLT). How do people guard their hearts? One way, is to be intentional to not think about things that are unbeneficial—such as entertaining ideas one shouldn't or focusing on things that foster resentment. Being selective about who one trusts is also important. It may be necessary to keep certain relationships at a distance. Ways to help guard the heart from being led astray include reading the Word of God and purposing in one's heart to follow Jesus every day. Each person who wants to experience God's best must be willing to yield to the Holy Spirit.

Yielding to the Holy Spirit is a daily decision. In 1 Corinthians 15:31, Paul said, "I die daily" (NKJV). In the Greek, what Paul actually said was that he faced death daily. Indeed, he did. Although he'd been zealous against Jesus and persecuted Christians, God revealed Himself to Paul in a profound way. This experience is recorded in the Book of Acts. After realizing Jesus was truly the Messiah, Paul dedicated his life to sharing the gospel, no matter what the cost. He encountered shipwrecks, beatings, imprisonment, and even a stoning. People tried to kill Paul for sharing the gospel and telling people about Jesus. So, it was very appropriate to say that he faced death daily. However, I like the way that Scripture reads in most translations, "I die daily," because the concept is still applicable that I need to die daily to my own selfish desires and embrace God's heart for me.

Often, when people want more of God and pursue Him, His desires become their desires. However, there are times when my flesh (desires or ungodly tendencies) tries to demand my attention. No matter what season I am in, it is important to surrender to the Holy Spirit and not let my flesh rule me.

God's desire is that His people reflect His image. "But we all, with unveiled face, beholding as in a mirror the glory of the Lord, are *being transformed into the same image* from glory to glory" (excerpt from 2 Corinthians

3:18, NASB). In other words, as someone spends time with the Lord and learns about God's heart, that person develops characteristics similar to the Lord and reflects who God is.

Encounters with God spark transformation in people's lives. During an encounter with the Lord, people may receive a revelation of God's goodness that inspires them to love Him more. An encounter with the Lord could also cause people to experience conviction about areas of their lives that are not yet surrendered to the Lord and behaviors they need to change. The Lord wants to continually mature believers in their faith. Believers are encouraged in 2 Peter 3:18 to "grow [spiritually mature] in the grace and knowledge of our Lord and Savior Jesus Christ" (AMP). As someone grows in his or her relationship with God, that person may begin to evaluate decisions more closely and change certain behaviors.

Sometimes people work against what God wants to do in their lives; even accidentally this can happen through pride or justifying certain decisions. However, if people are humble and ask the Lord to deal with them, He will. Humility is an important key to drawing close to God and receiving His grace. Grace refers to the goodness of God that's given to someone even when he or she doesn't deserve it. It's His grace that brings someone deliverance, forgiveness, and daily guidance.[3]

CARRYING GOD'S PRESENCE

When someone gives their heart to Jesus, the Holy Spirit comes to live inside of them. The more people acknowledge God and humble themselves before Him—being quick to admit fault and ask forgiveness when a bad choice is made—the softer their hearts are. In other words, being humble can help someone accept correction and make adjustments as needed. People with open hearts are more likely to be sensitive to the Holy Spirit, making it possible to experience more of God's presence than someone whose heart is hardened. Simply spending time with God also helps someone carry His presence.

Worshiping God is one way people may encounter a strong measure of God's presence, especially when they are worshiping with other believers. It is when I've been singing to the Lord or listening to worship music that I have had some of the most meaningful revelations. Many times, it's during a time of worship when God puts His finger on an area of my life that needs to change. Worship ushers in His presence, especially when singing songs that exalt and praise Him. This is because God inhabits the praises of His people (Psalm 22:3). Focusing on God and praising Him can create a sweet, intimate moment with the Lord and allow someone to have an encounter with Him.

I would be so bold as to say that when people routinely pursue God and encounter His presence, they carry a stronger measure of God's presence as a result. Where God's presence is, change can happen. If people spend time each morning in the presence of God, not only are they more sensitive to His voice throughout the day, but it could even happen that it impacts the people around them. Perhaps just being near someone who is carrying God's presence could cause a person to feel a particular sense of love, comfort, or conviction because of the Holy Spirit.

In Acts 5 it's records that people would try to have the Apostle Peter's shadow fall on the sick so they could be healed. Why? I believe it's because Peter carried God's presence to such a degree that change happened in those around him and healing and deliverance took place. I believe this happened because of Peter's deep intimacy with God and his commitment to follow the Lord.

Obedience to the Lord Leads to Intimacy

One way to draw close to the Lord and encounter His presence is through obeying Him. Years before we married, Jacob told me the Holy Spirit had said to him, "Obedience [to the Holy Spirit] leads to intimacy [with God]." It made sense. Since disobedience and sin distances someone from the Lord (until that person repents), I could see where obeying the Lord and submitting to the promptings of the Holy Spirit could help someone experience closeness with God.

A friend in the faith once told me she had been encountering God's presence in a much greater way after she started to obey what God was asking her to do. "I have never encountered His presence like I have recently. It is because I have *submitted* [to the promptings of the Holy Spirit]. I didn't *submit* before." She described the peace and joy she now had. As I spoke with her, it was evident her obedience to the Lord allowed her to experience a level of freedom greater than she'd previously known.

FRUIT OF THE HOLY SPIRIT

Growing in God means yielding to the Holy Spirit so He can bear in us the fruit of love, joy, peace, patience, kindness, goodness, faithfulness, gentleness, and self-control (Galatians 5:22-23). These fruit of the Spirit naturally become more evident in a person's life as they follow God and spend time with Him. I didn't understand how this process worked until one day when I was walking across my college campus. Frustrated, I was reflecting on an immature comment someone had just made. I spoke silently in my heart and began complaining, "Lord, it's hard to be a Christian. I am supposed to love everybody all the time, like the guy who made that inappropriate comment..." Before I could finish my complaint, the Lord interrupted me with the thought, *That is why I do it.* Instantly, I understood how the fruit of the Holy Spirit is produced. When someone is difficult to love, *God* loves them through me; it is not something I do all by myself. My response to convictions the Holy Spirit impresses upon me is what determines the spiritual fruit in my life. Love, joy, peace, patience, kindness, goodness, faithfulness, gentleness, and self-control come when I *yield* to the Holy Spirit and respond how He wants me to.

For example, let's say that a wife lies to her husband and really upsets him. In his flesh (natural reaction), the next time he sees her, he wants to verbally derail her because she purposely gave him wrong information. However, he obeys the prompting from the Holy Spirit not to repay evil for evil and restrains himself (practices self-control) and prays for her (showing love). That man is developing godly characteristics because he chose to yield to the Holy Spirit.

Promptings from the Lord could cause someone to change their lifestyle. Perhaps someone becomes more mindful of the language he or she uses and begins to refrain from using swear words. Maybe, instead of taking in harmful substances, someone decides to maintain a healthier lifestyle. Instead of watching unedifying things on television, perhaps a person makes a different choice about what to watch. Maybe another person, who is normally self-focused, decides to spend less time for self and more time serving others. Yielding to the Holy Spirit can produce changes in one's attitude and behavior.

In addition to bearing spiritual fruit and encouraging people, God desires to mature people in the faith and uproot those things that would hinder growth in Him. As people progress in their relationship with God, He works in people's hearts to direct them toward living a holy life which includes purity and absence of sin. He also seeks to develop His character in them.

IDENTITY

When I got married and took my husband's last name, I embraced the role of wife as part of an expanded identity, excited for what it encompassed. Then, when I got divorced, my role changed. But that didn't mean I was somehow less valuable. I knew I was still just as valued by God. If I let myself be entirely defined by being a wife, I would have felt a real sense of loss with regard to who I was as a person when I got divorced. Thankfully, as a follower of Jesus Christ, my primary identity as a child of God never changes.

What is a person's core identity? Ultimately, it is what God says which truly determines the identity of a person. Humans are created in God's image—He designed us! (Genesis 1:27). The Lord knows each person, even before they are born (Jeremiah 1:5).

Someone's *identity* is not the mistakes he or she has made, nor is it the failures or poor decisions of the past. However, many people live under that premise, thus embracing a kind of false identity. How a person thinks determines how they live and often determines what decisions they make.

I recognized my own insecurities and saw Jacob also needed to develop a greater understanding of his identity in the Lord. For Jacob, knowing and believing that he was truly loved and accepted by God was challenging for him. That lack of belief kept Jacob from embracing who he was in Christ. If he had embraced God's love it would have helped him to have victory over his struggles. The sin in Jacob's life, his misconceptions, and the negative way he viewed himself hindered him from walking in his true identity.

False Identity

A false sense of identity is created because of insecurities, misperceptions, and bondage. It causes people to equate themselves with unfavorable traits or sin, see themselves as lesser than others, or simply not realize their God-given potential. As a result, they flounder in life, not realizing who they are created to be. Thoughts and wrong beliefs about who someone is can form in response to various comments and experiences to which a person is exposed. In an attempt to understand or establish an identity, some search for value and belonging by entering into multiple intimate relationships, gangs, drugs, alcohol or other harmful things.

Demeaning comments like, "You'll never amount to anything," or "You aren't good enough," can cause a lot of heartache. Those statements can stay with a person for years and create a mentality where someone really believes they have nothing to offer or have no value. Whether or not people *feel* like they have something of value to offer—they do. *Everyone* is unique and is valuable. Even if the people in someone's life don't truly care, God certainly does!

True Identity

My marriage taught me that God establishes identity, but many people do not walk in their true identity because they don't know what it is. I would define identity as who someone truly is. Finding oneself and searching for meaning is not something limited to those in their teenage years. People of all ages search for their identity by assessing the value others place on them, trying to find their niche in life, and wanting to be sure they have purpose. When people continually search for meaning and purpose in life, it's often because they have not sought to understand the contents of the Bible—there, God describes who we are as His child.

Each person must have an understanding of what God says about them before being able to enter into the fullness of what God intended for their lives. In the Bible, God describes the purpose for every person, His love for mankind, and the gifts and talents He apportions to people. It is through spending time with the Lord that one understands the purpose of his or her life, which is to be in relationship with God and make a positive impact on others. Someone's *true* identity is not dependent on what others say, but on what God, the Maker, says.

Every person is unique, and loved by God. Individuals' unique characteristics—talents, gifts, gender, familial affiliations, profession, education, nationality, background, present environment—all feed into someone's identity. However, there is a core identity in Christ for a child of God, which everyone is intended to walk in. But not everyone walks in this identity, nor do all people realize this is who God created them to be!

When people enter into relationship with the Lord, they become a child of God and can find their value in the Lord and what He says about them! They can stand on the promises in the Bible. According to the Scriptures, they are loved, created with purpose, gifted, healed, set free, of a sound mind, forgiven, unafraid, hopeful, an extender of grace, redeemed, and victorious in Christ.

Below is a list of some characteristics a person has as a child of God, and the Bible verses to support them.

Characteristic	Scriptural support
Loved	John 3:16, 1 John 4:7
Created with Purpose	Exodus 9:16, Romans 8:28
Gifted	1 Peter 4:10, Romans 12:6
Healed	Isaiah 53:5
Set Free	Galatians 5:1
Of a Sound Mind	2 Timothy 1:7
Forgiven	Luke 6:37, Colossians 1:14
Unafraid	2 Timothy 1:7
Hopeful	Romans 15:13
Extender of Grace	Ephesians 4:7
Redeemed	Ephesians 1:7, Titus 2:14
Victorious in Christ	1 Corinthians 15:57, 1 John 4:4

Not all of those things are characteristics or experiences a person automatically has. Sometimes a person needs to contend for them! For example, forgiving others and extending grace is not always easy, but with the Lord it is possible. Fear has a grip on many people, but God doesn't want people to be afraid, "For God has not given us a spirit of fear but of power, of love, and of a sound mind" (2 Timothy 1:7, NKJV). Living to be the person God intended, can be a battle. Seeking God and leaning on Him, can guide someone to victory.

No one is on this Earth by accident. The Lord God created each person in his or her mother's womb. He knows everyone by name and has a plan and purpose for each person. God wants to be an integral part of each person's life!

The Bible says those who love and follow Jesus are holy, loved, and gifted; they are also part of His kingdom. Each person is loved by God, created with a purpose, and given gifts and talents. It would be a lie for someone to determine he or she has nothing to offer or has no value. To see oneself as not good enough or unworthy of love—despite whatever failures or disappointments one experiences—is a false perception.

In Jesus Christ, the mistakes of the past no longer define a person. Each person who chooses to make Jesus Christ their Lord and Savior, also has God as their Father. This makes them a child of God.

WHAT DOES GOD REQUIRE OF US?

The question is posed by the Prophet Micah, "What does the Lord require of you?" Micah then answers, "He has told you, O man, what is good; and what does the Lord require of you but to *do justice*, and to *love kindness*, and to *walk humbly* with your God?" (Micah 6:8, ESV).

How does one "do justice"? What is justice? Justice takes on many faces and may be defined differently by various people.

One view of justice could be people being punished for their wrongdoings. Setting innocent people free may be another description of justice. Freeing those who have been victims of human trafficking and child labor could indeed be a way to apply justice; this kind of thing is surely in alignment with God's heart. The Lord desires for the oppressed to go free (Isaiah 58:6). Another viewpoint of justice could be ensuring the prevention of wrongs being done against people, such as crime prevention or the rehabilitation of criminals.

God certainly wants to see the prevention and rectification of wrongs. He wants to minister to and heal the hearts of those who have been victims, as well as those who have committed wrongdoings. To everyone, God wants to reveal Himself and show them His love. The way He often does that is through inspiring or directing people to reach out to and love others.

"Loving kindness" could refer to the daily interactions with others—the verbal greetings, gestures, and facial expressions used. It can also refer to serving others and doing nice, thoughtful things. Kindness can be expressed in so many ways!

How does someone walk humbly with their God? Recognizing that God is all-powerful, and that man is to be subject to Him, is one way to be humble. Other ways to exercise humility include not thinking of oneself as higher than others, and being quick to admit when a mistake or bad decision has been made. God resists the proud but gives grace to the humble (James 4:6).

202

Humility can allow God to do great things in and through a person. In addition to being humble, walking with God also includes growing in the fruit of the Holy Spirit, surrendering to God, and living a life entirely unto the Lord.

LEGALISM

Since the day I received the prophetic word that I was being freed from legalism, I can feel that freedom in my life and am so thankful! Legalism refers to feeling obligated to do something God has not asked you to do in order to maintain a relationship with Him. This could be self-imposed, or it could be in response to what someone other than God has told a person he or she must do.

An example of living under a rule-based standard that is not God-ordered could include fasting. Let's say there is a follower of Christ, who has walked with the Lord for years, and has been convicted by the Holy Spirit to fast for two days a week. That is someone's *personal conviction* from the Lord, *not* something that must be applied to *every* believer. However, this person then tells a new believer that in order to maintain a relationship with God, it is necessary to fast for two days a week. Subsequently, the new believer in Christ then follows that rule—believing it is a requirement to please God—and feels guilty if a week goes by where there has not been two days of fasting.

The Bible does not say someone must fast twice a week. There are examples in the Bible of people fasting, but there is no direct command to all believers about how often it should be done. Examples exist in the Scriptures where some people were directed to fast for three days and a few people even went as long as forty days. How often or how long someone fasted varied from person to person. Pharisees were a very religious people group described in the Bible who would fast often. Yet, Jesus was known to rebuke the Pharisees for the state of their hearts. God is not looking for religious people. He is looking for people who will have a relationship with Him. Fasting for a certain amount of time, as determined by a person other than the Holy Spirit, is an example of living under someone else's conviction.

Feeling the constant need to live by someone else's conviction can cause someone to come under legalism. Legalism is a type of bondage.

Considering the convictions of others is not always wrong. If a believer in Christ explains to someone that sexual relations outside of marriage is wrong or that stealing, gossip, murder, or unforgiveness is a sin, this is not someone imposing a legalistic, non-biblical standard. Explaining what is clearly a sin according to the Bible would instead be an example of someone sharing life-giving truth with another person. Hopefully, any truth shared with another person is presented in a way that is loving. Otherwise, the messenger comes across as self-righteous and judgmental. When correction regarding sin is being shared with others, it *must* come from a place of love. Hard truths can be spoken while still demonstrating love for that person. Believers should love each other (and those outside of the faith) enough to tell them about the Truth and what it means to follow Jesus.

Since receiving the word from the Lord about being freed from legalism, I have gained insight into the guidance provided in John 14:15, "If you love Me, keep My commandments" (NKJV). I've learned you don't *prove* you love God by keeping His commandments. That's also legalism. The *evidence* of love is keeping His commandments. A person must keep God's commandments, but when a person loves God, his or her motivation for obeying is different.

ARE ALL PROMISES FOR EVERYONE?

Some promises are indeed for everyone who puts their faith in Christ, while other promises are for certain individuals. It's possible to be given a message, based on a passage of Scripture, that is not actually what God is saying to someone for his or her specific situation. To know when God is speaking it's important to have the discernment of the Holy Spirit. For example, let's say that a woman wants to have a child. Then, someone very well-intentioned says to them, "You will be like Hannah and have a child in your arms by this time next year" (Hannah is a woman in the Bible who wanted a baby and her prayer request was granted). This statement could either be a declaration of faith, a false word, or an accurate prophetic word.

If God really did say the woman would have a baby by next year, then it would be an accurate word. However, if someone knew or sensed what the woman was desiring and *assumed* it was God's desire to grant her a child within a year, to tell her that will happen, would be a false word. In the event the statement to the barren woman is a declaration of faith, one would expect a person to say something like, "*I am believing* that this time next year…"

Maybe it is God's heart to grant that woman a baby. Discerning the timing of when God wants to move in someone's life is not always clear. If someone is not sure it's truly God speaking, then great caution should be used and the situation should be prayerfully approached before telling someone, "I hear God saying…" If caution is not exercised or someone is not accurate in what he or she shares, the person who received the word may end up confused and very disappointed.

Perhaps the person made the statement about that woman soon having a child in her arms because a person saw in the Scriptures of the Bible (in 1 Samuel 1) that Hannah wanted a child and her prayer request was granted by the Lord. Therefore, that person thinks the Lord will always grant a child to everyone who is barren or having difficulty carrying a baby full-term. Not every example in the Bible, of when the Lord grants someone the desire of his or heart, is always applicable to someone else's situation. I believe God often wants to bring healing and do miraculous things in people's lives, but knowing for certain that's what God wants for a particular situation, takes discernment. Some Scriptures are specific to the individual's experience recorded in the Bible and are not meant to be universally applied.

Let's consider Moses as an example. Could God part the Red Sea through someone other than Moses? Sure. Anything is possible. However, not every person that approaches the Red Sea and wants to see it part will suddenly experience a supernatural parting of the Red Sea. That situation was specific to Moses. If God told someone to go to the Red Sea because He was going to part it, then the Red Sea would part if that person was obedient. However, the manifestation of the sea parting would be contingent on what God directed for that individual.

Conversely, there are Scriptures which are universally applicable to followers of Christ, such as the promise that God will give wisdom to those who ask (James 1:5).

OBEDIENCE

One way to express love for God is to obey Him (John 14:15). As people obey the Ten Commandments and other guidelines in the Bible, they are able to avoid sin, which would be obstacles to their relationship with God. Abiding by biblical principles helps people experience freedom from the bondage of sin and can position them to receive blessings.

In addition to obeying the general guidelines given in the Bible, it's also important to obey promptings from the Holy Spirit, which is how God speaks personally to each person. A few examples of things the Lord might ask someone to do could include talking to a certain person, praying for a situation, or serving in a particular capacity. It could be something small or big that God asks of someone. The Bible says obedience is better than sacrifice (1 Samuel 15:22). Obedience is key to growing in relationship with the Lord.

Possible Outcomes of Disobedience

Amazingly, God commissions followers of Christ to be His coworkers, which means certain things are only accomplished when they are obedient to what God is directing them to do. If someone ignores a prompting from the Lord such as speaking to a particular person, praying for someone, or doing a particular task, that opportunity could be lost. In that case, it is probably wise to not only ask God for forgiveness but also request that He restore the opportunity lost. If it seems unlikely that there will be a second chance to do that particular task, it could be good to ask God to send someone who will successfully complete it.

At times, there are blessings tied to obedience. Therefore, not obeying God could cause someone to miss out on a blessing, or to experience a delay before receiving it.

Not Responsible for Results

One task God might give to someone could be to share a message with a particular person or group of people. When sharing a message with someone that the Lord has directed, the messenger is only responsible to share the message—he or she is not responsible for the *outcome* of what happens. In other words, if God tells someone to deliver a message, the person delivering the message is not held responsible for the recipient's response. Not all people are receptive to words of guidance or correction.

One time in my spirit, I sensed I needed to share a Bible verse with a sister in the Lord, whom I did not often see. Obediently, I called her and shared with her the Scripture that the Lord had given me. I left her a voicemail explaining that the Lord disciplines those He loves and I sensed God was wanting her to discipline her child. This was not a comfortable phone call for me to make! I did not know her that well and barely knew her little boy. However, I really believed that word was from the Lord and its message certainly aligned with Scripture. As the days passed by, I hoped that perhaps she might touch base with me. She didn't return my call. I had done my part, now it was in the Lord's hands. I was simply responsible to be obedient by delivering the message.

Obedience Can Help People Experience God's Fullness

It's possible a person could receive a word from the Lord that is contingent upon their obedience to what He directs that person to do. For example, let's say the Holy Spirit prompts someone to share a message with a man, "Restoration is coming to the relationship between you and your parents." A couple days later, the Lord prompts the man to write a letter to his parents asking them to forgive him for the way he rebelled against them. However, the man doesn't write the letter. Subsequently, the relationship between his parents and him does not get restored. Experiencing what God wants to accomplish in a person's life can be dependent upon one's obedience.

God wants to work in each person's heart to bring healing, wholeness, and bear spiritual fruit. There are also blessings that God has in store. Disobedience can hinder the things God wants to do in people's lives, whereas obedience creates more opportunity to receive from God.

FILLED WITH THE HOLY SPIRIT

People receive a measure of the Holy Spirit when they confess with their mouth that Jesus Christ is Lord and believe in their heart that He rose from the dead. However, someone can ask for more of the Holy Spirit! Luke 11:13 says, "If you then, being evil, know how to give good gifts to your children, *how much more will your heavenly Father give the Holy Spirit to those who ask Him!*" (NKJV).

How does a believer get filled with the Holy Spirit? Simply by asking! Asking God to fill oneself to overflowing with the Holy Spirit can be a life-changing request! Becoming filled with the Holy Spirit is also known as the Baptism of the Holy Spirit because someone is baptized (immersed) in the Holy Spirit.

Throughout the Scriptures, when someone was filled with the Holy Spirit, their spiritual gifts were stirred (sometimes, if gifts aren't stirred up, they don't come to the surface). In addition, many people also received the ability to pray in tongues.

I was in love with the Lord for a year and a half before I experienced the Baptism of the Holy Spirit. In my case, someone prayed for me while I was attending a church service. There is power in coming into agreement with another person in prayer so it can be helpful for people to pray together when asking to be filled with the Holy Spirit. However, a person can also pray for this by himself or herself.

After learning the scriptural backing for the Baptism of the Holy Spirit and its associated advantages—a prayer language, the stirring of spiritual gifts, a greater sensitivity to hearing God's voice, and an increased power to resist temptations—I wanted to share this insight with others. Immediately, I began meeting with other Christians on my college campus to explain this simple but powerful concept of the Baptism of the Holy Spirit. I found that many people had been like me—unaware that this was available to them. As a result of sharing with them, I was privileged to see many people ask God for more of the Holy Spirit.

Over the years, I have come to understand there can be hindrances to accessing all the benefits of the Baptism of the Holy Spirit. Unforgiveness in particular, can hinder the flow of God's power as well as block the manifestation of the prayer language. If someone asks God for the Baptism of the Holy Spirit and wants to receive a prayer language but doesn't, that individual should ask God for it and seek Him as to why the prayer language has not yet come. It's possible there could be a sin such as unforgiveness in that person's life or a state of one's heart hindering the flow of the Holy Spirit.

I personally believe anyone who puts faith and trust in Jesus and asks God for the Baptism of the Holy Spirit can receive a prayer language. However, tongues is *not* indicative of salvation! I know many Christ-followers who love Jesus but don't speak in tongues; they are still saved and going to Heaven. For a Christ-follower to be saved, he or she does not *need* to have a prayer language. It is just a gift God gives many of His followers. One benefit to having this gift, is that when I use it I can be confident I am praying according to God's perfect will, because it's the Holy Spirit praying through me. Since the Holy Spirit is one of the three persons of God, He will never contradict what God the Father or Jesus want.

The Holy Spirit is able to use someone's prayer language to accomplish any of the following: exalting God the Father, proclaiming the works of Jesus Christ, strengthening people in their faith, and releasing God's will. Releasing God's will into someone's life could result in: encouragement, conviction, revelation of who He is, healing, provision, protection, or anything else aligning with God's character per the Bible.

If someone wants to be filled with the Holy Spirit, I would encourage them to ask the Lord for more of Him! Because there is power in spoken words, I recommend asking aloud. When people ask with a sincere heart for God to fill them, He delights in the opportunity to respond. Below is an example of what a believer might say when asking to be filled with the Holy Spirit:

Lord, I give You my heart.
I want more of You.
Please fill me with Your Holy Spirit, from my head to my toes.
I want You to overflow in me.
In Jesus' name, amen.

GAINING SUPERNATURAL INSIGHT

Using a means other than the Holy Spirit to obtain supernatural insights such as fortune-telling, mediums, palm reading, or astrology is not wise because those activities draw revelation from the enemy. For example, when psychics tap into the spirit realm to talk with the deceased, they are accessing something spiritual, but they aren't going to God. Leviticus 19:31 says, "Do not defile yourselves by turning to mediums or to those who consult the dead. I am the Lord your God" (NLT). The Lord wants to be the only source of supernatural revelation.

Practices of getting supernatural revelation from sources other than God Himself, can bring oppression into a person's life and lead someone into deception; this can draw a person away from God. If someone has tried to use various approaches to tap into the spirit realm or fortune-tell, it's possible be cleansed from that. As with any sin, the person simply needs to ask God for forgiveness and stop that behavior. It's also wise to get rid of whatever supplies were used (tarot cards, ouija board, numerology books, and other tools of the occult).

How Do I Know It's God

Recognizing God's voice can be difficult because one must discern where those thoughts originated from. There are questions one can ask to help determine if a thought or idea is from God.

Questions to ask could include:
- o   Were those thoughts one's own ideas?
- o   Was it from one's own intellect, emotions, or desires?
- o   Does it align with the Bible? Was it the Holy Spirit?

The enemy may insert a thought into someone's mind—to discourage, cause doubt, instill fear, stir up negativity, foster resentment, lead to sin, or any other attempt to detract from one's walk with the Lord—ultimately trying to lead people away from God. God's voice will lead people in the way of righteousness and may ask people to take a step of faith. Usually, God drops a word or phrase into someone's spirit, which then bubbles up as a thought. The Lord could also bring a picture to mind.

One way to hear from God is to spend time focusing on and talking to Him, paying close attention to the thoughts and images that come to mind. Especially if something comes to me that I was not just thinking, reading or talking about, I usually pay attention. These images or thoughts are usually from the Lord and come to mind because there are situations or people for whom I need to pray. Perhaps someone is in danger or in need of guidance, or perhaps there is an area of my life that I need to surrender to God. For me, when a thought comes in a way that interrupts my present thinking or conversation, I have come to realize that is often the Lord prompting me.

At times, there have been phrases, words, or dreams that I knew God gave me, but I did not know what to do with them. I needed more context. When this happens, God must be sought for the interpretation. It can be helpful to ask questions like:

o   Why did this come to mind today?
o   What would you have me to do with this?
o   Lord, why did I dream that last night?

If an answer does not come right away, don't give up. Fasting may be appropriate. It may also be a good idea to research the phrase or item that came to mind because that can increase one's understanding of what God is revealing. Even if I don't fully understand what the Lord is saying, I can still ask Him for more understanding and ponder the dream, phrase, or vision in my heart.

God has dealt with me on more than one occasion to write down what He speaks—this way, those things can be kept somewhere and referred to later. Sometimes, a message from the Lord can take years to come to pass. Reviewing what God has done or said may build someone's faith and be very helpful.

WAYS GOD SPEAKS:
THOUGHTS

Shortly after committing my life to Jesus Christ in college, I was in my dorm room one day and read Jesus' words captured in John 10:27, "My sheep hear My voice, and I know them, and they follow Me" (NKJV). Excitement and realization stirred within me. *I am one of the Lord's sheep. That means I can hear His voice. God is willing to speak to me!* Understanding that God was willing to speak to me was life-changing. In the years that followed, I believed that God *wanted* me to recognize His voice. As I continued my walk with the Lord, there were several instances when I did hear Him.

As the Alpha and Omega, God knows everything from the beginning to the end, and He may provide insights into my past, present, or future. This can be exciting to experience, but the intention of the prophetic is not to tell someone every detail of his or her future. It is to equip and encourage someone in his or her walk with the Lord. The ultimate purpose of anything God reveals is always to aid in the Lord's will being done, which often includes drawing people closer to Him and creating a better understanding of who He is.

Some people are very sensitive to what God is saying and may recognize His voice often. Others might feel like they rarely hear from God. Truth is, God wants to speak to everyone. He may speak directly to people, stir in someone's heart, or choose to speak a message through another person such as a friend, family member, pastor, coworker, or stranger. Having a message delivered through another person is usually an effective way to get someone's attention. The Lord can also use dreams, songs, movies, books, gifts, feeling a lack of peace, an overwhelming surge of emotion, journaling during quiet time with the Lord, or the items in someone's surrounding environment— even a billboard sign. It's possible the Lord would speak audibly to someone, though this seems to be rare. I know of several instances where someone has heard God speak audibly, but I have never known of anyone for whom this was the primary way God spoke to him or her. One of the best and most frequent ways to hear from God is to spend time reading the Scriptures.

Thoughts

The Lord says in Isaiah 55:9, "For as the heavens are higher than the earth, so are *My ways higher than your ways, And My thoughts than your thoughts*" (NKJV). So, when a thought comes which is very different from how I normally think, it could be the Lord bringing me that thought. Not every random thought is from God. However, when something suddenly comes to mind that I would not typically think of, I consider the possibility that it might be the Lord getting my attention.

Much of the time, God speaks through gentle nudges and subtle thoughts. Knowing which thoughts are from the Lord versus simply being one's own thinking can be extremely difficult to determine. A person could easily dismiss a prompting from the Lord, not realizing it was God nudging them.

Journaling

God wants to reveal Himself to people but waits until people seek Him. Jeremiah 29:13 says, "Then [with a deep longing] you will seek Me and require Me [as a vital necessity] and [you will] find Me when you search for Me with all your heart" (AMP). An effective way to seek God is by studying the Bible. Spending time talking with Him is also important.

Journaling one's conversation with the Lord—including the thoughts that come to mind during that conversation—can be a great way to hear from God. One way to do this could be to pose a question to God, then write down whatever thoughts come in response. Sometimes, those thoughts are the Holy Spirit speaking.

In *4 Keys to Hearing God's Voice*, Mark Virkler shares his experience of how God taught him to recognize His voice through journaling and suggests submitting those journals to mentors (trusted and seasoned Christians) for feedback. Then, the mentor can review the journal entries and identify anything that may seem contrary to God's heart.[1]

Images

Images that randomly pop into my mind could be from the Lord. I have learned not to dismiss random thoughts without checking with the Lord—especially when a person comes to mind. Asking, "Is that from You, Lord?" and praying for the person whose image just popped into my mind, or asking for understanding as to why that image appeared to me, helps me to respond appropriately to whatever God may have been showing me.

I've learned that when I see an image of a person, I should usually pray for that individual; if I don't pray, I may be missing an opportunity to invite the Lord's intervention at a critical time. Many people who come to mind, I have not seen in years, or may not have thought about in ages. To ensure that I don't miss an opportunity to partner with the Lord and pray at a strategic time, I ask God to help me discern when He wants me to pray for people and try be attentive to those promptings.

Symbolic

Sometimes images that come to mind is God showing me something symbolically. For example, in prayer one day I saw an image of a worm. I knew this was with regard to my friend and understood what it was symbolizing. After the image of the worm came into my mind, I described to her what I saw and explained, "A worm is used to break up hardened ground and make soil soft. This enables things to grow more easily. This is similar to how God uses you to break up the hardened grounds in people's hearts…" Did this word about worms pass the filter if tested against the Bible? Yes. The function of worms isn't described in the Bible, but there was scriptural backing for the word in Mark 4, where Jesus compares the heart to soil. When testing a word, the overall meaning cannot contradict the Scriptures (considered in context) in the Bible. However, the exact wording of the message, or the specific picture that comes up in someone's spirit, is not necessarily going to be found in the Bible. The overall message and concept of the word is what is tested.

After I received the Baptism of the Holy Spirit, I often saw all kinds of random images while praying. However, I rarely understood their significance at first. Finally, the day came where I realized I should ask the Lord what those images represent or what significance they have. So, I began to talk with the Lord about it, "This is what I am seeing. Why am I seeing this? What does it mean?"

If the Holy Spirit shows someone an image or speaks a phrase that is unfamiliar, He will often release the understanding for it, if He is asked. When the Lord is asked for the meaning, He may reveal it directly to the person; or He may have the person research the image or topic, and bring understanding that way.

God wants to be sought for revelation and understanding, so it is unlikely that He would bombard someone with revelation and give them every answer to every question they've ever had all at once. In my experience, when God reveals things, it is gradually. He may only speak one word or one phrase at a time.

One of the best ways to receive insights and hear from the Lord is to spend time with Him—reading the Bible, worshiping God, and praying. Prayer is extremely important. Since thoughts or experiences can come from multiple sources, to determine what's truly from the Lord it's very important to have the discernment of the Holy Spirit and be familiar with the Bible.

WAYS GOD SPEAKS:
DREAMS

Throughout my walk as a Christian, I've come to understand that God can use dreams to speak to people. Dreams can have direct, literal messages, or they can be symbolic. If Jesus spoke in parables and analogies while He walked on the Earth, why wouldn't God use parables to deliver a message in the night season?

In my life, dreams have been used by the Lord for a variety of purposes, such as providing:

o Promptings to pray for things
o A message of encouragement for a friend
o Understanding of the Scriptures
o Confirmation or guidance for an upcoming decision
o General wisdom
o Insight into an area of my life where repentance is needed

Not all dreams are from God. Many dreams contain elements of one's subconscious such as concerns, upcoming events, personal experiences, or recent topics discussed. Although dreams may have some elements from the subconscious, they may still contain a message that the Lord is trying to convey.

To determine whether a dream has significance, it is very helpful to journal them. Writing the dream down and reflecting on it helps identify if the dream was actually God speaking or influenced by information to which I was recently exposed. In addition to journaling, I also pray about the dream and ask God if it was from Him and, if it was, to please reveal the message of the dream to me.

Personally, I have found that even when I don't remember a dream upon waking, when it's a dream from the Lord, something happens in the day that triggers a memory of my dream.

When the Lord releases a dream, it should be prayerfully considered. Interpreting a dream without the insight of the Holy Spirit can bring someone to a wrong conclusion. If people use their own logic to explain the meaning of a dream, they may come up with a completely different message than what the Lord was trying to convey.

Unfortunately, it can be easy to ignore God's promptings when He is trying to get our attention. During college, I prayed earnestly that God would give dreams about Jesus to my friend who was skeptical about God's existence. Then one day, my friend mentioned to me that he didn't think dreams were anything more than the subconscious. Although it is true the subconscious can greatly influence someone's dreams, God can also be a source. I was very disappointed because I realized that no matter what dreams God may have given my friend, he had ignored them up to that point.

Interestingly, someone does not need to be in relationship with the Lord to hear from Him through a dream. Genesis 41 records a dream given to Pharaoh (who was not a follower of God) and how Joseph (who was a follower of God) interpreted the dream, revealing that there would be an upcoming drought. Pharaoh then took the precautions necessary and the food supply did not run out.

SPIRITUAL WARFARE

Spiritual warfare happens because there is an enemy. The influence of the enemy can be seen all over the world—with the devastation happening in the world around us, the terrible things on the news, and the bondages in people's lives. Everywhere, people battle evil influences. The spiritual world around us, where good forces such as angels and evil forces such as demons exist, is largely unseen and may seem kind of mysterious.

People who have certain spiritual gifts are able to see into this realm at times. To date, I have never *seen* an angel or a demon, although I know people who have. The effects and influences of demons, though, are something everyone can see. One needs only to turn on the news to see the works of the enemy and influence of evil. Although it's people who may be doing evil things, the real battle is in the spiritual realm, with the powers that influence people. "For we are not fighting against flesh-and-blood enemies, but against evil rulers and authorities of the unseen world, against mighty powers in this dark world and against evil spirits in the heavenly places" (Ephesians 6:12, NLT).

The reason the devil wreaks havoc on the Earth is because of sin. When Adam disobeyed God, he opened a door to sin which has permitted the devil to create problems in the world ever since. Sin is what gives the devil access. That's why people face spiritual warfare.

Warfare consists of trying to remove the enemy and his influence from various places—family relationships, health, personal thought-lives, work environments, government establishments, or any other situations where someone sees the enemy's influence—so that God can come in and have His way. What is God's way? God's way consists of revealing Who He is, showing people His great love, bringing healing, justice, holiness, provision, encouragement, and the other things associated with His character, as described in the Bible.

Weapons of War

How does someone fight a spiritual battle? By partnering with the Lord and using the Word of God. Items such as a cross necklace or other inanimate objects associated with the Christian faith don't serve as a means to protect someone or scare away the enemy. It's applying what's in the Word of the God and exercising faith in Jesus that allows someone to do battle spiritually. To effectively fight a spiritual battle one needs to know who God is and the authority He gives believers. The key to victory is to keep one's focus on God and not be discouraged by the enemy.

Weapons of warfare include:
- Praise: He inhabits the praises of His people (Psalm 22:3).
- Worship: This exalts God.
- Prayer: Releases God to move in powerful ways.
- Fasting: Can help bring breakthrough in a situation.
- Declaring Scriptures in faith: God's Word is alive and powerful, sharper than a double edged sword (Heb. 4:12).

Standing on what Scripture says—contending or fighting in prayer for the promises in the Bible to become a reality—is an example of warfare. Much of the battle people face takes place in the mind—debunking lies and resisting thoughts that lead to sinful behavior and discouragement. The enemy can use hardships, other people, and lies to influence people's thinking. He tries to steal people's joy and get their sight off of who God made them to be. This makes it easier for him to derail people from God's purpose for their lives.

Wielding the weapons of warfare—praise, worship, reading the Bible, and prayer—on a consistent basis helps one to fight not only the larger battles that one may face, but also the smaller, everyday battles.

CLOSING THE DOOR TO THE ENEMY

The enemy will go where he has an open door. Sin is what gives the enemy the right to come in—to someone's personal life or the surrounding environment. Each person chooses whether to give in to temptations or thoughts the enemy presents. Sometimes people respond out of their flesh or simply make a bad choice; this is not necessarily induced by an evil spirit. If a person sins (especially repeatedly) and does not repent, that prolonged behavior can invite a spirit—tied to that particular sin—into a person's life and bring the person into bondage.

Determining When Deliverance Is Needed
Not all bad behavior occurs because of evil spirits, some people simply give in to their sinful nature, which all humans have. Evil spirits, also called demons or unclean spirits, can be invited into people's lives through the poor decisions someone makes, or even through their environment. How soon an evil spirit gets involved varies. To know whether one is involved requires the discernment of the Holy Spirit. There are questions someone could ask to help determine if there is an unclean spirit involved in a behavioral situation, such as:

1. Is the person merely mimicking the behavior of others?
   If the individual behaves in the same unfavorable way when being in a different environment and around different people, then there *may* be a spirit causing that behavior.
2. Is the person sincerely wanting to discontinue the behavior but is not able to? If a person wants to stop behaving a certain way but feels like they just can't, this could be an indication there is a spirit involved. Although, it could also be possible the behavior is continuing because the person simply doesn't practice self-control or needs to learn how to act differently.

Fasting and praying for someone can help expedite a person's ability to get free from bondage. Additionally, spending time with the Lord, as well as reading the Bible and applying its wisdom can help a person overcome a struggle. Even though struggles surface at various times during one's life, there can be victory in Jesus.

The truth can set a person free. "And you shall know the truth, and the truth shall make you free" (John 8:32, NKJV). Jesus is the Truth; He is the one who purchased freedom, healing, and deliverance for people.

Jesus delivered people who were bound by evil spirits while He was in the flesh on Earth and, thankfully, He still does that today. Jesus gives authority to His followers to be coworkers with Him in administering deliverance. I have come to realize deliverance is not something to be feared. Anyone willing to repent and seek God can be delivered.

Repentance/Removing Legal Ground From Enemy

Repentance entails asking God to forgive sins that have been committed and discontinuing those behaviors. When an individual makes a poor choice and sins, there should be repentance because it cleanses that person from sin and allows him or her to be in right standing with God. Repentance removes sin, and sin is what gives the enemy a legal right, or permission, to be present.

After repentance, the evil spirit associated with that sin will either leave or have to obey when it is told to go. It no longer has the right to stay there. Repenting allows someone to be in a position where they can use their authority.

Cleansing a Home

If a person senses an evil spirit in one's own home, it is wise to ask God to reveal anything that has permitted the evil spirit to be there. Perhaps there are items in the house, a person's actions, or even another person's words or spiritual practices that may be giving the enemy the legal right to be present.

If there is a need to spiritually cleanse someone's home, nothing fancy is needed. One needs only to ask the Lord if there are any items which need to be removed from the home or any activities that need to be repented of, then follow His direction and repent for anything that has allowed the enemy access. Repentance is the key for cleansing anything—someone's own heart or one's physical home.

Authority

Thankfully, Jesus has authority over the devil. By Jesus dying on the cross and paying for sin, He purchased victory for those who come to Him so a person does not have to let sin rule his or her life. Jesus also grants authority, to those who follow Him, over the works of the devil. "Behold! I have given you authority and power to trample upon serpents and scorpions, and [physical and mental strength and ability] over all the power that the enemy [possesses]; and nothing shall in any way harm you" (Luke 10:19, AMP).

THE ENEMY'S TACTICS

The enemy is strategic. He has been trying to do harm to mankind for many years, and he is pretty skilled at it. The devil's primary objective is to steal, kill, and destroy. Some of the tactics he uses are: temptation, fear, deception, offense, and sickness.

Getting People Into Sin

When the devil, who's very cunning, tried to get Adam and Eve to first sin, he questioned what God told Eve, and lied to her about what would happen when she disobeyed God's instructions. The devil works the same way today, trying to get people to disobey God and presenting them with temptation—his goal is to discourage, disappoint, and ultimately destroy each person. Humans are made in God's image, and the devil hates them because of that. To keep people from getting into heaven, the devil wants to lead them into sin and deceive them about their need for Jesus Christ.

One of the ways the enemy causes deception is by speaking through thoughts, these may be negative in nature or prompt someone to engage in bad behavior. Whether a thought is derived from one's own flesh or comes to a person because an unclean spirit is trying to influence them, the person does not have to submit to that thought. The decision that individual makes is still within his or her own control.

Fear

The enemy tries to instill confusion and fear in people. That way, he can keep them from moving forward in what the Lord has for them. God doesn't want people to live in fear. Overcoming fear and walking in their authority is something Jesus wants for all people.

Deception

Demons can influence people's thought lives. A demon doesn't have to dwell in a person to have influence or speak lies to them. Lies that come into a person's head like, "I am not good enough," "I'm not valued," or "I am so unattractive," could be an unclean spirit trying to get that individual to doubt himself or herself. There are other lies the enemy also tries to get people to believe. Philosophies, such as "If you are a good person, you'll go to heaven," or "Everyone has their own path to God," can keep people from pursuing the Lord because they don't realize their need for Him. The devil is a liar, and he tries to keep people from fulfilling their God-ordained purpose and destiny.

The enemy can bring deception into a person's life in a variety of ways, even through spiritual experiences. Unless a spiritual experience brings someone closer to the Lord Jesus Christ and aligns with what's described in the Bible, it could be from the enemy, even if it seems like a positive experience. For example, 2 Corinthians 11 indicates that Satan can transform himself into an angel of light. The Bible warns that if anyone (even an angel of light) preaches a gospel contrary to Jesus Christ crucified, then that message must be rejected. Otherwise, someone could become deceived. Testing an experience against the Bible is the way to determine if something is really from God.

Sickness and Offense

What better way to bring destruction into someone's life than through sickness? The devil wants to rob people of health and wreak havoc—this can be effectively accomplished when people harbor emotions, such as bitterness, that are not healthy.

There are several things that bring chaos and negativity into someone's life. Some of these can be found in Ephesians 4:31, "Get rid of all bitterness, rage, anger, harsh words, and slander, as well as all types of evil behavior" (NLT). Harboring certain emotions can be detrimental to the body. Proverbs 14:30 says, "A calm and undisturbed mind and heart are the life and health of the body, but *envy, jealousy, and wrath are like rottenness of the bones*" (AMPC). If there is a spirit of bitterness someone has embraced in his or her life, then that bitterness not only affects behavior toward others, but can also have an impact on that person's physical body.

Unforgiveness can provide legal ground for the devil because it is a sin. It also keeps people from walking in the freedom, and the fellowship, God has for them. Katie Souza with *Expected End Ministries* discusses the importance of repenting from sin and forgiving others. In her teaching, *Stay Unoffendable*, Souza explains the importance of living unoffended. She shares several examples of how harboring offense, or unforgiveness, allows sickness and physical issues to creep into people's lives and linger. God has the power to heal, but believers in Jesus often don't tap into that power because they are holding onto offense.[1] One pastor, who has seen many people healed, shared about a turning point in his ministry when he heard the Lord say, "Faith moves Me, but forgiveness releases My power."[2] After the pastor began sharing this revelation, many people chose to forgive and were healed at his services.

Offense can include resentment, anger, frustration, or hurt feelings. Holding onto offense can prevent the healing work that God wants to do. When someone lets go of offense and asks Jesus' forgiveness for having held onto offense, the believer can then apply the *dunamis* (Greek word for *dynamite* and *power*) of the Holy Spirit to heal the wounds in one's soul; this can result in healing and deliverance. Souza shares multiple examples of where this has happened in people's lives.[1]

Is there *always* a spiritual root to *every* disease? There is not clear evidence in the Bible to indicate there is always a spirit associated with every disease. Neither is there evidence to indicate that all sickness is the result of someone's sin. On the contrary, some people experience physical or health challenges from birth. One could argue that perhaps there was sin in the family line which permitted the sickness or challenge to occur, others may say that things just happen, and some may think the ailment is God's will. Sickness and various challenges come as the result of living in a broken world. God can use the hardships people experience to strengthen them, but I believe God ultimately desires each person to be healthy and whole.

Whatever the reason for a disease or ailment, God is able to heal those. Psalm 103:2-3 says, "Bless the Lord, O my soul, and forget not all His benefits: *Who forgives all your iniquities, Who heals all your diseases*" (NKJV). The Lord is able to deliver people from not only sin, but disease as well. I realize the topic of healing is a tender subject because many people ask for healing and don't see the results they hope for. This has happened in my family too. It's possible the answer to a prayer for healing may be "No" or "Not yet." I personally believe that it is often God's heart to heal.

To pursue healing, a good way to begin is with repentance. Sinful tendencies, or associated consequences, can be passed down from one generation to another—this could potentially be a hindrance to someone's healing. When repenting, it's a good idea to repent not only of one's own sin, but also sin that's been in the family line. That way, when asking God to heal emotional/soul wounds and physical infirmities, any potential hindrances have already been removed. To build one's faith in the area of healing, a person can always ask God for an increase in faith and study Scriptures about healing. Healing is received by faith through Jesus—*nothing* is impossible with God.

TESTING A WORD

Coming to God in prayer and asking for confirmation or direction with regard to a decision invites God to release revelation that will provide helpful insight, wisdom, or clarity. *All* revelation and any prophetic words (whether the messages come directly into someone's heart and mind or are delivered through another person) should be measured against the Bible. Revelation 19:10 says, "…For the testimony of Jesus is the spirit of prophecy [His life and teaching are the heart of prophecy]" (AMP). This means a prophetic word that is truly from God will never contradict God's character or the Bible. In addition to searching the Scriptures, determining the source of a word takes discernment from the Holy Spirit.

Not all insights someone receives are necessarily meant to be shared; some are just so a person can be prayerful. Especially for new believers and those who have recently discovered their ability to recognize God's voice, it is wise to ask a seasoned follower of Christ (who is familiar with the prophetic) whether or not to share certain visions or prophetic words with other individuals. Gathering input from believers who can help discern if a word is really from the Lord is helpful for a few reasons.

It's possible that:

1. Revelation may have been released solely for the purpose of being prayerful
2. Revelation can be distorted (due to veils over the heart or idols in one's life)
3. The timing isn't right to share a word with someone

If prophetic words are not tested, people could become deceived, misguided, or be sorely disappointed, thinking a word was from God when it was not. The primary way to test the prophetic is to use God's Word as a filter. For *anything* God speaks, through whatever method He uses to reveal it—a friend calling to discuss a dream, a pastor prophesying at a conference, a picture that comes to someone in prayer, or any other method—He is always able and willing to provide scriptural support.

If there is no Scripture accompanying a prophetic word, it's imperative to use caution and ask the Lord for clarity. If the word is contrary to the Scriptures, then the word should definitely be rejected!

Key questions to ask when testing a word from the Lord or a message about the Lord include:

- o God, what scriptural support is there for this?
- o Does this contradict the Scriptures in any way?
- o Does this word line up with Scripture—in context?
- o Would doing (or claiming) this word be contrary to the heart of God?

If the answer to any of those questions is "Yes," then the word is not from God and should not be embraced.

A message delivered with the best intentions may still be inaccurate, due to a variety of reasons. Perhaps a message was not really from God. Or maybe it was, but the person delivering the message miscommunicated it or mixed in one's own advice with what he or she heard God saying, and subsequently misinterpreted it. Any of these mistakes can cause confusion.

When being given a message (even as part of a general audience), if it does not align with Scripture (or maybe there's a warning in one's spirit), it is wise to say aloud something like, "I do not receive that. That is not true and that is not my portion." Those words don't have to be loudly declared—it could just be a soft whisper— but making a verbal statement like that can help to prevent that message from taking root in one's heart or life.

I have seen people embrace things that were definitely not God and reject things that clearly are. It can be difficult to discern what is really from Him. If someone receives a message that might be from the Lord, it's always wise to pray about it and test it against the Bible, then respond accordingly.

After verifying a word is from the Lord—whether it came through another person or directly from the Holy Spirit—it is usually appropriate to pray for the word to come to pass. An exception to this would be if God reveals that someone will sin; in this case, it would be good to ask God to reveal any sin that's present (or will be) and to deal with the individual's heart, and to bring forth repentance and salvation.

WHAT IF SOMEONE IS WRONG
ABOUT HEARING FROM THE LORD?

Although there are many instances where I'm certain God *has* spoken and intervened in my life, not every time I thought God was speaking was actually Him. One time, I thought the Lord told me He was bringing my future husband into my life by a certain time frame—and it didn't happen. I was devastated. *How could this be?* As I contemplated the situation, I realized it is possible to embrace a desire so much that it can be the equivalent of an idol in one's heart. Idols can twist what God is trying to speak to someone, or can simply cause a person to draw inaccurate conclusions about what is from the Lord.

Discernment

When I asked the Lord how to increase my level of discernment, I was drawn to two Scriptures in Proverbs. Proverbs 8:12 says, "I, Wisdom, live together with good judgment. I know where to discover knowledge and discernment" (NLT). From this verse, I could see discernment was linked to wisdom. I also noted that fear of the Lord was critical to having wisdom, as I considered Proverbs 9:10, "Fear of the Lord is the foundation of wisdom. Knowledge of the Holy One results in good judgment" (NLT).

I concluded having a fear (deep reverence) of the Lord would bring me wisdom and increase my level of discernment. Another key component for acquiring discernment was having knowledge of the Lord—which could be obtained through reading the Bible, mentorship, and spending time with God. The Holy Spirit is the best source of discernment because He provides clarity as to whether or not something really is from God.

If a person discerns incorrectly and assumes something is from God, when it's not, then it's good to ask the Lord for forgiveness. It's also wise to ask God for His grace in the situation, as well as clarity and encouragement to the people who may have been impacted by the incorrect assumption.

Confusion

Confusion can come from the many voices (besides God's) that sometimes speak into one's life—friends, family, one's own self, the media, others in one's environment, and the enemy. The enemy includes the devil and other evil spirits who try to whisper things that stir confusion or direct someone's focus away from the Lord.

It can be difficult to discern what is from the Lord and what is not. God may speak to provide: warning, correction, wisdom, encouragement, clarity, or guidance. He may also provide insight into a past event or future situation. Sometimes, it can be very helpful to know things in advance, as it could prevent a wrong decision from being made. Other times, not knowing the details of certain events puts people in a place where they need to trust God and seek Him for guidance. There are times when people are supposed to take one step at a time while leaning on the Lord.

I don't know if God wanted me to know so soon after moving out that Jacob and I would not stay together. After asking God repeatedly for an answer about what would happen with my marriage, I received an answer indicating Jacob would leave me. Was that response influenced by the vision Belle shared with me? It's possible. Because of the possibility that the answer I received *might not* have been God, it would have been dangerous to decide the fate of my marriage based on only that experience and my friend's vision. It's possible I had such a strong desire to have a family soon, that it (the desire) could have been like an idol in my life and influenced what I heard from the Lord.

Keep Pursuing

Does my experience of being wrong when I thought God was bringing me my future husband mean that I should give up listening for God's voice? Should I choose not to respond to God, wallow in my disappointment, and be too afraid to step out in faith? Of course not. I should still consider what I think He is speaking.

I simply needed to be humble and ask God to reveal any idols in my life, or strong desires in my heart contrary to what He wants for me. After admitting I was wrong and asking Him to cleanse my heart, I asked the Lord to forgive me for having hope rooted in something that was not of Him. I also asked Him to forgive any inaccuracy I may have projected to others. Thankfully, God's Word says His grace is sufficient for whatever mistakes are made (2 Corinthians 12:9) and His mercies are renewed every morning (Lamentations 3:23).

Refusing to respond to any future promptings or revelation from the Holy Spirit would be an immature response—I would be hiding behind fear and accepting defeat. God desires His followers to be overcomers. "No, despite all these things, overwhelming victory is ours through Christ, who loved us" (Romans 8:37, NLT).

HOW DO YOU RECOVER FROM FAILURE?

Everyone has failures and disappointments to contend with in life. Fear of failure often keeps people from fulfilling what God wants them to do. Unfortunately, many people concentrate on their short-comings and develop a mindset of defeat and a feeling of low self-worth. Jacob focused on his downfalls and didn't have a good grasp on his true identity. He tried to base his self-worth on his successes; however, he remained focused on past failures instead. Thankfully, the past does not have to define a person and neither does someone's failures. God's mercies are renewed every morning. Each day can be a new beginning!

I've taken comfort in knowing that Jesus' death has paid not only for my sins but also my failures. Instead of facing failure and feeling like there is a brick wall that I can't see beyond or move past, each failure can simply be a stepping stone to collect wisdom during life's journey. Recovering from failure is not always easy, but whenever I fall down and reach out to God, I am able to get back up.

People could experience failure in a variety of ways. A few examples of failure could include: a broken relationship, a mistake made at work, or a goal in life that wasn't achieved. If failure comes from not achieving a particular goal, to rebuild confidence and self-esteem, it can be helpful to set a series of small, attainable goals. That will allow someone to have a feeling of success, take encouragement from those accomplishments, and continue to pursue their other goals. For any failure, coming to the Lord and asking for encouragement is helpful. He wants to minister to people in the midst of their failures and disappointments, and guide them to victory.

Listening for God

God wants His children to respond to His voice for many reasons. One reason is to build up those who are in need of His encouragement. If I don't do what the Lord is asking of me, I may miss an important opportunity to serve someone or draw closer to God. Ignoring God when He speaks could cause others to miss out on a blessing that God wants to bring them through me. It could also cause me to be in grave disobedience.

Focusing on the times I have been wrong is discouraging. Considering my disappointments, misinterpretations, or other mistakes could make it easy for me to justify not responding to the Holy Spirit. I could assume that because I've been mistaken in instances when I thought God provided me insight, I should never respond again when I think He might be speaking. Instead, I must choose to learn from all my experiences. I cannot let misinterpretations or my other mistakes weigh me down forever.

World-renowned neurosurgeon, Dr. Ben Carson, arrived at a similar conclusion when he looked at the big picture of life. After experiencing a failed surgical operation where two patients died, Dr. Carson was disappointed, but he knew good could come out of that failure. Dr. Carson recognized that he could learn from each mistake. Those lessons could equip him to better handle situations that might arise in the future.[1] Most days, I recognize, like Dr. Carson, I can also learn from my mistakes. But that does not mean I never feel discouraged.

Because it is so easy to become discouraged with regard to pursuing the Lord or stepping out in faith, it's important to be intentional with how I direct my thoughts. I also need to be intentional about encouraging myself. In the Scripture, there is record of a man named David who was possibly going to be killed by a group of angry men. He was in a terrible predicament, but David "strengthened himself in the Lord" (1 Samuel 30:6, NKJV). Spending time with the Lord can indeed be a great source of strength and encouragement. I am grateful I can always go to the Lord, but that does not mean I always *feel* like going to Him. That's where discipline comes in. I need to have the practice of spending time with Him, bringing Him my concerns, and listening for what He wants to speak to me.

Continuing to grow in my faith, serve God, and minister to others is too important for me to let a disappointment keep me from pursuing the Lord for His direction. Being quick to admit when I've been wrong and take ownership of the mistakes I've made is a sign of spiritual maturity. Thankfully I can approach the Lord anytime, knowing His grace and mercy are sufficient. After humbling myself before Him, I am able to continue moving forward in my journey with the Lord.

CONFIRMATION

Many times when I believed God placed something on my heart, confirmation came soon afterward. This verified the message or insight really was from Him. Seeking God for confirmation is one method to help determine if a word is really from Him. I believe when God speaks to someone that He is willing to confirm it—this often consists of God repeating His message in different ways.

Confirmation may be a message to someone directly or could come through interactions with others. Some examples of a confirmation someone may receive could be: a friend sharing a dream they had, which pertains to the situation; a fellow believer sharing a similar word from the Lord; a Christ follower having peace in their spirit when the word is relayed to them; or reading a passage of Scripture (or other book) that reiterates what God has spoken. I have seen confirmation come in lots of ways.

Below are several examples of God speaking and the confirmation that accompanied those instances:

Coffee
Standing in my kitchen one day, I thought it would be nice to do something for a couple friends, Sue and Jerry, whom I had not seen in a while. So, I asked the Lord, "Lord, what can I do to bless Sue and Jerry?" A picture of coffee popped into my mind. *Hmmm. That would make sense. They are the parents of small children. I bet they would appreciate some coffee.*

A month or two passed and I finally went to pick some coffee to drop off to them. I stood in the aisle at the grocery store and found myself growing anxious, *How do I know which kind I should get? Lord, which one should I get? There are so many different ones to choose from!* Finally, I took a breath and grabbed the hazelnut coffee. I didn't have any specific kind in mind to get, but I knew I liked hazelnut. I stopped by their house in the late afternoon. Jerry took a break from the construction on his closet and came to answer the door. Looking at Jerry, I explained, "I brought you coffee, but I didn't know what kind to get you, so I got hazelnut." He smiled and explained, "I was just telling Sue that I needed to go to the store to get coffee because we don't have any. She told me, 'You can go without coffee for a day.' And I told her, 'No I can't.' And we just ran out of hazelnut creamer." I laughed, *What timing!* Jerry could have survived without coffee, but God took delight in blessing him with coffee that day!

Semper Fi

One year, there was a Christmas play, *Semper Fi,* I was planning to attend. I asked the Lord who I should invite. An image then came up in my mind of my friend, Rosie, whom I had not seen in a long time. So, I contacted Rosie. Unfortunately she had a schedule conflict and could not attend the play. Puzzled, I went before the Lord in prayer, *Why would you tell me to invite Rosie when she can't even attend the play?* Then, I was reminded the name of the play was *Semper Fi.*

"Semper Fi" is a Latin term used by the United States Marines. Translated, this phrase means "Always Faithful." The message of the play was that God is always faithful. Making the connection, I called Rosie and said, "I believe God wants you to know that He is always faithful." Her response was warm, "That means so much. I just had a miscarriage. This was not the first either. My husband and I want to have children so much." My friend and I had not been in touch for quite a while, and I had known nothing about her miscarriages.

The next November, within a year of our phone conversation, I learned she gave birth to a healthy baby boy. I couldn't help but reflect on my conversation with Rosie the year before. Indeed, God had been faithful to her and her husband. Since that child, she has given birth to a second son, and a daughter. She is now the proud mother of three wonderful children. Whenever I see the phrase "Semper Fi" written on a bumper sticker, I am reminded of how God let Rosie know that He is always faithful and how He granted my friend the desire of her heart. As I look at her situation, I am reminded of Psalm 37:4 which says, "Delight yourself also in the Lord, and He shall give you the desires of your heart" (NKJV). What I thought was simply going to be an invitation to a play ended up being a message of hope to a friend who needed encouragement.

Carla

At the gym one day I was using a piece of exercise equipment and asked the Lord if He wanted me to pray for anyone before I left. Immediately after posing that question to the Lord, an image of Carla popped into my mind.

Carla was someone who worked the front desk at the gym. *She wasn't at the desk when I came in. I don't understand why I would be shown Carla if she is not here today. I guess I will look for her when I leave today.* As I approached the exit, I walked next to a gym member whom I did not know. She mentioned that her knee hurt so I thought I should offer to pray for her. She accepted my invitation to pray and we stepped aside, in the corner of the lobby.

We were ready to ask for the Lord's hand of healing on her knee and I asked, "What's your name?" She looked at me and said, "Carla." *Wow. The desk worker named Carla is not here, but the Lord wanted me to pray for <u>this</u> Carla.* Excited, I shared with her how the Lord told me to pray for Carla before leaving the gym. She felt so encouraged! Not only did her knee feel better after we prayed, but Carla knew that God had seen her, knew her circumstances, and orchestrated that divine appointment.

Pray for Her

One Saturday morning I was at breakfast with a friend and when I caught sight of the woman at the table next to us with a man, the thought came, *Pray for her.* I hesitated. If she were by herself at the table it would have been a little easier for me to justify approaching her. I told the Lord if the man she was with left the table, I would offer to pray for her. He didn't leave. My breakfast buddy was then ready to go, so we left, and I prayed silently, "God, I didn't offer to pray for her. If you want someone to do that, send another."

As we got into the truck and pulled out of the parking spot, I reflected on the scenario, *If that was the Lord telling me to pray and not just my own random thought, then I really should do this.* I told my friend, "I need to run back inside." I returned, interrupted the couple mid-conversation, and explained I'd been sitting near them and had the thought that I should offer to pray for them, "Would it be okay if I prayed for you?" The woman was very grateful, the husband was a bit stunned. Immediately, the woman teared up and she said, "I have cancer." Looking at her, I never would have known. Physically, she was not showing the effects that often accompany radiation and chemotherapy. After explaining I had a friend outside who would be happy to pray with us, I went out to the truck to get him. Together, we prayed for this precious woman. That simple act of obedience brought the couple a lot of encouragement and hope.

My friend discerned that the woman needed to hear cancer was not part of the Lord's original design for mankind—she didn't have this as a punishment from God. Thankfully, he was able to explain that to her. The woman was a believer in Christ and had a great support system in place. After the prayer, we left the restaurant, feeling she was in good hands.

COLLECTIVE SUMMARY

God loves every person and wants to be in close relationship with them. He cares about us and wants to guide us through life.

He designed marriage so people could have a helpmate. Marriage is intended to be much more than what some people experience. It is a sacred covenant between a man and woman where both spouses are meant to be partners who honor, encourage, and lift one another up. That means serving each other, listening to each other, and submitting to one another.

No marriage is without its difficulties, so it is important to invite the Lord's input and seek wisdom from others when challenges arise. Restoration in marriage should generally be pursued, unless it's an unsafe situation or the Lord directs otherwise. If divorce is imminent or has already happened, God will be faithful to meet each person right where they are in life, providing wisdom and guidance as He is pursued.

Through Jesus Christ, and asking for His forgiveness, a personal relationship with God is available to anyone who wants it! God is personal, and wants to be a part of each person's life.

Listening for what God is saying and responding to His direction are critical steps in maturing as a follower of Christ. The best way to get familiar with God's character and to hear from Him is to read the Bible. The Word of God is alive and powerful.

People hear the Lord when the Holy Spirit speaks to them. This could include bringing someone's attention to a particular Scripture. The Lord can also speak directly to a person, this often consists of the Holy Spirit inserting words or a picture into a person's spirit (which becomes a thought). The Lord may also speak to someone through another person.

Ways to hear from God, or understand His heart on a matter, could include: reading the Bible, praying, worshiping, a person sharing a prophetic word, seeking godly counsel, dreams, and journaling. Biblically, dreams were used to: warn people of danger, bring revelation, provide insights concerning the future, and reveal the state of someone's heart. Not every dream is from God, nor is every random thought, but God could speak through those avenues.

To determine if a word (a supposed message from the Lord) is really from God versus another source, such as oneself or the devil, one should evaluate the word against the Bible. God will *never* provide guidance that contradicts His character or the Word of God. Supernatural revelation can come from sources other than God. Testing revelation against the Scriptures when someone thinks God may be speaking is important—that way, false expectations, misguidance, and confusion do not arise.

God is able to release supernatural provision, pour out His favor into our lives, do miracles, and bring incredible healing, but this is not why we first come to Him. We first come to Him because we realize we need His forgiveness for the sin that has been in our lives. When we draw close to God and trust Him, we foster a personal relationship with Him. As we learn His heart and how He longs for people to be made whole, we are able to press in for His promises.

Every person needs healing during life's journey. All people experience hurt or hardship at some point. Receiving healing may be dependent upon forgiving others and bringing hurts to the Lord. It may also require a person to contend for God's promises to come to pass—which includes standing on what the Bible says, not on one's feelings.

We live in a broken world where we face all kinds of difficulties. When concerns or doubts arise we can take them to the Lord and discuss those with Him. Some questions may get answered, and some might not. It's important to determine in one's heart not to let lack of answers keep oneself from loving and trusting God.

We seek God not only for what He can do or provide but because of who He is. He longs to be in relationship with us. Sending His Son, Jesus, to be sacrificed was done so we could have God walk beside us in this life and be with Him in Heaven for all eternity.

Ignoring the promptings and convictions of the Holy Spirit can delay someone's spiritual growth and hinder the transformation process that God wants to do in a person's heart. God's desire is for people to exhibit His character. "But we all, with unveiled face, beholding as in a mirror the glory of the Lord, are being transformed into the same image from glory to glory, just as from the Lord, the Spirit" (2 Corinthians 3:18, NASB). In other words, as someone spends time with the Lord and learns about God's heart, that person develops characteristics similar to the Lord and reflects Who God is.

HOPE

With God's help, you can have the guidance needed for whatever situations you face. God's heart is that each person would know His love, be in close relationship with Him, and experience restoration in various areas of life.

Beloved, I pray that whenever disappointment arises or unexpected ends come into your life, you still take heart because Jesus has overcome the world. Jesus said in John 16:33, "In the world you will have tribulation. But take heart; I have overcome the world" (ESV). I also pray that God blesses you, in Jesus' name.

References

Chapter 1-4, 6, 9-12, 16-17—no sources referenced.

Chapter 5, Hindsight is 20/20
1. Eggrichs, Emerson. *Love and Respect*. 2004. Thomas Nelson Inc. Nashville, Tennessee. Print.

Chapter 7, The Pursuit Continues
1. "The Who Lyrics, Behind Blue Eyes." http://www.azlyrics.com/lyrics/who/behindblueeyes.html Accessed on January 15, 2015.
2. "Pink Floyd Lyrics, Comfortably Numb." http://www.azlyrics.com/lyrics/pinkfloyd/comfortablynumb.html Accessed on January 15, 2015.

Chapter 8, Encouragement Through A Dream
1. Kreiger, Janice and Hunt, Rose. *The Master Builder's Apprentice*, 2013. Create Space, North Charleston, SC. Print.

Chapter 13, Easter Weekend
1. Net Bible. "Paraclete." http://classic.net.bible.org/dictionary.php?word=Paraclete Accessed on January 14, 2015.
2. Ironside, Andrew. *Prosperous Soul*. Andrew Ironside Ministries. Road to Life Church. Fall, 2012.

Chapter 14, Onyx Ring
1. Menendez-Ferrell, *Seated in Heavenly Places*. Shippensburg, PA. Destiny Image. 2009. Print.

Chapter 15, Cutting The Ties
1. Glory, Shekinah *Live Shekinah Glory Ministry*. "Yes Reprise." Released Dec. 6, 2004. Kingdom Records. 2007.
2. Kirkwood, Kerry. *The Power of Blessing*. 2010, Shippensburg, PA. Destiny Image Publishers.

Chapter 18, Deliverance and Restoration
1. Hammond, Frank, and Hammond, Ida Mae. *Pigs in the Parlor: The Practical Guide to Deliverance*. Kirkwood, Mo.: Impact Christian, 2008. Print.
2. "Blasphemy", http://www.merriam-webster.com/dictionary/blasphemy *Web*. June 4, 2015.

3. "Bless" http://dictionary.reference.com/browse/bless?s=ts. Web. December 21, 2014.

Chapter 19, Humbling Myself
1. Eggrichs, Emerson. *Love and Respect*. 2004. Thomas Nelson Inc. Nashville, Tennessee. Print.

Post Script, The Ultimate Relationship
1. Burke, John. *Imagine Heaven*. Grand Rapids, MI: Baker Books, 2015. Print.
2. Strobel, Lee. *The Case for the Resurrection*. Grand Rapids, MI: Zondervan. 2009. Print.
3. Lewis, C.S. *Mere Christianity*. New York, NY: Harper Collins, 2001. Print.
4. The Nazarene Way of Essenic Studies, "The Birth and Death of Jesus" http://www.thenazareneway.com/date_of_birth_and_death_of_j esus.htm Accessed on June 4, 2015.
5. Bouchard, Michael. Kensington Church. "Beyond the Veil: Two Gates" http://player.kensingtonchurch.org/watch/series/beyond-the-veil Accessed on May 19, 2017.
6. Bevere, John. Drawing Near: A Life of Intimacy With God. 2004. Thomas Nelson.

Marriage Reflections

Love and Respect
1. Eggrichs, Emerson. *Love and Respect*. 2004. Thomas Nelson Inc. Nashville, Tennessee. Print.
2. Feldhahn, Shaunti. *For Women Only: What You Need to Know about the Inner Lives of Men*. Sisters, Or.: Multnomah, 2004. Print.

Criticism: Love Test
1. Drinkard, N. Personal Interview. July, 2006.

Control
1. Morris, Rob, Love 146, *The Justice Event*. October, 2014.

Pornography
1. The Aquinas: Pornography as a drug. Feb. 27, 2015. http://aquinas.scranton.edu/2015/02/27/pronography-as-drug Accessed on March 10, 2016.

Blessing
1. "Bless" http://dictionary.reference.com/browse/bless?s=ts. Web. December 21, 2014.

Perception and Self-Esteem
1. Peters, William. "A Class Divided." 26 March, 1985. PBS. *Http://www.pbs.org/wgbh/pages/frontline/shows/divided/etc/view.html.* WGBH Educational Foundation. Web. 18 Dec. 2014.
2. *Facing the Giants.* Sony Pictures Home Entertainment, 2007. DVD.

Brokenness
1. Wilson, Dave. Kensington Church. "Made: Shaped by God." July, 2013.

Faith Insights

Surrender
1. *I Surrender All,* http://www.azlyrics.com/lyrics/cecewinans/isurren derall.html. Accessed on December 18, 2014.
2. *Fireproof.* Sony Pictures Home Entertainment, 2009. DVD.
3. All About… "Definition of God's Grace" http://www.allaboutgod.com/definition-of-gods-grace-faq.htm Accessed on January 20, 2016.

Forgiveness
1. Baker, John. *Life's Healing Choices.* Howard Books, 2007. New York, New York. (pg. 170)
2. Zarbough, Chris. "Forgiveness." Beyond Divorce Recovery Class, November 2015.

Ways God Speaks
1. Virkler, Mark. *4 Keys to Hearing God's Voice.* Shippensburg, PA: Destiny Image, 2010. Print.

The Enemy's Tactics
1. Souza, Katie. "Offenses." It's Supernatural. September 10, 2012. http://sidroth.org/television/tv-archives/katie-souza-offenses. Web. Dec. 22, 2014.
2. "Brian Adams." Feb. 28, 2011. http://sidroth.org/television/tv-archives/brian-adams/ It's Supernatural. Web. 15 Sep. 2016.

Although the author of this book was already familiar with the song lyrics referenced throughout the text, the lyrics were validated via the website www.azlyrics.com, "AZLyrics."

Web sites used for obtaining Scriptures, looking up key words, and comparing translations include:

- Bible Gateway, http://www.biblegateway.com
- Bible Hub, http://www.biblehub.com

Recommended Bible Translations:
Most Bible translations are probably fine to use, however, the several referenced throughout this book are ones that I would most recommend. Translations such as the Jehovah's Witness Bible should be avoided due to omissions of important information, such as Jesus being the Son of God.

To view additional resources please visit:
www.anunexpectedend.com

Please visit the website for *An Unexpected End* to see a list of recommended Bible studies, Christian books, as well as resources for abuse, codependency, addiction, faith, marriage, and other topics addressed in this book.

ABOUT THE AUTHOR

My walk of intimacy with Christ began in 2002, during college, when I went through a difficult time and was encouraged to join a Bible study. It was then that I began to read the Bible for the first time. God became very real to me during that season of my life and I have never been the same since!

I got engaged my senior year of college. A month after graduating with my teaching degree, I was married. Soon after, I started teaching science for middle school and high school.

I am quite close with my family and am grateful for the many ways the Lord has blessed us. I'm the oldest of four kids. There are some family traits that my siblings and I all share, like we all tend to have a lot of compassion for others and almost always wear mismatched socks—we started doing that before it was fashionable!

Alexa C. Faith is a pseudonym strategically chosen because of the play on words: "Alexa" (the name I chose to represent me) "sees" (notices, experiences) "faith" (trust in the Lord and His power). Also, choosing a pseudonym was done to protect the identity of my ex-husband.

My heart in writing this story is to share what have I learned through my marriage of four and a half years, the divorce that followed, and my walk with the Lord. Hoping to encourage others to find hope, grace, and forgiveness no matter what they have been through, I am very honest in portraying my experiences. My deepest desire is that anyone who reads my story will come to personally experience God's love and grow in relationship with Him. I share examples of how God can speak through dreams, songs, Scriptures, others in the Church, and directly into our thoughts.

The Lord sees every heart and every broken dream. He desires for all to come to Him and wants to restore each person, bringing them to a place of healing and wholeness.

Only when calling on Jesus and following Him can one truly find freedom.

Please visit my website:
www.anunexpectedend.com

www.ingramcontent.com/pod-product-compliance
Lightning Source LLC
Chambersburg PA
CBHW051416090426

42737CB00014B/2694